Activation Policies for the Unemployed, the Right to Work and the Duty to Work

P.I.E. Peter Lang

Bruxelles · Bern · Berlin · Frankfurt am Main · New York · Oxford · Wien

Elise DERMINE and Daniel DUMONT (eds.)

Activation Policies for the Unemployed, the Right to Work and the Duty to Work

Work & Society
Vol. 79

This publication has been peer-reviewed.

No part of this book may be reproduced in any form, by print, photocopy, microfilm or any other means, without prior written permission from the publisher. All rights reserved.

© P.I.E. PETER LANG S.A.
Éditions scientifiques internationales
Brussels, 2014
1 avenue Maurice, B-1050 Brussels, Belgium
info@peterlang.com; www.peterlang.com

ISSN 1376-0955
ISBN 978-2-87574-232-2
eISBN 978-3-0352-6495-1
D/2014/5678/98

CIP available from the Library of Congress (USA) and the British Library (GB).

Bibliographic information published by "Die Deutsche Nationalbibliothek".

"Die Deutsche Nationalbibliothek" lists this publication in the "Deutsche National-bibliografie"; detailed bibliographic data is available on the Internet at <http://dnb.d-nb.de>.

Acknowledgements

The origins of this book lie in an international symposium held at the European Trade Union Institute, in Brussels, on the 15th of March 2013. The symposium was the result of collaborative efforts between the Interdisciplinary Research Centre on Work, State and Society (CIRTES) and the Interdisciplinary Research Centre on Law, Enterprise and Society (CRIDES) at the Université Catholique de Louvain, and the Centre for Public Law (CDP) at the Université Libre de Bruxelles.

The editors wish to thank the European Trade Union Institute for its hospitality; Philippe Pochet, Bea Cantillon, Filip Dorssemont and André Nayer for agreeing to chair the various working sessions that led to the four parts of this book; Pascale Vielle, Paul Van Aerschot and Virginia Mantouvalou for their presentations on the day of the symposium; and the many participants for their questions and interpellations. The editors also wish to express their gratitude to the organisations and institutions without the financial support of which this adventure could not have happened: the Belgian National Fund for Scientific Research (FNRS), Wallonie-Bruxelles International, the Belgian Federal Minister of Social Affairs, the Minister of Employment of the Brussels-Capital Region, the Minister of Employment of the Walloon Region, and the research centres that co-organised the symposium.

Table of Contents

Acknowledgements 7

INTRODUCTION

Activation Policies for the Unemployed, the Right to Work and the Duty to Work: Which Interactions? 11
Elise Dermine and Daniel Dumont

I. HISTORICAL AND PHILOSOPHICAL APPROACHES TO THE RIGHT AND THE DUTY TO WORK

1848 and the Question of the *droit au travail*. A Historical Retrospective 23
Fernand Tanghe

Political-Philosophical Perspectives on the Duty to Work in Activation Policies for the Unemployed 33
Renaat Hoop

II. NATIONAL ACTIVATION POLICIES FOR THE UNEMPLOYED AND THE DIFFERENT UNDERLYING CONCEPTIONS OF THE RIGHT AND THE DUTY TO WORK

Activation Policies for the Unemployed in the United States: Work First 59
Daniel Dumont

Activation Policies for the Unemployed in France: "Social Debt" or "Poor Laws"? 77
Diane Roman

III. ACTIVATION POLICIES FOR THE UNEMPLOYED AND THE HUMAN RIGHT TO WORK

Activation Policies for the Unemployed and the International Human Rights Case Law on the Prohibition of Forced Labour 103
Elise Dermine

Activation Policies for the Unemployed and the International Human Rights Case Law on the Right to a Freely Chosen Work 139
  Elise Dermine

Right to Work and Individual Responsibility in Contemporary Welfare States. A Capability Approach to Activation Policies for the Unemployed 179
  Jean-Michel Bonvin and Eric Moachon

IV. DEBATING IDEAS: THE BASIC INCOME GUARANTEE AND THE EMPLOYMENT GUARANTEE

The Tensions of Welfare State Reform and the Potential of a Universal Basic Income 209
  Yannick Vanderborght

Securing the Right to Work and Income Security 223
  Philip Harvey

CONCLUSION

Activation Policies for the Unemployed: Redefining a Human Rights Response 255
  Olivier De Schutter

Contributors 279

INTRODUCTION

Activation Policies for the Unemployed, the Right to Work and the Duty to Work: Which Interactions?

Elise DERMINE and Daniel DUMONT

"The freedom of [society's] weaker groups, such as the unemployed, is a benchmark for the degree of real freedom for all citizens."[1]

Since the 1990s and the 2000s, social protection systems in European and North American countries have all experienced a turn towards activation.[2] This turn consists of the multiplication of measures aimed at bringing those who are unemployed and in receipt of social benefits closer to participation in the labour market.[3]

It must be stressed from the outset that the link between social security and the labour market has been, since their very foundation, a structural feature of all national social protection systems. Thus, the granting of unemployment benefits has always been conditioned upon compliance with certain legal requirements such as being available for work, accepting any suitable job offer and making an effort to find employment. Generally speaking, all social protection systems are characterised by a form of subsidiarity of the intervention of the community with respect to the steps that people can accomplish by themselves to provide for their own subsistence. Because of this subsidiarity, social benefits have always displayed a more or less "conditional" nature across countries and over

---

[1] J. Van Langendonck, "The Social Protection of the Unemployed", *International Social Security Review*, Vol. 50, No. 4, "Unemployment and Social Security", 1997, p. 40.

[2] For a comparative overview, see for example J.-C. Barbier and W. Ludwig-Mayerhofer, "The Many Worlds of Activation", *European Societies*, Vol. 6, No. 4, 2004, pp. 423-436; A. Serrano Pascual and L. Magnusson (eds.), *Reshaping Welfare States and Activation Regimes in Europe*, Brussels, P.I.E.-Peter Lang (Work & Society), 2007; W. Eichhorst, O. Kaufmann and R. Konle-Seidl (eds.), *Bringing the Jobless into Work? Experiences with Activation Schemes in Europe and the US*, Berlin, Springer, 2008.

[3] For this definition, D. Dumont, *La responsabilisation des personnes sans emploi en question*, Brussels, La Charte, 2012, p. 421.

different periods of time.[4] However, contemporary activation measures are intended to develop and strengthen the links between social security and the labour market, so as to increase transitions from the first to the second.

Though these measures may take the form of improving the assistance provided by public employment services, developing personalised support for jobseekers or investing in vocational training, they consist most often in strengthening the conditions that must be met in order to receive social benefits. Consequently, the intensity of active job searching to which unemployment and social assistance benefits are subjected tends everywhere to be reinforced through an ever tighter jobseekers monitoring system. Similarly, in many social protection systems, the notion of suitable employment, which defines the section of the labour market for which jobseekers must show their availability, is undergoing a process of flexibilisation, in order to compel those concerned to lower their expectations or to accept the first job that comes their way. In some countries, especially Anglo-Saxon ones, social benefits recipients are even required to perform socially useful work in order to continue receiving their benefits – it is workfare. Besides these various measures, the activation of beneficiaries is also sometimes embodied by a reduction in both the amount of social benefits and the period of time for which they are granted.

It is in this well known general context that the authors involved in this book wanted to take a closer look at the relationship between activation policies for the unemployed and the coupling of the right and the duty to work. If one understands how activation measures are likely to increase transitions toward the labour market – which leaves open the question of the quality of the jobs to which access is thereby provided[5] – we can also make the assumption that these measures may, particularly when they are marked with the seal of coercion, hinder or dramatically reduce the right to freely chosen work.[6] In such circumstances, the realisation of

---

[4] J.-C. Barbier and M. Knuth, "Of Similarities and Divergences: Why There Is No Continental Ideal-Type of 'Activation Reforms'", Paris, Université Paris I Panthéon-Sorbonne, Centre d'économie de la Sorbonne, *CES Working Papers*, No. 2010-75, 2010, p. 4; D. Dumont, "Activation rime-t-elle nécessairement avec stigmatisation?", *Droit et Société*, No. 78, 2011, pp. 449-456.

[5] On this issue, see among others S. Borelli and P. Vielle (eds.), *Quality of Employment in Europe. Legal and Normative Perspectives*, Brussels, P.I.E.-Peter Lang (Work & Society), 2012.

[6] In this sense, see the precursory warnings, on the continental side, of J. Freyssinet, "Plein emploi, droit au travail, emploi convenable", *Revue de l'IRES*, No. 34, 2000, pp. 27-58 and J. Van Langendonck, "De 'actieve' welvaartsstaat", in B. Raymaekers and G. Van Riel (eds.), *Hoe dichtbij is de toekomst?*, Leuven, Universitaire Pers Leuven, 2005, pp. 241-254. Meanwhile, certain bodies monitoring compliance with

the "right to work", which is often the stated aim of those who promote activation, tends in practice to be reduced to an increasing pressure being exerted on the unemployed. In this case, it is actually the duty to work that is particularly reinforced.

The following words clarify this hypothesis by reinscribing the turn towards activation and its impact on the coupling of the right and the duty to work in a diachronic perspective. This will be followed by a brief presentation of the structure of the book, of which two transversal features are multidisciplinarity and a combination of Anglo-Saxon and Francophone traditions of thought.

Activation Policies Facing the Coupling of the Right and the Duty to Work

Since modernity, work in our societies has had the moral status of both a duty and a right (A.). But it was not until the establishment, in the 20th century, of social protection systems, that this duty and this right received a precise legal significance, and their respective extents were thus determined (B.). It is this balance that mass unemployment and contemporary activation policies for the unemployed have disturbed, reopening the old debate regarding societal arbitration that needs to be settled between the right and the duty to work (C.).

A. *Work in Modern Societies, a Duty as much as a Right*

Modernity has invested the work value with multiple functions. It is the coexistence of these functions that explains why work has been considered ever since, on ethical grounds, both as an individual's duty and as a right *vis-à-vis* society.[7]

---

the international conventions that proclaim the right to work also began to formulate warnings, noting that the development of activation measures is likely to negatively impact the right of social benefits recipients to freely choose their employment. See, on the side of the Council of Europe, European Committee of Social Rights, *Conclusions 2004, on the Application of Article 1, § 2 of the 1961 ESC*, Sweden, 31st of April 2004 and *Conclusions XVI-2, on the Application of Article 1, § 2 of the 1961 ESC*, Latvia, 30th of June 2004; and, on the side of the International Labour Organization, Committee of Experts on the Application of Conventions and Recommendations, *General Survey Concerning Social Security Instruments in Light of the 2008 Declaration on Social Justice for a Fair Globalization*, International Labour Conference, 100th session, 2011, pp. 93-95, especially § 228.

[7] On this evolution correlated to the emergence of modernity, see D. Méda, *Le travail, une valeur en voie de disparition*, Paris, Aubier (Alto), 1995, chapters III et IV. See also J. Elster, "Is There (or Should There Be) a Right to Work?", in A. Gutmann (ed.), *Democracy and the Welfare State*, Princeton, Princeton University Press, 1988, p. 57.

On the one hand, work is collectively framed as the main vector for social cohesion and peace. It is indeed associated with the promise of making relations more peaceful through the increase of wealth and well-being. In this perspective, individuals are seen as interdependent and complementary in the act of production: they all depend on the work of others in order to meet their own needs. From the moment that society in its entirety revolves around work, each of its members has a moral duty to participate, through his work, in increasing productive activity and, more generally, in the proper functioning of society.

At the same time, work is also seen as an essential human dimension. First, historically, for its instrumental function, i.e. as a way for individuals to earn income and a place in society. But later on also for its intrinsic function, i.e. as a good in itself, allowing everyone to express their individuality and to blossom. Adorned with these functions, work integrates the sphere of human rights. Without work, the most fundamental of all rights, the right to life, remains devoid of effectiveness – be it that this right is seen as the right to subsistence or as the right to personal development. That is why the moral duty to work that weighs on individuals, on behalf of the maintenance of social cohesion, is doubled by a reciprocal ethical requirement on the part of society: that of ensuring to all its members the effective possibility of finding a job in which they can blossom.

B. The Construction of Social Protection Systems, or Achieving a Balance between the Right and the Duty to Work

Obviously, the various functions assigned to work do come into tension. On the one hand, employment must be freely chosen in order to enable the individual to deploy his skills and to achieve personal development. But, on the other hand, social cohesion requires individuals to set aside, at least to a certain extent, their personal aspirations, because it is, from this perspective, on everyone's participation in productive activity that the proper functioning of society depends. Our social representation of work thus appears marked by the conflicting demands of freedom of choice, motivated by the ideal of personal emancipation, on the one hand, and collective constraint, justified by the concern of general interest, on the other.

The practical realisation of freely chosen full employment therefore represents an oxymoron. Since the beginning of the 19th century, it was constantly confronted with the following dilemma. If public authorities intervene to provide work to each member of society, they risk heavily negating individuals' free choice of employment, and strengthening, in an excessively coercive manner, their duty to work (legal constraint). But if public authorities refrain from intervening, in the name of preserving freedom of choice, then the right to access the labour market and to freely choose one's professional orientation is at risk of remaining purely formal, so that in the end numerous individuals will be *de facto* coerced, in order to ensure their survival, into accepting any work conditions (economic constraint). Liberals – proponents of laissez-faire – and socialists – supporters of a planned economy – competed concerning these arguments for nearly two centuries, without being able to escape the dilemma.[8] Both camps were claiming to be proponents of the right to work and accusing the other of wanting to reduce this right to a mere duty.

At the end of the First World War, and even more so at the end of the Second World War, Western European and Northern American countries succeeded in overcoming this impossible equation and in easing the hitherto insoluble tension between the right and the duty to work. The gradual conversion to Keynesianism and the parallel construction of social security systems enabled Western states to flirt with full employment while protecting the freedom to choose a job, according to the way advocated by Beveridge in his famous book *Full Employment in a Free Society*.[9]

Full employment achieved in the economic field actually gave substance to the right to work. Throughout the post-war boom, a very high proportion of the workforce had a job, and even a stable job. In addition, individuals who were temporarily deprived of work were supported through social security while they were searching for a new job. The right to unemployment benefits thus appears to be a substitute for the right to work. However, this right is not unconditional. It carries within it an expression of the duty to work that individuals have *vis-à-vis* society, since the granting of benefits is conditional upon being available for work. Only people who are and who remain involuntarily deprived of work have the right to be compensated. But the duty to work – and this is how the balance was achieved – is itself circumscribed,

---

[8] For a detailed analysis of the debates around this issue in the French National Assembly in 1848, see F. Tanghe, *Le droit au travail entre histoire et utopie*, Brussels-Florence, Publications des Facultés Universitaires Saint-Louis, 1989. On the similar political battles between states of the Eastern bloc and states of the Western bloc that took place a century later, during the elaboration of the Universal Declaration of Human Rights, and then of the International Covenant on Economic, Social and Cultural Rights, see, respectively, J. Morsink, *The Universal Declaration of Human Rights. Origins, Drafting, and Intent*, Philadelphia, University of Pennsylvania Press, 1999, pp. 157-190 and M. Craven, *The International Covenant on Economic, Social, and Cultural Rights. A Perspective on its Development*, Oxford, Clarendon Press, 1995, pp. 194-203.

[9] W. Beveridge, *Full Employment in a Free Society*, London, Allen & Unwin, 1944.

because unemployment compensation systems legally limit the general condition of availability for work to jobs that are considered suitable and to individuals deemed able-bodied. In doing so, they mitigate the economic obligation to reintegrate into the labour market and provide some effectiveness to the right to freely chosen work.

Thus, within social protection systems, a compromise is made between the right and the duty to work, and therefore between the affirmation of freedom of choice as a condition of the possibility of personal development and the imposition of a certain constraint on behalf of social cohesion. Of course, each national system of social protection shapes this compromise in its own manner. It is in this respect that these systems are, to quote Esping-Andersen's famous analysis, more or less "decommodifying": it is a matter of degree.[10] Nevertheless, despite this diversity, every system contains a surpassing of the opposition between the liberal and socialist conceptions of the right to work that competed throughout the 19th century and the beginning of the 20th. Legally, the right to work realised by Keynesianism and social security is indeed not reduced to the mere formal freedom, proclaimed by liberals in response to corporatism, to exercise a profession. But it also does not take the form, once considered necessary by socialists in order to actually achieve full employment, of providing work to each individual through a planned economy.

In its post-Second World War version, and as it was enshrined in the international human rights instruments, the right to work legally consists of two sides: on the one hand, the (positive) right of access to the labour market and to have a job, embodied by Keynesian macroeconomic policies and the supplementary right to unemployment benefits; on the other hand, the (negative) right to free choice of employment, guaranteed by the prohibition of forced labour and the construction of the concept of suitable employment. The former corresponds to the right to work in the strict sense, the latter to what is usually called, at least in the French tradition, the "freedom of work" (*liberté du travail*). In legal terms, it should be noted that the international conventions consider these two sides, positive and negative, as two inextricably linked facets of a single right.[11]

---

[10] G. Esping-Andersen, *The Three Worlds of Welfare Capitalism*, Cambridge, Polity Press, 1990.

[11] See Article 23, § 1 of the Universal Declaration of Human Rights ("Everyone has the right to work [and] the right to free choice of employment"); Article 6, § 1 of the International Covenant on Economic, Social and Cultural Rights (the right to work is defined as the "right of everyone to the opportunity to gain his living by work which he freely chooses or accepts"); the preamble to the ILO Convention No. 122 of 9 July 1964 Concerning Employment Policy (reference is made to the need for an "economic expansion on the basis on full, productive and freely chosen employment"); the preamble

C. Activation Policies for the Unemployed: What Impact on the Relationship between the Right and the Duty to Work?

The emergence of mass unemployment in our societies, following the crisis of de-industrialisation in the 1970s, has deeply shaken the balance between the right and the duty to work achieved during the post-war boom. With the disappearance of full employment, the right to work in its positive dimension is hardly ever fulfilled. Or more accurately, it is reduced to the (in principle) supplementary right to unemployment benefits in the absence of suitable employment, or even to the right to means-tested social assistance for those unemployed individuals who either could not qualify for contributory benefits or have exhausted their benefits. As long as unemployment was reduced to its frictional component, the granting of benefits to individuals temporarily deprived of a job was enough overall to protect their freedom to choose their employment: the unemployed were compensated during the few months they needed to find a job that corresponded to their qualifications. But with the transformation of unemployment into a structural and long or very long-term phenomenon, the guarantee of financial support from social security can no longer effectively secure the right to freely chosen work.

It is in this context that, since the 1990s and the 2000s, a broad consensus has gradually been reached in Western countries: social security systems cannot limit themselves to ensuring the financial autonomy of unemployed individuals out of the labour market. They must also play the role of a springboard into employment. This is viewed as necessary for the maintenance of social cohesion, which depends on the widest possible participation of the population in the labour market. It is viewed as necessary too for the achievement of personal development and self-realisation for the victims of underemployment, since although the payment of social allowances allows them to provide for their subsistence, it does not offer the virtues usually associated with work.

---

of the ILO Convention No. 168 of 21 June 1988 Concerning Employment Promotion and Protection against Unemployment (reference is again made to "the promotion of full, productive and freely chosen employment"); Article 1, § 1 and 2 of the European Social Charter ("With a view of ensuring the effective exercise of the right to work, the Parties undertake to accept as one of their primary aims and responsibilities the achievement and maintenance of a as high and stable level of employment as possible, with a view to the attainment of full employment" and "to protect effectively the right of the worker to earn his living in an occupation freely entered upon"). *Adde* Committee on Economic, Social and Cultural Rights of the United Nations, "General Comment No. 18: The Right to Work", 35th session, 24 November 2005, E/C.12/GC/18, § 1 ("The right to work contributes at the same time to the survival of the individual and to that of his/her family, and insofar as work is freely chosen or accepted, to his/her development and recognition within the community").

Since then, countries have been reforming their social protection systems in order to develop activation measures for social benefits recipients. It is known that the nebula of activation covers a wide range of measures – from skills training and paid internships to the obligation to carry out free community service, and including more or less of an increase in the coercion exerted on social benefits recipients. Such measures are now commonplace in unemployment insurance and social assistance systems. Traces of the activation logic are also beginning to be seen in programmes dealing with work disability.

Because of their heterogeneity, these measures have widely varying impacts on the balance between the right and the duty to work. When they consist in supporting professional reinsertion, and while they are not accompanied by a tightening of the rules governing compensation, they can help to give greater effectiveness to the right to work, understood in the sense of the right to access a freely chosen work. Contrary to a recurrent analysis,[12] we indeed do not believe that activation policies are *per se* synonymous with authoritarian re-commodification of social benefits recipients. In addition to the fact that, as we have pointed out, social security systems have always maintained strong links with the labour market, activation policies may seek to strengthen these links while preserving, for the unemployed, a certain leeway and a certain autonomy in relation to the market.

But it is likely true that in fact, because of the strong tendency to emphasise above all the duties assigned to allowances recipients and at the same time to reduce the extent of social benefits, activation often tends to restrict the individual freedom to determine one's professional orientation. As has been said, the hypothesis that led to this book is that this exacerbation of coercion, because it is done at the expense of the negative facet of the right to work, i.e. the possibility for those concerned to assert their personal aspirations, reduces the right to work essentially to a duty to work. In this case, we can speak of a re-commodification of the unemployed.

* * *

Based on this hypothesis, the contributors to the present book have sought to highlight from different angles the relationship between activation policies for the unemployed, the right to work and the duty to work.

The book is structured in four parts. The first offers an historical and philosophical perspective on the issue. To begin with, courtesy of

---

[12] In this vein, see typically I. Lødemel and H. Trickey (eds.), *'An Offer You Can't Refuse'. Workfare in International Perspective*, Bristol, Policy Press, 2001.

Fernand Tanghe, we are taken back to the very rich and informative debates that, in the middle of the 19th century, surrounded the first manifestations of the idea of consecrating a "right to work". This retrospective is followed by a political theory analysis, in which Renaat Hoop maps out the multiple justifications that are formulated nowadays in favour of or against the strengthening of the duty to work for the unemployed.

The second part contributes to documenting the diversity of the interplay between the right and the duty to work that underpins contemporary activation policies, by means of a double case study. Diane Roman reports on the legal and political developments observed in France, while Daniel Dumont focuses on another iconic country: the United States.

The third part looks at the fundamental right to work, in order to identify the specific criteria by which to assess the conformity of national measures promoting the return to employment, first with respect to the international instruments protecting said right, and then with respect to the philosophy that underlies this right. In her two contributions, Elise Dermine dissects the case law – largely unknown – of the bodies supervising the application of the international conventions that, as regards civil and political rights, prohibit forced labour and that, as regards economic, social and cultural rights, enshrine the right to freely chosen work. In doing so, she identifies the legal limits resulting from each type of convention that can be opposed to the exacerbation of the duty to work of beneficiaries. In a complementary way, Jean-Michel Bonvin and Eric Moachon mobilise the work of the Nobel Prize winner for economics Amartya Sen as well as comparing social protection systems, in order to identify ways that are likely to improve the effectiveness of the right to work of the unemployed, on both its positive and negative sides.

Finally, by way of contribution to the debate of ideas, the fourth and final part, which is more prospective, is devoted to the critical presentation of two proposals at odds with the coercive variant of activation. Yannick Vanderborght defends the idea of guaranteeing to every individual, in a completely unconditional manner, a universal basic income, while, in his contribution, Philip Harvey delivers a plea to secure the guarantee of a decent job for every jobseeker.

The book ends with the concluding reflections of Olivier De Schutter, in which he proposes to redefine the human rights approach to activation policies and formulates several proposals in this perspective.

* * *

Activation Policies for the Unemployed, the Right to Work and the Duty to Work

In a recent inventory of empirical research in social security law, Michael Adler regretted that the legal features of activation policies and their impact on the node of rights and duties remain relatively unexplored.[13] The editors of this volume hope that it will help to fill this gap and encourage new research in this direction.

---

[13] M. Adler, "Social Security and Social Welfare", in P. Cane and H. Kritzer (eds.), *Oxford Handbook of Empirical Legal Research*, Oxford, Oxford University Press, 2010, p. 421.

I. Historical and Philosophical Approaches to the Right and the Duty to Work

1848 and the Question of the *droit au travail*
A Historical Retrospective

Fernand Tanghe

Before anything else, and in order to avoid any misunderstandings, it should be made clear that while in French there is a distinction between the *droit au travail* and the *liberté du travail*, in English there is only one expression for both: the right to work (see the introduction to this volume). And while in French, the two expressions have very different, even opposing meanings, they are concealed – one could even say repressed – by the apparent univocity of the English formula. Therefore, in what follows, we will use the French expressions in order to avoid confusion.

Those who make a clear distinction between *liberté du travail* and *droit au travail* usually have a false idea of the origins of the latter. They associate it with the rise of syndicalism and the labour movement. In this respect, the *droit au travail* appeared only relatively recently: at the end of the 19th century and the beginning of the 20th. When related to human rights, it should indeed be conceived as belonging to the so-called "second generation" of these rights (and thus is of a later date than its first generation – the *droits-liberté* of the bourgeois revolutions). But in fact, the *droit au travail* actually emerged much earlier, as this contribution will show, with the principal date being 1848, and the context being the revolution that was happening at that time in France (the expression *droit au travail* and its distinction from the *liberté du travail* is thus related to French history). All the arguments, pro or contra, that have since been called upon in the discussion of this right were already present in the debate that took place that year in the French National Assembly.[1] One could even argue that all subsequent debates on the subject are merely footnotes to that "moment 48". This observation implies that an anamnesis of the content of that debate could stimulate, in a very important way, contemporary discussions on activation policies for the unemployed.

---

[1] I have analysed in detail the arguments used in that debate in my book *Le droit au travail entre histoire et utopie*, Brussels-Florence, Publications des Facultés universitaires Saint-Louis, 1989. The present article is based on it.

I. Precursory Ideas

Before 1848 there had already been some revealing "anticipations" of the matter. Perhaps the most important example is the preamble, written by the "physiocrat" Turgot, to the edict of 1776 concerning the abolition of the *jurandes et communautés de commerce, arts et métiers* (i.e. the corporatist organisation of labour).[2] In fact, Turgot's efforts would first fail, before being successfully renewed during the French Revolution. Admittedly, in his preamble Turgot employs the expression *droit de travailler* (the right to engage in work): there is neither mention of the *droit au travail* (the right to work) nor of the *liberté du travail* (the freedom of work) and there is no question of any opposition between them. In fact, Turgot's liberalism is inspired by a naïve optimism (a characteristic, for that matter, of the "enlightened" liberalism of his time): its presupposition is that the liberation of labour relations, through deregulation, would automatically ensure full employment – a credible presupposition at that time given that liberalism had not yet undergone the "test of reality". Nonetheless, one can say that Turgot's *droit de travailler*, considered the reasoning sustaining his defence of it, virtually contains the *droit au travail*.

Indeed, in his preamble, Turgot states: "the right to engage in work (*droit de travailler*) is the property of every man and that property is the first, the most sacred and the most imprescriptible of all".[3] The enjoyment of this right must be ensured above all else for those who are especially in need of it: the people whose only property is their work and for whom it constitutes the sole resource of their subsistence. Thus, the *droit de travailler* is intimately linked with the most fundamental right: the right to live. If there exists a property that has to be guaranteed for all men, it is the property of work, because for the poor work is the only means – given the fact that it is their sole property – of achieving their right to live. Alluding to the conceptions of taxation that obliged the individual to pay preliminary duties in order to obtain permission to work, Turgot places emphasis on the incompatibility between the corporatist organisation of labour and the guarantee of the right to live: "Some people have even said that the right to engage in work is a royal right, a right that the king can sell and that the citizens must buy. We insist that we reject such a kind of maxim [...]. In consequence, we want to abrogate those arbitrary institutions that do not allow the poor to make a living from their work".[4]

---

[2] The text of the preamble can be consulted in A. Franklin, *Dictionnaire des arts, métiers et professions*, Paris, Welter, 1906, pp. 293 et seq.

[3] "Le droit de travailler est la propriété de tout homme et cette propriété est la première, la plus sacrée et la plus imprescriptible de toutes".

[4] "On a été jusqu'à dire que le droit de travailler était un droit royal, que le prince pouvait vendre et que les sujets devaient acheter. Nous nous hâtons de rejeter une

So, Turgot does not define the *droit de travailler* as a liberty but as a property. This is significant, given that this manner of presenting things undeniably has social implications. Indeed, on the one hand the State has a duty to protect everyone's property; on the other hand, work is the first property, and, for the poor, the indispensable means to ensure their right to live. This property is maintained through the possibility to dispose of one's body, of the ability to work that it implies and of what it yields by its work. In relation to it, the status of the property of things is thus a subordinate one: to be able to dispose of things is an indispensable condition for maintaining life, and especially for the poor, it is a necessary instrument for the conservation of the body as a labour force. From this viewpoint, things are merely, as products, an extension of the "working body". Meanwhile, to dispose of them, to consume them, constitutes a vital necessity, in order to reproduce that body. Consequently, one needs to ensure for everyone a real capability to dispose of that part of the world of things constituted by the means of consumption required for the satisfaction of vital needs.

But more precisely, the poor are owners of their work only insofar as their body represents a potential labour force. In the absence of a job, they cannot enjoy "their" property. As their sole resource is their potential work, they do not dispose automatically or evidently of the things that ensure at least the conservation of their body. Now, if on the one hand the right to live requires that the property of work guarantees that everyone disposes of that part of the world of things corresponding to the necessity of the process of life, and if it is a duty of the State to protect the property of all citizens, and if on the other hand the life of the poor can only be maintained by the property of work, then it follows that the State, in order to protect that property, must prevent the poor from being jobless, and, if necessary, supply them with a job when circumstances require it. To guarantee the right to live of the poor, to ensure that they are able to reproduce their labour force, has thus an undeniable implication. In case they do not succeed in hiring out their labour force on the market, i.e. if the market fails to procure them the necessary jobs, the State itself will have to supply them, in a direct manner, with a job. In other words, the *droit de travailler* contains the germ of the *droit au travail* – even if Turgot, given his optimistic view of liberalism, does not effectively realise that the latter is implied in the former.

This conclusion will impose itself a few years later, in the course of the French Revolution. Admittedly, while the *droit au travail* for the able-bodied poor does then become an issue, in practical terms the results

---

pareille maxime [...]. Nous voulons en conséquence abroger ces institutions arbitraires qui ne permettent pas à l'indigent de vivre de son travail".

are rather meagre. The reason being that its discussion is not really a priority at the time. There are more urgent problems, and the question of the *droit au travail* is drowned out amidst an ocean of other reforms and revolutionary measures. Nevertheless, even Le Chapelier, in the presentation of his famous "loi anti-ouvrière" (anti-poor laws), leaves no doubt on the subject: the abolition of the corporatist organisation of labour should not cause fears concerning the subsistence of the people, for "it is the nation that has to supply jobs for those who need them for their subsistence".[5] This is moving clearly in the direction of the *droit au travail*, even if this implication will soon be suppressed. Indeed, during the 19th century the *loi Le Chapelier*, which abolished corporations, was mostly being used as a tool to ban strikes and other forms of trade unionist struggles, and even to forbid the mere existence of trade unions. That it has been considered retrospectively as a weapon against the working class rests nonetheless on a one-sided interpretation.

II. *Droit au travail* Versus *liberté du travail*

While the *droit au travail* is merely a minor detail in the dramatic course of events of the great French Revolution, in 1848 it represents what is really at stake in the change of regime that is by now taking place (following the overthrowing of the *Monarchie de Juillet*, installed in 1830). Its immediate cause is an economic crisis related to the recent industrial revolution and its consequences, which has translated into massive unemployment among the working class. Initially the provisional government of the time employs some measures to supply work for the unemployed. By way of the *ateliers nationaux* (national workshops), as they are called, it tries to respond to what constitutes the priority of the moment. But because these measures inevitably take an improvised form, they provoke a lot of criticism. They arouse unanimous disapproval among leftist politicians, who say that the "ateliers nationaux" serve only to make a mockery of work. In the words of Proudhon, work in these ateliers is reduced to *remuer de la boue* (indeed it consisted mainly of levelling soil).[6] In other words, all this improvisation is merely *aumône déguisée* (disguised charity).[7]

Louis Blanc, a member of the provisional government and a socialist, had in fact recommended a very different approach: he had supported

---

[5] "C'est à la nation de fournir des travaux à ceux qui en ont besoin pour leur existence" (quoted by H. Hatzfeld, *Du paupérisme à la sécurité sociale*, Paris, Colin, 1971, p. 193).

[6] See F. Tanghe, *Le droit au travail entre histoire et utopie, op. cit.*, p. 65.

[7] L. Blanc, *Histoire de la révolution de 1848*, Vol. II, Paris, Marpin & Flammarion, 1880, p. 127.

the creation of *ateliers sociaux* (social workshops) within which the workers would fulfil, instead of some kind of unskilled labour, a job that corresponded to their professional qualifications. According to Blanc, these workshops would be the presages of a new organisation of labour. But opponents to the *droit au travail* sowed confusion by presenting the *ateliers nationaux* as the practical application of a socialist doctrine. In doing so, they tried to discredit the left, and they succeeded: in the eyes of a large part of the population, the *droit au travail* soon became synonymous with subsidised idleness. After a few months of provisional government, elections heralded a victory for the conservative forces and once in government the new majority soon decided to close down the *ateliers nationaux*. The decision provoked an insurrection of the workers, which in turn was followed by a ferocious repression by the army and the national guard. It is against this backdrop that, during the autumn of 1848, the parliamentary debate around the new Constitution takes place, particularly concerned with the question of whether or not the *droit au travail* should be part of it.

During this debate, the *droit au travail* and its implications are discussed from every conceivable angle. As two frankly opposed camps take form – its supporters versus its adversaries ("socialists versus liberals" in what follows)[8] – every argument for or against the *droit au travail* that has ever been used since is scrutinised. In the eyes of the liberal camp, the *droit au travail* destroys the *liberté du travail*, whereas for the other camp the former is a condition of the realisation of the latter. While the first camp pretends that the *droit au travail* is incompatible with the right to property, the second is convinced it is the condition of its generalisation. The liberals denounce the *droit au travail* as an undue "juridification" of moral demands, and call it insane because it undermines the moral value of behaviours. The socialists answer this reproach by saying that an economic system that does not recognise this right turns immorality into an inescapable law, for it stifles every moral commitment from the side of the workers. According to liberals, the *droit au travail* stands in the way of economic growth and is thus a stumbling block to progress, while according to the socialists it furthers both.

In fact, all these arguments, for and against, bear witness to an emerging awareness: the realisation that the "enlightened" liberalism such as that which had been supported by, and since, Turgot, contained insurmountable antinomies. 1848 sees the antinomic character of this "well-tempered" kind of liberalism of the Enlightenment finally come

---

[8] In fact, the opposition was a bit more complicated: a coalition of the socialists and republicans of that time on the one hand versus a coalition of liberals and conservatives on the other.

into focus. This also explains why its inheritors split into two opposing camps. What is more, it is interesting to note that both of these camps invoke Turgot in order to strengthen their position. They both highlight certain implications of Turgot's vision but, as they do it in a selective way, the incompatibility of these implications and their contradictory nature is exposed. In other words, one witnesses the breaking up of enlightened liberalism through the emergence of two kinds of rights and their opposition, the *droits-liberté* and the *droits-créance*. The opposition of the *liberté du travail* and the *droit au travail* is a privileged example of this scission. I will concentrate the rest of this text on these two (and leave out the other aspects of the debate).[9]

Let us first consider the point of view of the liberals: that the *droit au travail* destroys the *liberté du travail*. In the first step of their argumentation, they note that the *droit au travail* implies a claim on the State that is incompatible with the reciprocity required by contractual relations. The workers acquire a right to demand from the State that it supplies them with a job, whereas the State has no right to demand that they look for a job by themselves in order to provide autonomously for their subsistence. Thus, it is a unilateral duty imposed by the working class on the State, not a contract committing two parties. The State is exclusively the servant, while the working class becomes the master. The *droit au travail* creates a privilege (in the sense of the *Ancien Régime*, i.e. of a lasting nature) in favour of a particular class and at the expense of the rest of the citizens. In other words, an *aristocratie des prolétaires* (aristocracy of proletarians) would emerge. This could only stimulate a mentality of selfishness and egocentrism among the workers. The *amour du travail* (love of work) will vanish and personal effort will give way to a spiralling development of demands ending up in civil war. Indeed, the *droit au travail* not only favours class struggle, it is also itself an awesome weapon for its pursuit. It gives the workers a collective right over the State, transforming it into the exclusive instrument of their interests. In doing so, the State becomes their representative *vis-à-vis* the class that detains the means of production, with the inevitable result being the expropriation of capital.

In the second step of their argumentation, the liberals draw attention to the negative effect that the *droit au travail* will have on the workers themselves. From a privilege it will soon turn into their enslavement. Indeed, if the State must guarantee them a job, this will only be possible through the complete regulation of labour (and thus economic planning). The State will become the sole entrepreneur. This implies, as a fatal

---

[9] For a more detailed approach, I may refer to my book *Le droit au travail entre histoire et utopie, op. cit.*

consequence, that the formation and repartition of the labour forces will be imposed from the top, by authoritarian means. A monopolistic State will decide which kind of work people will have to perform, where and when they will be hired, with this all depending on needs that are defined exclusively by bureaucrats. Thus, no more free choice of profession and contractual partnership, no more free mobility of labour forces, no more consideration of individual merit and distinction of talent. The result for the workers will be the unconditional subjection to regulations over which they will not have the slightest control. At the end of this road, every kind of work metamorphoses into forced labour, comparable to that imposed in penitentiaries. In other words, society would transform itself into an immense prison.

Let us look now at the arguments from the other camp. According to the viewpoint of the socialists, the *droit au travail* is the only way to give the *liberté du travail* any effective content. Contrary to what the liberals pretend, it is an indispensable condition for making this liberty universal. Indeed, in the absence of the *droit au travail* the so-called *"liberté" du travail* consecrates the domination of a capitalist class, leaving the workers with no other choice than to experience conditions of work and wages dictated by their boss or else face death by deprivation. In fact, in such circumstances, for the working class, the *liberté du travail* masks a denial of the right to live. So this right is no longer a universal right, guaranteed for all men. Moreover, the power relationships in the factories are such that the bosses can impose on the workers conditions of labour that are tantamount to camouflaged homicide. No invocation of the *liberté du travail* or of contractual liberty can justify such violations of the right to live, which moreover annul all real liberty. In the absence of the *droit au travail*, the *liberté du travail* conflicts with the right to live, which is precisely the preliminary condition of all liberties, and thus also of a real *liberté du travail*. Louis Blanc summarises this way of thinking as follows: if some people monopolise the means of production and thus the power to fulfil the right to live, then humanity splits into two classes of people, with one selling life and the other reduced to buying it. Here we can see an analogy between this reasoning and that of Turgot: for the latter, the evil consisted of the fact that the poor were forced to buy their right to work, and thus to live, from the sovereign. In the eyes of Blanc, it resides in the fact that the worker is forced to buy his right to work, and thus to live, from the capitalist classes.[10]

So then, the *liberté du travail*, in the absence of *droit au travail*, is merely a pseudo-liberty for the workers. The employment contract is a weapon that the capitalists use in order to destroy the liberty of the weak.

---

[10] J.-M. Humilière, *Louis Blanc*, Paris, Editions ouvrières, 1982, pp. 96 and 117.

The worker, by hiring out his labour force, not only forfeits the right to dispose of the product of his work; he sells himself, his own person, to the capitalist, for he becomes a thing consumed by the latter. The capitalist, indeed, is the only one who disposes of the body of the worker in the course of the working day and so, the worker is no longer a subject with rights, but an ingredient of capital abandoned to their employers' despotism. In this way, it is not only the free disposition of one's work that disappears; even one's health and physical integrity are threatened with annihilation. Contractual liberty conceals the waste and destruction of the labour forces. And even then, the worker must first succeed in selling that force. The *liberté du travail* is not even a dependable way to provide alienating work, for the logic of competition entails involuntary unemployment. It is thus not enough for the worker to be simply disposed to work. Even if he does not ask for any better, competition on the labour market will very often prevent even alienating work. The murderous nature of the laws of competition will force the workers to kill each other. Under these circumstances, the *droit de travailler* is no longer a right, for the *liberté du travail* turns into a privilege. So, if one wants to generalise Turgot's *droit de travailler*, one must admit the *droit au travail*; and if the *liberté du travail* supposes that everyone is really able to work, then the *droit au travail* is a condition *sine qua non* of that liberty.

III. Work or Suitable Work?

For its supporters, replacing the *droit au travail* with a *droit à l'assistance* (right to assistance) disconnected from the exercise of a job is not an issue either: there is no equivalence between them. As Louis Blanc writes, "on what can the right to assistance be based? Obviously on the principle that every man received by birth the right to live from God. Now, it is exactly that principle that bases the right to work. If men have the right to live, obviously they must have a right to the means of preserving their life. And what is that means? Work. To admit the right of assistance but not the right to work is to recognise the right of men to lead an unproductive life, whereas in the meantime one refuses them the right to lead a productive life; it means that one consecrates their existence as a burden and refuses it as employment, which is a noteworthy absurdity".[11]

---

[11] "Sur quoi peut reposer le droit à l'assistance? Evidemment sur ce principe que tout homme, en naissant, a reçu de Dieu le droit de vivre. Or, voilà le principe qui, justement, fonde le droit au travail. Si l'homme a droit à la vie, il faut bien qu'il ait droit au moyen de la conserver. Ce moyen, quel est-il? Le travail. Admettre le droit à l'assistance et non le droit au travail, c'est reconnaître à l'homme le droit de vivre improductivement, quand on ne lui reconnaît pas le droit de vivre productivement; c'est consacrer son existence comme charge, quand on refuse de la consacrer comme

This problem had already been discussed during the French Revolution with the conclusion being more or less the same: concerning the able-bodied poor, a right to assistance without work was out of the question. Doing so would have meant granting them a *droit à l'aumône* (right to charity), where instead it should be a matter of supplying, in case of and in times of necessity (involuntary unemployment, economic crisis), some kind of work. But this point of view was, at that time, inspired by the suspicion that the jobless able-bodied poor were idlers, or even parasites, or at least that there existed among them an undeniable penchant for avoiding steady work. In this perspective, pretending that the State must supply them with work was part of a discourse aimed at legitimising the repression of mendicancy. On the other hand, the only aim of the work supplied by the State was to satisfy the elementary needs of the poor: it was conceived merely as a means of survival. From that point of view, the nature or the content of the work was not important at all: it was supposed to guarantee merely an impersonal right to survival, and as such any unqualified or rudimentary job fitted its purpose. There was no need for more or better.

Concerning the content of work, the landscape profoundly evolves in 1848. Supporters of the *droit au travail* no longer suspect the workers of being an idle class, on the contrary: the workers themselves reject the *droit à l'aumône* as humiliating. Consequently, they claim the right to live as productive subjects, as if they had interiorised their devotion to work to the point of seeing it as an obvious sign of nobility. For instance, Félix Pyat makes clear, in the name of the workers, that work is neither a servitude nor a divine punishment or disgrace. It is, in his words, "a gift from God to men in order to improve themselves. When God said to them: you will work, it is as if He had said: you will fulfil yourselves, you will be the sons of your work, the creator of yourselves. Work is thus a divine means that frees the worker from deprivation, makes him master of nature and raises him up to the majesty of the Creator".[12]

Obviously, from this point of view, work can no longer be conceived simply as a means to satisfy man's elementary needs, in order to merely survive. From this point forward, the aim of life is the self-realisation of

---

emploi, ce qui est d'une remarquable absurdité" (L. Blanc, *Le socialisme. Droit au travail*, Paris, Bureau du Nouveau Monde, 1849, p. 54).

[12] "Un don que Dieu a fait à l'homme pour le perfectionner. Quand Dieu a dit à l'homme: tu travailleras, c'est comme s'il lui avait dit: tu t'achèveras, tu seras le fils de tes œuvres, ton propre auteur. Le travail est donc un moyen divin qui l'affranchit [l'ouvrier] du besoin, qui lui soumet la nature, et qui l'élève jusqu'à la majesté du Créateur" (quoted in J. Garnier (ed.), *Le droit au travail à l'Assemblée nationale. Recueil complet de tous les discours prononcés dans cette mémorable discussion*, Paris, Guillaumin, 1848, p. 407).

the individual. Hence, work becomes the means *par excellence* of the latter, the high road to the self-fulfilment of man, and consequently man's most fundamental need. This perspective implies that the *droit au travail* is different from and much more than a simple right to subsistence. It becomes the right of every individual to suitable work, i.e. work that takes into account their training, their capacities and their talents. This point of view, moreover, is shared by the liberal camp: although they reject the *droit au travail* for other reasons, for the liberals it makes sense only if it is conceived as an individual right responding to the profession of its beneficiary and including the recognition of one's talents – also in terms of remuneration.

One could wonder if, in this perspective, the *droit au travail* also supposes that one accepts the social division of work in its existing form and its "spontaneous" development. In this case, as Adolphe Thiers remarks, one should even provide a sufficient clientele, for example, to lawyers and doctors in cases wherein this would appear necessary. To proceed otherwise in such circumstances would be a discrimination.[13] On the other hand, if one reasons in the perspective of their social utility, many kinds of work seem rather questionable. Should one recognise for every individual (poor or rich for that matter) the right to a job that suits him, howsoever whimsical it may be, under the pretext that it is his own way of self-fulfilment? The alternative – certainly not very appealing – consists of an authoritarian definition of needs in the context of a planned economy, with the consequence being that self-fulfilment must be reduced to the development of a limited number of aptitudes and socially desirable talents.

If one considers the way things have evolved since 1848, one must admit that the left – or at least its social-democratic wing – has refused this alternative, and in so doing has implicitly subscribed to the demands of a productivist logic and of a consumer society, including the implications of these concerning the way one defines the *droit au travail*. But that is another story...

---

[13] J. Garnier (ed.), *Le droit au travail à l'Assemblée nationale, op. cit.*, p. 216.

Political-Philosophical Perspectives on the Duty to Work in Activation Policies for the Unemployed

Renaat Hoop

Introduction

The Western welfare states, which were structurally developed after the Second World War, came under ideological fire at the end of the 1970s and the beginning of the 1980s. The debate concerning the scope and the appropriate shape of the welfare state has not stopped raging since and has resulted in multiple attempts to remodel the arrangements of the social security system at the backbone of that welfare state.

Since the 1990s, most of the suggestions put forward in this respect have revolved around active labour market policies and activation.[1] The central idea of this new policy paradigm is that the welfare state should not limit itself to passively granting benefits but should actively strive to get the unemployed (re)integrated into the labour market. With the help of employment services, one wants to encourage jobseekers to become more active in their efforts to find work and improve their employability. Key examples of activation programmes are requirements for unemployed people to attend intensive interviews with employment counsellors, to independently search for job vacancies and apply for jobs, to participate in the formulation of an individual action plan, to participate in training or job-creation programmes. In this way, one hopes to kill two birds with one stone: more people in work serves the economic viability of the system as a whole and leads to an increase in social participation.

At first glance this strategy seems perfectly sound. It may not even be considered very innovative, since the willingness to look for a job and to become self-supporting again has long been a basic principle of our welfare

---

[1] See for instance W. Eichhorst, O. Kaufmann and R. Konle-Seidl (eds.), *Bringing the Jobless into Work? Experiences with Activation Schemes in Europe and the US*, Berlin/Heidelberg, Springer-Verlag, 2008; A. Serrano Pascual and L. Magnusson (eds.), *Reshaping Welfare States and Activation Regimes in Europe*, Brussels, P.I.E.-Peter Lang, 2007; L. Lodemel and H. Trickey (eds.), *An Offer You Can't Refuse: Workfare in International Perspective*, Bristol, The Policy Press, 2000.

arrangements, especially in the arrangements based on the insurance principle, like most unemployment benefits schemes.[2] However, a certain wariness seems to be in place for activation programmes differing from free public employment services in that the mandatory character of the participation in these programmes is more clearly and explicitly stressed and sanctioned. Key features of such strategies are to reinforce and expand availability for work and mutual obligation requirements, meaning that benefit recipients are expected to engage in active job searching and improve their employability, in exchange for receiving efficient employment services and benefit payments. "These strategies aim to apply the principle of 'mutual obligations', and in particular to monitor benefit recipients' compliance with eligibility conditions and implement, when necessary, temporary sanctions or benefit exclusions".[3] This so-called mutual obligation approach of the activation policies clearly comes down to a reinforcement of the duty to work for those who receive social benefits and hence entail a possible redress of the balance between rights and duties for benefit recipients.

But activation policies also imply, at least in principle, an increased commitment from public employment services: they are given a more active role themselves as well. Their main task is not only to guarantee the correct payment of legally defined benefits but also to help the unemployed to (re)integrate in the labour market by offering them tailor-made solutions and programmes to overcome any observed impediments thereto. Their role seems to be remodelled, from redistributor to stimulator and regulator.

Finally, activation programmes seem to be focusing very one-sidedly on paid work in the formal labour market. In this respect, one should not forget that the existence of social security schemes (and even of the welfare state in general) has until now often been described (and even justified) as a way of protecting citizens from the negative impact and the inequalities caused by the market mechanism within a capitalistic production method and as a means of ensuring them financial autonomy outside the labour market. An element of decommodification seems to

---

[2] D. Pieters, *Aan het werk... Beschouwingen over het arbeidsethos in het socialezekerheidsrecht van vandaag en morgen*, Deventer, Kluwer, 1986, p. 5. In social security arrangements that are not based on the principles of insurance and contributions by employees such as the social assistance schemes, conditionality in terms of availability for work requirements is much less self-evident. Since these minimum provisions were set up to protect all residents or citizens from poverty for the sake of human dignity, requirements set by way of reciprocity could also be directed at other activities than paid work in the formal labour market such as informal and volunteer work, care, etc. or could even be totally absent.

[3] OECD, *Employment Outlook 2007*, Paris, OECD Publishing, 2007, p. 208.

have been an essential element of our welfare state construction.[4] The inevitable (and according to some even necessary) economic inequalities caused by the axioms of competition and individual self-reliance of the market are tempered or compensated (and therefore acceptable) by a certain equality outside the market, i.e. by the social rights acquired and guaranteed via our membership to society, that is, as a citizen.[5] If the main goal of social security schemes becomes a forced orientation towards the labour market – an evolution, a moving away from decommodification to recommodification – as seems to be the case in activation strategies, this compromise between economic efficiency and social justice might be at jeopardy.

In short, the possible changes brought about by activation policies appear to be more than mere technical adjustments of welfare programmes. They may represent new ideas about the goals of public policy and the respective role and commitments of public services and benefit recipients. For that reason, some critical reflection is in place. In this contribution, I want to present a political-philosophical approach as an assessment framework for critically reflecting on the activation policies and the reinforced duty to work they lead to, for it is my conviction that policy choices, especially in the social domain, are implicitly or explicitly, consciously or unconsciously, determined or influenced by underlying philosophical or ideological views. When, as in the case of activation policies, a policy choice is felt as an important shift, it may be useful to check to what extent the underlying philosophy or ideology has equally changed in order to be able to fully assess the impact of the policy change. Therefore, I have selected four major schools of thought in political philosophy – liberalism and social liberalism, communitarianism and republicanism – and I have tried to distinguish between their visions on citizenship. Defined as the double relationship between the citizen and his government and between the citizen and his fellow citizens, citizenship is a useful concept to bring back these larger political-philosophical or ideological views into a well-defined citizenship ideal and to bring to the fore the concrete expectations these views hold with regard to the actual behaviour of citizens.

---

[4] Decommodification is a concept used by the Scandinavian social scientist G. Esping-Andersen in his typology of welfare states. If people have to turn to the market in order to provide for themselves, they are commodified; if they are not dependent upon the market, he talks about decommodification: G. Esping-Andersen, *The Three Worlds of Welfare Capitalism*, Cambridge, Polity Press, 1990, pp. 35-54.

[5] One of the oldest and most elaborate analysis of this kind can be found in T.H. Marshall's well-known essay *Citizenship and Social Class* presented in 1949 in Cambridge: T.H. Marshall, "Citizenship and Social Class", in T.H. Marshall, *Class, Citizenship and Social Development* (1950), Westport, Greenwood Press, 1976, pp. 65-122.

In the following section, I will first elaborate on my use of the concept of citizenship and then describe the citizenship views that I deduced from the earlier mentioned schools of thought in political philosophy (I.). In a subsequent section, I will use these citizenship views as the framework for a critical analysis of the activation policies for the unemployed (II.). I will end my contribution with some general concluding remarks.

I. Political Philosophies and Views on Citizenship

By selecting only four major schools of thought in political philosophy, I have of course chosen not to retain some views and theories as distinct or relevant schools of thought. This is not problematic in my view, however, since what is important for my purpose is not to be able to present an accurate categorisation of all political-philosophical views,[6] but to dispose of a number of distinct and coherent lines of reasoning that sufficiently represent the dominant contemporary views in political philosophy and can function as an adequate framework for assessment. Since the liberal-communitarian debate has been dominant in political philosophy for the last few decades, choosing liberalism and communitarianism as relevant schools of thought was quite obvious. I have supplemented these with social liberalism, an important and popular variant of liberalism, and with republicanism, which has gained increasing attention in recent years. I believe that these four schools of thought sufficiently cover the dominant lines of reasoning in today's Western societies.

Moreover, even if a certain view or tradition is not mentioned as a distinct political philosophy, its main arguments or viewpoints may well be (partially or wholly) incorporated in the schools of thought that I have distinguished.[7] I am also fully aware of the fact that I have done great

---

[6] This seems to be in any case an almost impossible task since there exists no broad agreement on the exact categorisation of political-philosophical theories. For instance, republicanism can be dealt with as a separate school of thought but can also be seen as a variant of communitarianism (M. Bovens, "Het communitarisme als catch all stroming", in M. Bovens, H. Pelikaan and M. Trappenburg (eds.), *Nieuwe tegenstellingen in de Nederlandse politiek*, Meppel/Amsterdam, Boom, 1998, pp. 146-164; W. Kymlicka, *Contemporary Political Philosophy. An Introduction*, 2nd edition, Oxford, Oxford University Press, 2001, p. 298), while others even consider it a type of, or at least consistent with liberalism (R. Dagger, *Civic Virtues: Rights, Citizenship and Republican Liberalism*, Oxford, Oxford University Press, 1997). The same accounts of course for attempts to categorise different authors within these lines of thinking since certain authors have been claimed by more than one of them at the same time.

[7] Socialism, for example, is not present in my framework as a distinct political philosophy but its viewpoints with regard to the welfare state are to my opinion sufficiently incorporated and represented by what I describe as social liberalism. Since socialism has evolved towards social democracy, its distinction from liberal egalitarianism or left-liberal democracy has faded. Indeed, John Rawls himself, who I myself will describe as a

injustice to the different nuances that exist in every school of thought and that probably not everyone will agree with my delimitations. But in order to be able to use them as an evaluative instrument, I had to reconstruct these philosophies into forms of ideal types and look for the greatest common denominator. I have tried to do this by deriving from these philosophies their view on citizenship because, as I will demonstrate, this concept makes it possible to concentrate on the expectations philosophies hold with regard to the actual behaviour of citizens. For that matter, citizenship has been a popular concept both in political philosophy and in sociological literature on the welfare state.

In sociology, citizenship has always been a central idea in studies of the welfare state. This is mainly due to the British sociologist T.H. Marshall, who conquered the concept, as it were, for social sciences and, by adding a social element, directly related it to the origins of the welfare state. But also in more recent writings concerning the crisis of the welfare state, citizenship and civic duty have been omnipresent concepts.[8] And rightly so. When the welfare state constitutes an arena that involves, more than anything, questions of social structure and processes of social reproduction, the defining of the relationship between government, society and citizenry, and the establishment of the living conditions of citizens,[9] citizenship is truly the perspective from which to tackle these matters.

In political theory and philosophy, citizenship acquired a renewed interest in the 1990s.[10] Kymlicka gives a twofold explanation for this

---

social liberal, has said that his conception of justice can be described as either left liberal or social democratic (J. Rawls, *Political Liberalism*, New York, Columbia University Press, 1993, p. 416). Conversely, many social democratic parties have explicitly cited Rawls in developing and defending their platforms (W. Kymlicka, *Contemporary Political Philosophy, op. cit.*, p. 195). Note, however, that also republicanism is said by some to "look promising as an inspiration for a post social critique" and to be able to constitute "a restatement of socialist criticisms of market society" (G.F. Gaus, "Backwards into the Future: Neorepublicanism as a Postsocialist Critique of Market Society", in E.F. Paul, F.D. Miller and J. Paul (eds.), *After Socialism*, Social Philosophy and Policy, volume 20, part 1, Cambridge, Cambridge University Press, 2003, pp. 64-65). Pettit as well seems convinced of "the socialist attractions of the republican ideal" and indicates that "the ideal of freedom as non-domination ought […] to be congenial to socialists" (P. Pettit, *Republicanism. A Theory of Freedom and Government*, Oxford, Oxford University Press, 1997, pp. 142-143).

[8] For example, H. Coenen and P. Leisink, *Work and Citizenship in the New Europe*, Aldershot, Edward Elgar, 1993; L. Mead, *Beyond Entitlement: the Social Obligations of Citizenship*, New York, Free Press, 1986; M. Roche, *Rethinking Citizenship. Welfare, Ideology and Change in Modern Society*, Cambridge, Polity Press, 1992.

[9] J.M. Roebroek and M. Hertog, *De beschavende invloed des tijds. Twee eeuwen sociale politiek, verzorgingsstaat en sociale zekerheid in Nederland*, Den Haag, Vuga, 1998, p. 17.

[10] R. Beiner (ed.), *Theorizing Citizenship*, Albany, State University of New York Press, 1995; A. Hemerijck, J. Simonis and P. Lehning, "De herontdekte burger", in J. Simonis,

"explosion of interest".[11] First of all, citizenship provides a concept that is able to integrate the demands of liberal justice and community membership and can mediate the ongoing debate between liberals and communitarians. Secondly, interest in citizenship has also been sparked by a number of political events and trends – amongst which is criticism of the welfare state and welfare dependency – that have made clear that the health and stability of a modern democracy also depends on the qualities and attitudes of its citizens. In short, also in political philosophy the concept of citizenship seems to have given an impetus for a new dynamic of ideas that can serve as a frame of reference to thoroughly discuss actual social problems.

But what does the notion of citizenship exactly stands for? Citizenship has mostly been conceived of as a rather passive status of rights, referring to the citizen in his relationship to the government (citizenship-as-legal-status). Citizenship then merely stands for a bundle of rights the citizen can claim *vis-à-vis* his government. But when we want to use this concept in order to illuminate underlying expectations with regard to a citizens' practice, we need to broaden it and add a more active component that also gives room for the possible responsibilities and virtues of the citizen towards his fellow citizens (citizenship-as-desirable-activity).[12] In this vision, citizenship refers both to a vertical axis (the position of the citizen in his relationship with the authorities) as to an horizontal axis (the relationship with his fellow citizens or the community) and thus reflects a triangular relationship between citizen, community and government.[13] A vision on citizenship then gives a prescriptive and specific interpretation of this vertical and horizontal relationship. It holds an idealistic expectation with regard to the concrete conduct of the citizen in this double relationship.[14] Where a political philosophy offers a global view on the way society and state should ideally be organised, the citizenship view we can extract from it holds an idealistic picture of a citizen practice based on the two aforementioned axes.[15]

  A. Hemerijck and P. Lehning (eds.), *De staat van de burger. Beschouwingen over hedendaags burgerschap*, Meppel, Boom, 1992, pp. 9-24; W. Kymlicka and W. Norman, "Return of the Citizen: a Survey of Recent Work on Citizenship Theory", *Ethics*, Vol. 104, No. 2, 1994, pp. 352-381.

[11] W. Kymlicka, *Contemporary Political Philosophy*, op. cit., pp. 284-285.

[12] W. Kymlicka and W. Norman, "Return of the Citizen: a Survey of Recent Work on Citizenship Theory", *op. cit.*, pp. 353-355.

[13] In the same sense, R. Lister, *Citizenship: Feminist Perspectives*, London, Macmillan, 1997, p. 3; D. Van Houten, *De standaardmens voorbij. Over zorg, verzorgingsstaat en burgerschap*, Maarssen, Elsevier/De Tijdstroom, 1999, p. 42.

[14] In this sense, H. Van Gunsteren, *Eigentijds burgerschap*, Den Haag, Sdu, 1992, p. IV.

[15] However, this does not mean that each citizenship view will accept the necessity or desirability of this twofold relationship. It is perfectly possible that a citizenship view

It is a basic assumption in this contribution that social policies and changes in social legislation are not neutral but are influenced by and reflect this kind of citizenship views. In the 20th century, Western states evolved from night-watchman states towards modern welfare states, which implied that governments came to actively intervene in ever more fields of society since states wanted to play a key role in the protection and promotion of the economic and social wellbeing of their citizens.[16] The ambition was to mould and modify society or, to use my own terminology, to favour the realisation of a citizen practice. The law has been the instrument *par excellence* in pursuing this goal. Indeed, social (security) law is distinct from other areas of law because of its undeniably steering character. In this area of law, the instrumental use of law and the interpretation of the state as an active intervening state are most clearly visible.

It is my conviction that the public behaviour of citizens (i.e. their behaviour in relation to the government and in relation to their fellow citizens) can be influenced by the way society – through law – has been organised,[17] for social policies and social legislation create possibilities and constraints with regard to the actions of individuals and by consequence favour certain practices at the detriment of others. How we organise our society through legislation changes patterns of behaviour and generates a citizen practice. Major changes in law may be expected to generate or at least favour new citizen practices. As I suggested (in my introduction) that the activation paradigm represents more than a mere technical change in social security arrangements, it is to be expected that this new policy will generate a new citizen practice as well, irrespective of whether this was a deliberately pursued practice or not. An approach of the activation paradigm in terms of citizenship views may clarify what kind of practice(s) this could be.

In order to be able to perform this cross-reference in the next section, I shall here describe and compare these views on the points activation

---

favours a notion of citizenship in which only one of the two axes is established or considered worthwhile. But each view will have to take a stand with regard to this double relationship.

[16] F. Ewald, *L'Etat providence*, Paris, Bernard Grasset, 1986; A. De Swaan, *Zorg en de staat. Welzijn, onderwijs en gezondheidszorg in Europa en de Verenigde Staten in de nieuwe tijd*, Amsterdam, Bert Bakker, 1996.

[17] The extent to which this is the case in reality is a question for sociologists, but the number of sociological studies that focus on the relationship between citizenship and the welfare state (see *supra*, footnote 8) confirms that this interaction is a fact, even if the ascertained practice is not always the one that was expected or hoped for. See for example about the "disincentives" and "adverse effects" of welfare state arrangements: C. Murray, *Losing Ground. American Social Policy 1950-1980*, New York, Basis Books, 1984 and C. Schuyt, *Tegendraadse werkingen. Sociologische opstellen over de onvoorziene gevolgen van verzorging en verzekering*, Amsterdam, Amsterdam University Press, 1995.

policies are likely to effect as I described in my introduction. First, I shall outline the specific ideal of citizenship that is central to each view. Then, I shall examine the general attitude they adopt concerning social security, the welfare state and social rights, both in respect of their existence and their scale, and in respect of their conditional or unconditional nature. I shall also examine to what extent work and participation are relevant issues in the different views on citizenship and what value and meaning is attributed to them in case they are considered relevant.

A. *Liberalism and Social Liberalism*

Classic liberalism as a political philosophy finds its origins in the 17th century ideas of John Locke and has experienced a revival in recent decades, especially in the Anglo-Saxon world, in the form of neo-liberalism or libertarianism through authors like Robert Nozick and Ayn Rand. Social liberalism is a variant of liberalism that became dominant after the Second World War,[18] but that is rooted in the writings of J.S. Mill and disposes over a respectable tradition through authors such as T.H. Green, L.T. Hobhouse, J.A. Hobson, J. Dewey, W.H. Beveridge and J.M. Keynes.[19] John Rawls and Thomas Humphrey Marshall can be cited as the most prominent representatives of social liberalism. The first, because he defended this line of reasoning against its critics in the most fundamental and systematic way;[20] the second, because he described the historical development[21] of the concept of social citizenship from a sociological perspective.[22]

---

[18] R. Voet, "Citizenship and Female Participation", in J. Bussemaker and R. Voet (eds.), *Gender, Participation and Citizenship in the Netherlands*, Ashgate, Aldershot, 1998, p. 13.

[19] J. De Beus, "John Rawls: de burgerlijke samenleving als democratie", in B. Van Klink, P. van Seters and W. Witteveen (eds.), *Gedeelde normen? Gemeenschapsdenken en het recht*, Zwolle, W.E.J. Tjeenk Willink, 1993, p. 81; G.A. van der List, "Het liberalisme na de Franse Revolutie", in P.B. Cliteur, A.A.M. Kinneging and G.A. van der List (eds.), *Filosofen van het klassiek liberalisme*, Kampen, Kok Agora, 1993, p. 181.

[20] B. Van den Brink, "Het recht van de moraal. Liberalisme en communitarisme in de politieke filosofie", in B. Van den Brink and W. van Reijen (eds.), *Het recht van de moraal. Liberalisme en communitarisme in de politieke filosofie*, Bussum, Dick Coutinho, 1994, pp. 10-11; R. Voet, *Feminism and Citizenship, op. cit.*, p. 31.

[21] Marshall divides citizenship rights into three categories, which he sees as having taken hold in England in a progressive and cumulative way in three successive centuries: civil rights, which arose in the 18th century; political rights, which arose in the 19th century; and social rights, which have become established in the 20th century. By guaranteeing civil, political and social rights to all, the liberal-democratic welfare state ensures that every member of society feels like a full member of society, able to participate in and enjoy the common life of society. Where any of these rights are withheld or violated, people will be marginalised and unable to participate.

[22] W. Kymlicka and W. Norman, "Return of the Citizen: a Survey of Recent Work on Citizenship Theory", *op. cit.*, p. 354; R. Voet, *Feminism and Citizenship, op. cit.*, p. 34.

The equal possibility for individuals to autonomously realise their personal life plans is the central value of liberalism and constitutes the heart of its citizenship view. This individual liberty is vital and in its protection lies the *raison d'être* of the government, which should remain neutral in all other respects. No intrinsic value is given to community life and social or political participation is seen as a matter of personal choice. Liberals believe in a spontaneous organisation of society by means of the market mechanism whose laws force the individual to moderate his preferences and to rationally (re)consider them.[23]

Liberalism also leaves it to market forces to decide what work is or can be, whereby work ultimately means paid work. Here, work mainly matters as a key to social trading, as an instrument for obtaining the necessary means to realising one's personal life plan. Although work takes a central position in the liberal view, it is not awarded any intrinsic value nor is it subject to any fundamental assessment. However, one should not lose sight of the fact that the market mechanism also entails some kind of public acknowledgement of what work can mean. Only work that leads to the production of goods and services that are wanted by the market will ultimately matter; work that lacks this characteristic will be marginalised or even completely disappear.

Where the function and meaning of work is concerned, there is no substantial difference between classic liberalism and social liberalism.[24] These lines of thought only maintain different perspectives with regards to the existence of social rights. While classic liberals interpret freedom as negative freedom – that is, the absence of coercion, force or suppression, a freedom *from* – social liberals recognise a notion of positive freedom[25] as the extent to which a person is actually able to make well-considered choices, to lead a self-chosen life – a freedom *to*. To that end, a formal guarantee of freedom is not enough; the material conditions for it should also be fulfilled.[26] And since all citizens have equal rights, the government should guarantee the availability of these necessary resources. In the social liberal view, civil and political rights are by consequence supplemented by social rights.

---

[23] A.A.M. Kinneging, "Inleiding", in P.B. Cliteur, A.A.M. Kinneging, and G.A. van der List (eds.), *Filosofen van het klassiek liberalisme, op. cit.*, p. 16.

[24] With regard to this point, there is however a difference between socialism and social democracy on the one hand and classic and social liberalism on the other. Socialism and social democracy seem to relate better with the communitarian intrinsic moral dimension of work (see *infra*) than with the instrumental liberal view.

[25] For the distinction between positive and negative liberty, see I. Berlin, *Four Essays on Liberty*, London, Oxford University Press, 1969.

[26] J. De Beus, "John Rawls: de burgerlijke samenleving als democratie", *op. cit.*, p. 81; R. Voet, *Feminism and Citizenship*, London, Sage Publications, 1998, p. 33.

Social liberalism can thus be seen as the philosophy or view that best offers a justification for our modern welfare states, since social liberals believe that the government has a role to play in helping individuals realise their own life-plan by making sure that they disposes of a minimum of means thereto. For them, the liberal notion of freedom – notwithstanding the priority of personal responsibility – also implies a guarantee of this minimum of means, regardless or separate from the individual's market position. The social liberal citizenship view undeniably contains an element of decommodification. Classic (and neo-)liberals consider any trade-off between positive and negative freedom unacceptable. They are not prepared to provide anything further than a minimum system of social security in which the emphasis must be on people's own responsibility and ability to manage for themselves. Where classic liberalism leads to a strong conditionality with regard to social benefits, this is not the case for social liberalism. I will further elaborate on this topic of conditionality.[27]

B. *Communitarianism*

The word "communitarianism" refers to a group of authors who, from the 1980s onwards, explicitly reacted against some of the basic assumptions of liberalism that had been given new impetus in John Rawls' *A Theory of Justice*.[28] As a counter-movement, communitarianism is a less consistent and unequivocal school of thought than liberalism.[29] However, creditable attempts have been made to bundle the communitarian ideas into one consistent theory.[30] As important representatives of this school of thought, the following are considered: A. Etzioni, A. MacIntyre, M. Sandel, Ph. Selznick and C. Taylor.

Communitarians focus on the citizenship ideal of making an active contribution to the reinforcement of community life. Here, self-realisation means discovering one's proper place and role within the community, and acquiring and identifying with its traditional values and virtues. This is only possible by taking part in existing practices, by way of social participation.[31] In communitarianism, the perfect citizen is the one

---

[27] Cf. II.A.
[28] J. Rawls, *A Theory of Justice*, Cambridge, Harvard University Press, 1971.
[29] For an overview of this debate between liberals and communitarians: S. Avineri and A. de-Shalit (eds.), *Communitarianism and Individualism*, London, Oxford University Press, 1992; B. Van Klink, P. van Seters and W. Witteveen (eds.), *Gedeelde normen? Gemeenschapsdenken en het recht*, Zwolle, W.E.J. Tjeenk Willink, 1993.
[30] For instance, H.B. Tam, *Communitarianism. A New Agenda for Politics and Citizenship*, London, Macmillan Press, 1998.
[31] R. Voet, *Feminism and Citizenship, op. cit.*, p. 17; I. De Haan, *Zelfbestuur en staatsbeheer. Het politieke debat over burgerschap en rechtsstaat in de twintigste eeuw*, Amsterdam, Amsterdam University Press, 1993, pp. 136-137.

who assumes his responsibilities and engagements as a member of the community, who helps to preserve this community by showing solidarity with his fellow citizens. Contrary to liberals, communitarians do not conceive of the community as the result of a freely concluded contract but they underline its constitutive role for the identity of individuals.

It is that same community that preferably has to enable the provision of mutual care in solidarity, instead of anonymous state authorities. Communitarians believe that by too strongly guaranteeing social rights, the government could undermine the community's ability to provide community care and, hence, endanger its stability. In any case, reciprocity and social responsibility remain keywords. Hence, social rights cannot be unconditional: from each member of the community, an active contribution towards that community is expected. Communitarians call for a greater recognition by citizens of their obligations to society and to one another.[32]

Work is, by consequence, a response to one's social duty; a possibility to express the social responsibility one assumes as part of the community. Work will be relevant and valued when it constitutes a contribution to the development of sustainable forms of community life; when it helps in creating positive effects in terms of social cohesion and inclusion. In communitarianism, activities become work when they need to be accomplished within the specific context of community relations, when they respond to a social need. Our existing labour order can be seen as such a work-creating context, but also accounts for family and social life. Wherever people forge community relations, activities arise that have to be accomplished. For communitarians, work has not only an instrumental value as a means of existence for both the individual and the community at large, but is also a source of recognition. Through our participation in socially relevant work, we can feel appreciated by the community and develop a feeling of self-esteem and a goal in life. On top of the (instrumental) economic dimension comes an intrinsic moral dimension of work.[33] The protection of the latter is important and even takes precedence over a purely materialistic conception of work, since only meaningful work can lead to the communitarian values of social inclusion and self-fulfilment.

---

[32] On this communitarian balance between rights and obligations: A. Etzioni, *The New Golden Rule. Community and Morality in a Democratic Society*, New York, Basic Books, 1997.

[33] H.B. Tam, *Communitarianism. A New Agenda for Politics and Citizenship, op. cit.*, p. 85.

C. Republicanism

Republicanism or civic humanism is largely inspired by the ancient Greeks and Romans and finds its historic roots in authors like Aristotle and Machiavelli. Its contemporary representatives are H. Arendt, B. Barber, A. Oldfield, Ph. Pettit and H. van Gunsteren.

Like the communitarians, republicans highly value community and participation but they confine it to the political community and to political participation.[34] In republicanism, the ability to participate autonomously in public deliberations on the *res publica* is the highest attainable goal. But contrary to communitarianism, republicanism does not expect citizens to share some pre-political cultural practices or traditions. The common good, to be promoted through political participation, is the intrinsic value of political participation itself.[35]

As in liberalism, liberty and equality are important values. But here, equality refers to equality as a public person: the recognition of one's capacity for political judgement and participation. And liberty stands for (collective) self-government (instead of personal independence and civil liberties), also known as the liberty of the ancients, to govern and being governed.[36] An alternative interpretation of this republican version of freedom is liberty as non-domination, put forward by Philip Pettit.[37] According to Pettit, the conception of freedom republicans endorse does not denounce the evil of interference (like liberals do) but rather the evil of domination. Domination means that there is a dominating party that *can* interfere on an arbitrary basis with the choices of the dominated; the dominating party *can* practise interference at will and with impunity. In this sense, one can suffer an absence of freedom even if one does not undergo any actual interference; domination requires only that someone have the capacity to interfere arbitrarily in your affairs.[38] A situation of

---

[34] H. Van Gunsteren, "Vier concepties van burgerschap", in J. Simonis, A. Hemerijck and P. Lehning (eds.), *De staat van de burger. Beschouwingen over hedendaags burgerschap*, op. cit., p. 52; Voet, R., "Citizenship and Female Participation", op. cit., pp. 20-21.

[35] W. Kymlicka and W. Norman, "Return of the Citizen: a Survey of Recent Work on Citizenship Theory", op. cit., pp. 362; W. Kymlicka, *Contemporary Political Philosophy. An Introduction*, op. cit., p. 298.

[36] W. Kymlicka, *Contemporary Political Philosophy. An Introduction*, op. cit., p. 295.

[37] P. Pettit, *Republicanism. A Theory of Freedom and Government*, op. cit., p. 21.

[38] Nor does interference always equals unfreedom in the republican sense since interference can occur without domination. This is the case "...when the interference is not arbitrary and does not represent a form of domination: when it is controlled by the interests and opinions of those affected, being required to serve those interests in a way that conforms with those opinions", such as in "the properly constituted law". P. Pettit, *Republicanism. A Theory of Freedom and Government*, op. cit., p. 35.

non-domination or republican freedom is realised then when a person is more or less immune to arbitrary control.[39]

Access to this republican notion of citizenship (which clearly situates itself in the public domain) requires the possession of some specific virtues. One of these is the ability to detach from the sphere of necessity, the private domain of work and family, because it is supposed to corrupt one's judgement on the political forum. In classic republicanism, work for the purpose of making a living was therefore regarded as an impediment to such participation and was consequently valued negatively.[40] Modern republicans however have proven more moderate and come to the conclusion that inequalities outside the public domain are only acceptable to the extent that they do not block access to and participation in the public sphere. Some corrective action by the authorities in the field of work and social security can thus be justified.[41]

In today's context, paid work or replacement incomes can be considered the functional equivalent of the property requirement that republicans traditionally apply as a condition for the attainment of

---

[39] According to Pettit the importance of democratic participation and control in the republican tradition does not come from any definitional connection with liberty but from the fact that it is a means of furthering liberty as non-domination. P. Pettit, *Republicanism. A Theory of Freedom and Government, op. cit.*, p. 30.

[40] E. MacGilvray, *The Invention of Market Freedom*, Cambridge, Cambridge University Press, 2011, p. 29.

The ancient Greeks like Plato and Aristotle made a distinction between *praxis* and *poièsis*. *Poièsis* was the work done in service of human needs, out of necessity. *Praxis* represented the political and ethical action in the *polis*, the only activity worthy enough to be performed by the true and free citizen.

[41] I. De Haan, *Zelfbestuur en staatsbeheer. Het politieke debat over burgerschap en rechtsstaat in de twintigste eeuw, op. cit.*, p. 175; H.R. Van Gunsteren, *A Theory of Citizenship: Organizing Plurality in Contemporary Democracies*, Boulder, Westview Press, 1998, pp. 106-109; H.R. Van Gunsteren, *Eigentijds burgerschap, op. cit.*, p. 54; P. Pettit, *Republicanism. A Theory of Freedom and Government, op. cit.*, p. 163. However, there seems to be no agreement among republicans with respect to the extent and the manner in which this corrective action should take place. The positions regarding a universal basic income are illustrative in this respect: while van Gunsteren stresses that his neo-republican concept of citizenship does not imply a universal basic income, other republicans rather seem to be in favour of it: I. De Haan, *Zelfbestuur en staatsbeheer. Het politieke debat over burgerschap en rechtsstaat in de twintigste eeuw, op. cit.*, p. 206; B. van Stokkom, *De republiek der weerbaren. Burgerschap, publieke actie en sociaal-democratie*, Houten, Bohn Stafleu Van Loghum, 1992, pp. 137-138; D. Raventos and D. Casassas, "Republicanism and Basic Income: the Articulation of the Public Sphere from the Repoliticization of the Private Sphere", in G. Standing (ed.), *Promoting Income Security as a Right. Europe and North America*, London, Anthem Press, 2004, pp. 229-251.

citizenship status.[42] However, they have added the stipulation that the republican principles of self-government, deliberation and non-domination are also to be respected in the sphere of work. The same applies for social security schemes: a policy that aims to promote citizens' socio-economic independence can only be assessed positively from the perspective of the republican notion of autonomy as long as the facilities in question are not themselves characterised by the possibility of domination or arbitrariness.[43] This means that the way in which welfare is provided should "not foster the dependency mentality or dependency culture of which critics of the welfare state sometimes complain", but also "that welfare be made available under well-established routines, even law-like restraints, not at the discretion of particular authorities".[44]

As mentioned already, the classic republican view on work greatly contrasts with our contemporary view, since work for the purpose of making a living is seen as an impediment to civic virtue. But also for modern republicans like the German-Jewish Hannah Arendt, economic life is still subordinate to political life. Arendt distinguishes three types of activity in the active human life and relates them with different degrees of liberty and humanity.[45] Labour (performed by the *animal laborans*) is merely oriented towards the preservation of life, a biological necessity mankind shares with animals. It is production aimed at immediate consumption. Also work, the activity by which man creates long-term material tools, represents only a limited freedom, since this activity is still subjected to the laws of necessity and characterised by instrumentality. Work creates a kind of public sphere though, a market place where the produced goods can be exchanged. Only action gives room to the ultimate domain of liberty, self-realisation and revelation to others. Action stands for the activity on the public domain where man engages in conversation with others, where he deliberates and ultimately jointly takes action and shapes the human interest by founding and preserving political bodies. Only in this sense can work be a goal in itself.

---

[42] H.R. Van Gunsteren, *A Theory of Citizenship: Organizing Plurality in Contemporary Democracies*, op. cit., pp. 103-104. See E. MacGilvray, *The Invention of Market Freedom*, op. cit., pp. 159-166 for a historical reconstruction of the debate around the question of whether the enjoyment of republican freedom is possible under modern economic conditions after the rise of industrial capitalism.

[43] I. De Haan, *Zelfbestuur en staatsbeheer. Het politieke debat over burgerschap en rechtsstaat in de twintigste eeuw*, op. cit., p. 205; H.R. Van Gunsteren, *A Theory of Citizenship: Organizing Plurality in Contemporary Democracies*, op. cit., p. 108; P. Pettit, *Republicanism. A Theory of Freedom and Government*, op. cit., pp. 161-162.

[44] P. Pettit, *Republicanism. A Theory of Freedom and Government*, op. cit., pp. 160 and 161.

[45] H. Arendt, *The Human Condition*, Chicago, University of Chicago Press, 1958.

By consequence, Arendt is very critical of our modern welfare states in which the *animal laborans* rules and the political domain of action have been completely swallowed up by the private sphere of labour. In her opinion, true human liberty has been destroyed in this way. Other republicans share this criticism and have formulated suggestions to have republican principles introduced in the domain of work and social security. Production should be targeted at social desirable goals and we should organise work in a way that gives more room for autonomy and the taking up of responsibility for the democratic community.[46] With regard to social security, Van Stokkom for example argues that our working status should no longer be the central criterion for claims on benefits and services but that the project of equality, based on the rights and duties of employees in a community of work, should be replaced by a new project of equality, based on the rights and duties of citizens in a political community. In his opinion, this could mean introducing a partial basic income with supplements for those who participate in civilian services or training programmes.[47]

II. Critical Analysis of Activation Policies for the Unemployed

What lessons can be learnt from this comparison of citizenship views based on the main political philosophies? What is their critical potential with regards to activation policies and the elements of our social security system that such policies are likely to affect as distinguished in my introduction: the conditional character of benefits (A.), the focus on labour market participation (B.) and the role of public employment services (C.)?

A. *Conditionality*

A first observation made with regard to the activation paradigm in social policy was the stricter conditionality of benefits: welfare rights are conditional on all kinds of job seeking efforts and benefit recipients are expected to actively engage themselves with the broad offer of services and programmes.

Only social liberalism could be understood as a justifying philosophy for a more comprehensive welfare state in which unconditional benefits are granted. Indeed, it is generally accepted that the social liberal concept

---

[46] I. De Haan, *Zelfbestuur en staatsbeheer. Het politieke debat over burgerschap en rechtsstaat in de twintigste eeuw*, *op. cit.*, p. 200.

[47] B. Van Stokkom, *De republiek der weerbaren. Burgerschap, publieke actie en sociaal-democratie*, *op. cit.*, pp. 137-138.

of citizenship focuses on rights and not duties and considers these rights as unconditional.[48] However, since welfare dependency became an issue from the 1990s onwards, it is remarkable to see how authors have discovered that the principles of personal responsibility and social obligation have actually also always been present in social-liberalism[49] and socialism.[50] Still, it is irrefutable that social liberalism's focus has been on rights and entitlements rather than on obligations or duty.

At first sight, a stricter conditionality could thus be interpreted as an evolution away from a social liberal approach. All other citizenship views accept, or even promote, the conditionality of our welfare state regimes, albeit for different reasons. Consequently, the interpretation of the stronger emphasis on conditionality in terms of my citizenship views will depend on the arguments put forward for it in public discourse.

Classic (and neo-)liberals state that a welfare state should not lead to dependency but should focus on the responsibility to earn a living and support oneself, which is considered a common obligation of all members of society. For that reason, social rights should be limited to a minimum and have strict obligations tied to them. The redress of personal responsibility and self-sufficiency is central here.[51] Indeed, the liberal ideal is precisely to be self-reliant and not be dependent upon anyone's solidarity. Imposing strict obligations oriented at finding paid

---

[48] L.C. Becker, "The Obligation to Work", *Ethics*, Vol. 91, No. 1, 1980, p. 39; J.H. Carens, "Rights and Duties in an Egalitarian Society", *Political Theory*, Vol. 14, No. 1, 1986, p. 31; W. Kymlicka and W. Norman, "Return of the Citizen: A Survey of Recent Work on Citizenship Theory", *op. cit.*, p. 365.

[49] S. White, "Social Rights and the Social Contract. Political Theory and the New Welfare Politics", *British Journal of Political Science*, Vol. 30, No. 3, 2000, pp. 509-512.

[50] G. Mulgan, "Citizens and Responsibilities", in G. Andrews (ed.), *Citizenship*, London, Lawrence & Wishart, 1991, p. 39; R. Plant, "Social Rights and the Reconstruction of Welfare", in G. Andrews (ed.), *Citizenship, op. cit.*, pp. 60 and 63. Carens argues that even if a form of positive social duty is compatible with (and according to him even required by) the principles of egalitarian liberalism, this liberal version of social duty still differs in important ways from the socialist ideal. From a socialist perspective, social duty is an intrinsic good, something that we wish to affirm, not merely endure. Commitment to the community and development of one's talents both for oneself and for others are seen as essential elements of the good life because people are seen as interdependent and morally tied to others. In egalitarian liberal theories (like Rawls's) where people are considered independent and self-seeking, a social duty merely serves as an engine of motivation for production and simply represents a necessary evil, not an intrinsic good (J.H. Carens, "Rights and Duties in an Egalitarian Society", *op. cit.*, p. 32 and pp. 45-46). At this point, the socialist perspective seems again to be closer to communitarianism than to social-liberalism.

[51] W. Kymlicka and W. Norman, "Return of the Citizen: a Survey of Recent Work on Citizenship Theory", *op. cit.*, pp. 355-356; L. Mead, *Beyond Entitlement: the Social Obligations of Citizenship, op. cit.*, p. 240.

employment makes sense in a liberal perspective because liberals believe that the productive capacity of persons should be restored as soon as possible and to prevent that one would get something for nothing.

Communitarians for their part will support the conditionality because they value reciprocity and social responsibility very highly. Just like membership of a community cannot be unconditional, neither can social rights. However, the responsibility expected in return is not of an individual nature as in liberalism, but is a social one. Recipients should not prove themselves to be self-supporting but to be supportive of the community. So when communitarians ask benefit recipients for something in return, they would probably accept any activity or service that can be considered a valuable contribution to society.

Also, contemporary republicans support the view that a certain balance is necessary between rights and obligations. The preservation and good functioning of democratic institutions also depends on the qualities and virtues of the citizens who should make responsible use of them. This also applies to the institutions of the welfare state.[52] Republicans do warn, however, of obligations that would endanger the citizen's autonomy or self-governance. Since the republican justification for welfare arrangements or social rights lies exactly in the aim to establish an equal access to the public sphere of deliberation and self-government by erasing disturbing inequalities and dependencies outside this sphere, these arrangements may not themselves be characterised by possible arbitrariness, dominance or a slavish dependency. Republicanism argues for legally or even constitutionally enshrined social rights[53] or as Pettit puts it, "a mode of delivering welfare that is independent of political vagaries and bureaucratic whims, [...] and independent equally of the caprice of any other agents that may be involved".[54] An activation policy

---

[52] B. Van Stokkom, "Een volk van engelen? Een eigentijdse visie op burgerdeugden", in J. Simonis, A. Hemerijck and P. Lehning (eds.), *De staat van de burger. Beschouwingen over hedendaags burgerschap*, Meppel, Boom, 1992, pp. 62-77.

[53] I. De Haan, *Zelfbestuur en staatsbeheer. Het politieke debat over burgerschap en rechtsstaat in de twintigste eeuw*, op. cit., p. 205; P. Pettit, *Republicanism. A Theory of Freedom and Government*, op. cit., pp. 158-162; H.R. Van Gunsteren, *A Theory of Citizenship: Organizing Plurality in Contemporary Democracies*, op. cit., p. 108; G. Mulgan, "Citizens and Responsibilities", in G. Andrews (ed.), *Citizenship*, op. cit., p. 46.

[54] P. Pettit, *Republicanism. A Theory of Freedom and Government*, op. cit., p. 162. Pettit himself gives the example of an employer who is given incentives to hire otherwise unemployed people and states: "The requirement we are discussing would argue against giving such an employer the right to hire and fire at will, with all the other arbitrary powers of petty intrusion that such a right would bestow. And it would argue for this restriction, even though employers might be willing to take on more employees in its absence" (p. 162).

that would render basic social rights such as minimal social assistance schemes precarious as a consequence of too strictly applied conditions does not seem justifiable from a republican perspective. Obligatory activation measures should minimally also demonstrate a certain level of legal predictability and contain procedural safeguards.

B. *Labour Market Participation*

A second element of the activation paradigm I distinguished in my introduction was the focus on participation in the labour market. When activation policies are being justified under reference to the important value of paid work and labour market participation, both for the individual and the society at large, they seem to be based on citizenship views that award an intrinsic meaning to work or participation. However, the citizenship views that do stress the intrinsic value of work and participation are rather sceptical when it comes to awarding this feature to paid work.

Communitarians value participation and integration in community life very highly and can, in principle, accept work as an important way of expressing one's responsibility as a member of the community, since work has been defined as a response to a social duty. By consequence, they could approach our existing labour order in a positive way and accept involvement in the formal labour market as a sufficient demonstration of social integration and participation. After all, in accepting a paid job one apparently responds to an existing social need. A further step then would be to protect and strengthen this formal labour order and to engage as many people as possible in it. In policy terms, this could mean establishing a right to work, creating employment or starting an activation policy for paternalistic reasons.[55] Other communitarians however have started to doubt the capacity of the labour market in realising its social integrating function, since increasingly more people remain without worthy work and the others have to work harder than ever. Tam, for example, stresses that the quality of the work is also important in order to create "inclusive communities". He clearly denounces a purely materialistic concept of work and gives precedence to the intrinsic moral dimension of it: "It would [...] be quite unacceptable to insist that work that is demoralizing and alienating should be carried out relentlessly for the sake of making society wealthier".[56] At the same time, these communitarians point out that the social integrating character of other

---

[55] In this sense, see for example A. Van de Putte, "Burgerschap, arbeidsbestel en recht op arbeid", *Tijdschrift voor Filosofie*, Vol. 59, No. 4, 1997, pp. 662-663.
[56] H.B. Tam, *Communitarianism. A New Agenda for Politics and Citizenship, op. cit.*, p. 88.

work constitutive contexts seems to have been neglected. Tam seems to refer to what Illich has named "shadow work"[57] when he states that the productivity of a community depends on more than simply paid work and that both categories, paid and unpaid workers, should have the possibility to cooperate together in generating output to enhance the quality of life for the whole community.[58]

Also, republicans situate intrinsic work and participation first and foremost outside the formal labour market: the activity of collective self-government by public and rational deliberation. They clearly set requirements on what work can be and how it should be organised or done. Even modern republicans only value paid work because of its instrumental value as a functional equivalent to property as a condition for the attainment of citizenship status.

Where communitarianism and republicanism can provide support for a clear conditionality with regard to social rights, this is not equally the case for the way this conditionality is specified. Since communitarians are especially committed to the values of social integration and solidarity, there is no reason why they would only accept participation in paid labour as a way of expressing or adhering to these values. From their perspective, involvement in informal work such as volunteering or unpaid care work could also count as a way to show one's responsibility towards one's fellow citizens. For an activation policy, this could mean that a trade-off can be considered between economic participation through paid work and social participation in a broader sense, through the function of which activity could better lead in a particular case to a feeling of self-esteem and appreciation by the community; to individual fulfilment and social integration. The proclivity to judge work by its intrinsic value and to be more critical about the positive effects of paid work, is also – and even more – present in republicanism. In the words of Hannah Arendt, work should regain some characteristics of action to the detriment of the characteristics of labour. An obligation to engage in work seems only to be justified when the work concerned is considered worthy or meaningful enough, and activation policies should make sure that what they offer meets this condition.

In classic and social liberalism on the other hand, paid work does come to the fore, but as we have seen, their citizenship views award no intrinsic

---

[57] The expression designates all forms of unpaid work that constitute in an industrial society a necessary condition for the production of paid goods and services. I. Illich, *Schaduwarbeid*, Weesp, Het Wereldvenster, 1985, p. 93.

[58] H.B. Tam, *Communitarianism. A New Agenda for Politics and Citizenship, op. cit.*, pp. 86-87.

meaning to work or participation. Work is only important in liberalism as a means to obtain the resources one needs to pursue one's own life plan. Relevant work then automatically means activities that produce these resources, activities other market participants are willing to pay for, or in short: paid work. Also social or political participation is for liberals a matter of personal choice. Contrary to communitarians, they do not aim at fostering community ties or solidarity and unlike for the republicans, political participation is no end in itself. Taking into account the liberal citizenship ideals of liberty and self-reliance, activation measures will by definition have to be aimed – directly or indirectly – at paid work since only paid work can lead to economic independency.

C. *Public Employment Services*

A third characteristic of activation policies is a different form of government intervention. The role of government bodies seems to have been remodelled, from redistributor to stimulator and regulator. The main goal of welfare arrangements is no longer to guarantee and pay sufficient benefits but to arm the unemployed to face the competition on the labour market and bring them to the starting line in the best possible condition. The rights of the citizens are now formulated in terms of an appropriate offer in the field of reintegration rather than as an entitlement to a benefit. This also means that the intervention of the government and the obligations it subsequently imposes will probably be of a more immaterial character, since the aim is to adjust, to transform and train benefit recipients by means of obligatory activities of (re)schooling, work experience, job offers, etc., in order to make them fit (again) for the demands of the labour market.

Where the simple guarantee of a benefit can be considered neutral with respect to personal conceptions of a good life, this is much less the case for this type of activation measure. The latter could lead to a certain standardisation and disciplining and create a major tension with the liberal values of a self-chosen life plan and the right to personal liberty and privacy of the persons involved.[59] The probability of suffering these kinds of intrusive measures will surely increase as

---

[59] Also, Desmond King has noticed that some policies in liberal democracy assume illiberal characteristics insofar as they violate the two core principles of liberalism, that is, equality of treatment and respect of individual freedom. Through an investigation of historical examples of the illiberal social policies adopted by British and North American governments, King argues that these kind of policies are intertwined with the creation of modern liberal democratic institutions and are, paradoxically, justified in terms of the liberal democratic framework itself (D. King, *In the Name of Liberalism. Illiberal Social Policy in the United States and Britain*, Oxford, Oxford University Press, 1999).

the situation of the person involved is judged more problematic, since a more comprehensive investigation will appear necessary in order to be able to define the most adequate approach and its concomitant services. In other words, the most vulnerable welfare recipients will probably be most affected by them.

The evolution from redistributor to stimulator could, for administrative bodies, entail an evolution from a commitment to results (paying a legally determined benefit) to an obligation to make efforts (supporting reintegration by providing services), while the opposite evolution will apply for welfare recipients: instead of having to engage in a generally formulated obligation to try to find employment again, welfare recipients will possibly be confronted with well-targeted and tailor-made obligations and procedural demands, the fulfilment of which can be frequently and precisely checked and sanctioned. Indeed, if the activation philosophy allows a personal approach in helping welfare recipients (with tailor-made offers and individual action plans), it also holds the danger of contractualisation, of conceiving the relationship between welfare provider and recipient as a contractual one, which would create the suggestion that we deal with parties with a comparable negotiating position.

Republicans seem most alert to these kinds of problems. They stress that social policies should always be shaped in a way that promotes the autonomy and the self-government of the person concerned. This is clearly not the case when one's security of existence is at stake in a negotiation with administrative bodies. The recognition of the dependency of welfare recipients should not be a pretext for imposing more and stricter obligations on them; on the contrary, it should be a reason to build in more guarantees for the protection of their personal autonomy. De Haan believes that in all institutions that shape the identity of citizens and divide life chances, the republican principles of self-government – equal participation, equal treatment and deliberative rationality – should be pursued. The equality of the social citizenship concept should therefore not only apply to the division of social rights themselves, but also encompass the debate over the reform of the welfare state institutions and the way social rights are awarded.[60] Some kind of institutional involvement of welfare recipients, be it on a collective or an individual level, could indeed be envisaged as a counterpart for the more intrusive way in which welfare services are able to operate under the banner of activation. To the extent that this participation could have

---

[60] I. De Haan, *Zelfbestuur en staatsbeheer. Het politieke debat over burgerschap en rechtsstaat in de twintigste eeuw*, op. cit., pp. 175-176.

a bearing on the establishment and content of the policies themselves, it could open up opportunities for public deliberation that go beyond the protection of proper interests.

Conclusion

Activation policies are bound to have an influence on important aspects of our social security arrangements, in particular on the respective rights and duties of the recipients and the administrative bodies involved. The establishment of a number of distinct citizenship views has allowed me to interpret these possible effects and to critically analyse them not as isolated facts but as possible parts of a more coherent and comprehensive view with regard to the existence and the organisation of our welfare state and the concomitant expectations with respect to the behaviour of citizens. This exercise, it is hoped, will appear fruitful since it makes it easier to understand or to see in which way and to what extent the emergence of activation policies should give rise to caution.

I want to end this contribution with some concluding considerations.

As a general conclusion to my citizenship analysis, one could say that the emergence of activation programmes can be described as an evolution from a social liberal to a more classic or neo-liberal approach in social policy. As I have indicated, social liberalism can be seen as the philosophy or view that best offers a justification for a comprehensive welfare state that guarantees all its citizens a minimum of means regardless or separate from their position on the market. Undeniably, the social liberal citizenship view contains an element of decommodification. Activation policies now tend to replace or at least supplement this guarantee function by an activation function that comes down to a stricter focus on the labour market. This means an evolution from decommodification to recommodification. Stressing the importance of labour market integration fits well in a classic liberal approach, where the individual is deemed capable of obtaining the necessary means of existence via the market as long as the access to it isn't hindered and a minimum of liberty of action is guaranteed.

From a liberal perspective, the observed shift from benefits to work can be interpreted as a shift from ends (having means of existence) to means (paid work) or as a compromise between a purely classic liberal approach and a more social liberal one. The social liberal elements, such as state intervention and a positive notion of freedom, remain, but are interpreted in a different – more classic liberal – way: a minimum of means is not guaranteed by welfare arrangements but the (classic) liberal way to get them, i.e. the unconditional market access to acquire them. The object of the guarantee function becomes the activation function. This is a shift from a welfare ethic (where the allocation of scarce means in society is based on needs) to a work ethic (which affirms the primacy of personal liberty and takes self-sufficiency as the main guiding principle).[61] In this way, a closer connection is found to the (classic) liberal conviction that means ought to be obtained by proper labour and trade and not by an imposed redistribution. Labour participation then becomes the central element, not only with regard to the duties of the beneficiary but also with regard to his rights.

This liberal work ethic, however, is of a materialistic nature, since the underlying norm is not that people should be active and hardworking – the traditional work ethic – but that they should be able to independently make a living.[62] When activation policies are stimulated under reference to a work ethic or to a balance between rights and duties, we should be aware of this nuance because this discourse could be misleading. Indeed, this discourse may suggest that, by receiving and accepting a benefit, a debt arises that has to be paid off towards society. In other words, the principle of reciprocity is put forward. Responding to this principle should be possible by every contribution that is judged valuable to society, especially in social assistance schemes where there is no predetermined link with paid labour. But this will not be the case when the invoked work ethic appears to be a materialistic one, when the underlying norm is not to give something back to society, but is on the contrary not having to rely on society. Only paid work can correspond to this type of work ethic; informal unpaid work cannot. The proclaimed norm of reciprocity will then miss its target. Rather than creating among citizens a sense of duty, it will probably only evoke feelings of frustration, powerlessness or even humiliation, since a lot of people will feel excluded from the possibility of giving something in return.

The aforementioned shift from benefits to work is also in danger of making the cause of distress disappear from view. Since government institutions will focus on the (re)adaptation of the persons drawing benefits (or the supply side of the labour market), they might lose sight of the fact that the discharge of workers is somehow inherent to our economic system. The services that are offered by activation policies try to fix the maladjustment to the labour market and reduce a social-political problem to an individual one. This again seems to fit more in a liberal approach where the inability to hold oneself in the labour market can be interpreted as a personal failure in terms of a lack of productivity or holding too many or expensive preferences. However, one should not

---

[61] I. Sewandono, "Theorie achter de verzorgingsstaat", in J. Van Doorn and C. Schuyt (eds.), *De stagnerende verzorgingsstaat*, Meppel, Boom, 1978, pp. 52-53.

[62] D. Pieters, *Aan het werk... Beschouwingen over het arbeidsethos in het socialezekerheidsrecht van vandaag en morgen*, op. cit., pp. 73-74.

forget that the establishment of our welfare state precisely started with the observation that due to the changes in our economic system, the citizen had lost individual control over the guarantee of his subsistence and social security. This insight should not be forgotten when realising activation schemes.

II. National Activation Policies for the Unemployed and the Different Underlying Conceptions of the Right and the Duty to Work

Activation Policies for the Unemployed in the United States: Work First

Daniel DUMONT

Introduction

In the European public opinion, the United States is seen first and foremost as the country of "unbridled capitalism", a country with, as a consequence, very limited social protection policies. In the same vein but from a more academic perspective, i.e. in the field of comparative social policy, the United States is systematically referred to as the most typical example of a so-called "residual" welfare state, that is, a social protection system dominated by basic assistance for the poor and limited universal programmes, which have to be complemented – for those who can afford it – by private insurance.[1] In short, the U.S. welfare state is clearly seen as a "laggard" compared to Europe.[2] When one analyses American social policies with a European eye, it is indeed quite striking that the U.S. welfare state is, if not minimal, at least quite incomplete by European standards. In relation to the issue at stake in the present book, the key point is this: despite having always been more incomplete and less decommodifying than its European counterparts, the American social protection system, like the systems on this side of the Atlantic, has also been confronted with the phenomenon of pressurisation of the unemployed.

Without seeking to encompass all U.S. social welfare programmes, which falls out of the scope of this article,[3] what this chapter will try to do is to outline a synthetic overview of the various sectors of the

---

[1] As is well known, this view was pioneered by Gøsta Esping-Andersen in his famous book *The Three Worlds of Welfare Capitalism* (Cambridge, Polity Press, 1990).

[2] See for example the various authors quoted by J. Alber, "What the European and American Welfare States Have in Common and Where They Differ: Facts and Fictions in Comparisons of the European Social Model and the United States", *Journal of European Social Policy*, Vol. 20, No. 2, 2010, pp. 102-103.

[3] For this type of exercise, see D. Dumont, "A European View on the American Welfare State", *European Journal of Social Law*, Vol. 3, No. 1, 2013, pp. 4-36, on which this contribution largely builds.

American social protection system that have the strongest links with the labour market and that, for this reason, are of particular interest for the issue of activation. To this end, it will first address the two most relevant social insurance programmes, namely the unemployment system and disability insurance. Then, it will successively cover four different means-tested transfers, that is, the benefits specifically targeted to the poor. For each scheme, the key aspects regarding its origin and organisation, its eligibility conditions and the benefit level of generosity will be highlighted. Generally speaking, emphasis will be put on the major effects that the various benefits have for claimants and recipients, and especially for the poorest of them. The outline will also include some comparative insights, in order to put the American case into an international perspective.

Throughout this descriptive review,[4] it will be shown that the type of activation policy for the unemployed that is implemented in the United States is what could be labelled, as has been suggested, a "negative" one.[5] It can be referred to as a negative-style activation, in the sense that in the U.S., it mainly takes the form of retrenchment. Over the last two decades, the American social safety net – which, again, has always been quite meagre in comparative perspective – has been subject to very severe cutbacks, in the name of a political fight against "dependency". Deployed in a legal framework characterised by the absence of a constitutional recognition of fundamental social and economic rights, this retrenchment move *de facto* forces recipients as well as claimants to take a job as quickly as possible. But in parallel, low-income workers are financially supported by means of an earnings subsidy mechanism. Roughly speaking, the overarching motto guiding American social policies could be said to be "no salvation without work". In this respect, the United States offers a particularly vivid example – probably the most radical one in the whole of Europe and North America – of the so-called "work first" strategy. Overall, this strategy has clearly induced a shift in the balance between the right and the duty to work in the direction of the latter pole.

In terms of sources of information, besides the references relating to each programme that will be mentioned, the survey that follows largely relies on what is informally known in the United States as the "Green Book". It is a vade mecum of the major American social welfare policies

---

[4] For (very) critical perspectives on American social policies, see, among many others, J. Handler and Y. Hasenfeld, *Blame Welfare, Ignore Poverty and Inequality*, New York, Cambridge University Press, 2007.

[5] B. Quade, C.J. O'Leary and O. Dupper, "Activation from Income Support in the U.S.", in W. Eichhorst, O. Kaufmann and R. Konle-Seidl (eds.), *Bringing the Jobless into Work? Experiences with Activation Schemes in Europe and the U.S.*, Berlin, Springer, 2008, p. 348.

combining legal and empirical data that is periodically updated by the staff of a committee of the U.S. House of Representatives.[6]

I. Unemployment Insurance: Limited Benefits for the Involuntarily Unemployed

In most countries, the unemployment insurance system is, understandably, one of the sectors of social protection that attracts the most attention regarding the issue of activation. This is less the case in the United States, for various relevant reasons.

Whereas old age pensions and health care for the elderly – the two largest social insurance programmes in the U.S. – are entirely managed by the federal government, the Unemployment Insurance (UI) system is mainly regulated, organised and funded at state level. This feature has a historical origin. The first unemployment insurance schemes were established at the beginning of the 1930s by just a few states. Along with Workers' Compensation, the scheme covering occupational injuries and illnesses, they constitute the oldest component of the American social safety net. At the time of the New Deal, the first "big bang" in U.S. social policy, Franklin Roosevelt proposed building on the experience gained by those pioneering few states to establish a joint federal-state partnership that would mean substantial autonomy at the local level. As a consequence, only limited federal requirements were included in the famous Social Security Act of 1935.[7] Each state has since developed its own unemployment insurance programme. Accordingly, eligibility conditions and benefit amounts vary widely across states. Each administers its own programme under the supervision of the U.S. Department of Labor, which monitors compliance with federal norms. The states also finance the cost of the benefits themselves, by imposing a wage tax on employers. The federal government only meets part of the expenses relating to the administration of the system.

---

[6] U.S. House of Representatives, Staff of the Committee on Ways and Means, *Background Material and Data on the Programs within the Jurisdiction of the Committee on Ways and Means*, 110th Congress, 2008 (hereinafter the *Green Book*), available at <http://democrats.waysandmeans.house.gov/singlepages.aspx?NewsID=10490> (accessed August 1, 2013). Note that the document, in its nineteenth edition, is no longer accessible on the official Committee's website since the Republicans took control of the House in the midterm elections of 2010. A twentieth edition was released in 2011, but in a format totally different from that of the previous editions: it only consists of a selection of web links to various online resources. See <http://greenbook.waysandmeans.house.gov> (accessed August 1, 2013).

[7] J. Hight, "Unemployment Insurance: Changes in the Federal-State Balance", *University of Detroit Journal of Urban Law*, Vol. 59, No. 4, "Long Lines and Hard Times: Future Unemployment Insurance Alternatives", 1982, pp. 616-617.

Under federal law, almost the entire salaried labour force is covered by these unemployment programmes. However, whereas the unemployment insurance system has a fairly broad scope of application, the risk provided for is defined rather restrictively. All state programmes indeed share two key features that are striking in a comparative perspective. The first relates to the eligibility requirements for the benefits, the second to the maximum period they are granted.

As elsewhere, eligibility requirements can be divided into two categories: monetary and non-monetary. To qualify for the benefits, claimants must first have worked in covered employment for a certain time and must have made a minimum amount of earnings during this period, called the base period (monetary requirements). Second, they must also be and stay involuntarily unemployed, which means complying with the classic set of conditions: (i) to be able to work, (ii) to not have quit one's job without good cause, (iii) to not have been discharged for work-related misconduct, (iv) to not refuse an offer of suitable employment and (v) to be available for and actively seeking work (non-monetary requirements). Regarding the criteria for suitable work, claimants are generally required to accept a wider range of jobs as the length of their unemployment rises. Although the principle of these diverse eligibility requirements is familiar, almost all states have strongly tightened their terms over time, particularly in the 1980s,[8] under the Reagan presidency. They have sharply raised the minimum earnings that applicants must have made in the base period. Concurrently, they have significantly toughened the sanctions for voluntary unemployment, by increasingly replacing the temporary loss of the allowance with definitive disqualification.

As a result of these two parallel evolutions, an average of only about a third of the unemployed population are actually receiving unemployment benefits.[9] The ratio of compensated unemployed to unemployed is thus peculiarly weak in the U.S. Many of the working poor do not succeed in fulfilling the monetary requirements, because they work intermittently and for very low wages. This risk is especially salient for women and people of colour. As a matter of fact, numerous involuntarily unemployed people, especially single mothers, depend – or more precisely, as we shall see, used to depend – on social assistance,[10] which is far more meagre than an unemployment benefit.

---

[8] See L. Williams, "Unemployment Insurance and Low-Wage Work", in J. Handler and L. White (eds.), *Hard Labor. Women and Work in the Post-Welfare Era*, Armonk (NY)-London, M.E. Sharpe, 1999, pp. 160-164.

[9] *Green Book, op. cit.*, pp. IV-4 and IV-5.

[10] L. Williams, "Unemployment Insurance and Low-Wage Work", *op. cit.*, pp. 159, 162 and 163.

The second striking characteristic of the American unemployment system is that states usually limit the benefits to a maximum period of 26 weeks, i.e. six months. It must be added that a permanent federal-state mechanism provides for the payment of "extended benefits" for up to 20 additional weeks in states where unemployment is particularly high. The federal government covers half the cost of those extended benefits. Additionally, Congress and the administration have a practice of enacting supplemental temporary aid, this time fully federally funded, in cases of major nationwide economic recession. During the Great Recession of the late 2000s for example – the worst economic crisis endured by the United States since the Great Depression of the 1930s – the total maximum duration was extended to an unprecedented 99 weeks. In this respect, the U.S. unemployment insurance system shows some responsiveness to economic fluctuations. However, this extension was not intended to last and was progressively reduced along the timescale of the economic recovery. Yet the six months' ceiling applicable under normal circumstances is quite low.[11]

By comparison, what can be said of European countries? Since the 1990s, there has clearly been a trend to reduce the maximum duration of unemployment benefits. Yet, considerable variation remains between, for instance, the Americanised United Kingdom, where "jobseeker's allowance" may be claimed for only 26 weeks, and the unique case of Belgium, where contributory unemployment benefits are as a rule not subject to any time limit. Between these two extremes, unemployment benefits are typically available for a maximum length of one and a half to two years.[12] Thus, while Americans discuss the duration of benefits in terms of weeks, Europeans rather discuss it in terms of months, or even years. Maybe even more significantly, many European countries also have an unemployment assistance system, which provides an allowance, sometimes means-tested, to unemployed persons who have exhausted their benefits. In terms of amount, these unemployment assistance benefits are usually somewhere halfway between those of unemployment insurance and those of social assistance. Nothing like that exists in the United States. As a result, the 30 to 45% of unemployed Americans who

---

[11] Moreover, one should not forget that in the United States, the worker who loses his job often loses his health insurance in addition to his wage, as medical coverage is usually tied to employment (in this connection, see the reflections of S. Glied, "The Employer-Based Health Insurance System. Mistake or Cornerstone?", in D. Mechanic *et al.* (eds.), *Policy Challenges in Modern Health Care*, New Brunswick (NJ), Rutgers University Press, 2005, pp. 37-52). Consequently, a lay-off in the U.S. has much harsher repercussions than elsewhere.

[12] G. Burtless and T. Gordon, "The Federal Stimulus Programs and Their Effects", in D. Grusky, B. Western and C. Wimer (eds.), *The Great Recession*, New York, Russell Sage, 2011, p. 266.

exhaust their benefits every year without having found a new job[13] must basically rely on themselves.

In sum, the unemployment that is implicitly considered legitimate, the one that public authorities financially compensate, is defined quite restrictively in the U.S. Limited accessibility to benefits and the short duration of their granting explain why it devotes only between 0.3 and 0.5% of its GDP to its unemployment policy, versus 2 to 3% in nearly all other member countries of the OECD. This modest figure also reflects the fact that investment in vocational training and employment services – two key aspects of activation policies in many countries – is very limited in the U.S.[14]

II. Disability Insurance: Incapacity for Work Benefits

Disability schemes are often somewhat overlooked in the study of activation policies. They constitute, however, an important dimension of the related legal environment, to the extent that incapacity for work benefits can, in some cases, offer a fallback solution to the jobless deprived of their unemployment benefits.

In the United States, disability insurance is part of a larger programme named Social Security. Established by the 1935 Social Security Act in the framework of Roosevelt's New Deal, this programme initially consisted of an old age pension system. But Social Security was expanded in 1956 when the Disability Insurance (DI) programme was added, a scheme covering incapacity for work. Like the retirement pensions, Disability Insurance is financed by payroll taxes and managed by the Social Security Administration, as part of the broader Old-Age, Survivors, and Disability Insurance (OASDI).

For our purpose, the Disability Insurance programme's most notable features are the very stringent eligibility requirements to which disability benefits are subject. Besides the rule that applicants must have worked and contributed for at least five of the last ten years, they must prove, in order to be administratively considered "disabled", that they are no longer able and will not be able to perform any substantial gainful activity for at least one year. Concretely, proving a complete inability to hold any employment requires substantial medical documentation. Unlike other countries, the U.S. disability scheme thus does not rely on a gradual

---

[13] *Green Book*, *op. cit.*, p. IV-17.
[14] B. Quade, C.J. O'Leary and O. Dupper, "Activation from Income Support in the U.S.", *op. cit.*, pp. 352-353. On job search assistance, see also C.J. O'Leary, "State UI Job Search Rules and Reemployment Services", *Monthly Labor Review*, Vol. 129, No. 6, 2006, pp. 27-37.

approach of work incapacity, but on a binary one: it is "all or nothing". Hence, only very severe work incapacity is compensated by benefits and warrants an exemption from the workforce.[15]

* * *

Let us turn now to means-tested transfers. More of these schemes than on the social insurance side need to be reviewed with regard to the position of the jobless and their activation. By definition, all the benefits that will be successively dealt with are subject to an income test. And as we shall see, the U.S. official poverty measurement methodology is often used in the determination of monetary eligibility.[16] In short, this methodology was developed in the first half of the 1960s, in the context of the so-called "War on Poverty" initiated by the Democratic president Lyndon Johnson, the (only) other period of major expansion in U.S. social policy following the New Deal. Since then, the official poverty threshold has been defined as the cost of a subsistence food budget multiplied by three. The point of reference is fixed and does not evolve with changes in standards of living, so that its real value has remained exactly the same for fifty years. Owing to economic growth and the rising of inequalities, the relative value of the threshold has strongly declined over time. It currently amounts to less than 30% of the American median income,[17] while in comparison the European indicator of at-risk-of-poverty is set at 60% of the national median income. Therefore, it has to be kept in mind that the U.S. official poverty line is particularly meagre. Finally, as for their funding means-tested benefits are not funded by payroll taxes, but by state and federal general revenues.

III. Supplemental Security Income: Cash Aid to the Needy Elderly or Disabled

The first means-tested scheme for us to focus on is named Supplemental Security Income. Better known in the United States as SSI, it is a federal programme that provides cash assistance to the needy aged or disabled.[18] It was introduced under Nixon in 1972. Although he was a Republican, Nixon expanded the social policies of the War on Poverty

---

[15] On this choice, see M. Diller, "Entitlement and Exclusion: The Role of Disability in the Social Welfare System", *UCLA Law Review*, Vol. 44, No. 2, 1996, pp. 361-465.

[16] On the American poverty indicator, and for a comparison with the European one, see D. Dumont, "A European View on the American Welfare State", *op. cit.*, pp. 6-10.

[17] T. Smeeding, "Poor People in Rich Nations: The United States in Comparative Perspective", *Journal of Economic Perspectives*, Vol. 20, No. 1, 2006, p. 71.

[18] For an overview, see M. Daly and R. Burkhauser, "Left Behind: SSI in the Era of Welfare Reform", *Focus*, Vol. 22, No. 3, 2003, pp. 35-43.

in several ways, pushed by a Democrat-controlled Congress. Nixon's aim was to replace pre-existing state assistance programmes initiated by the Social Security Act that differed widely in terms of eligibility requirements and benefit amounts, in order to create a national income maintenance system for poor senior citizens and the impaired. In a landscape rather marked by the weight of previous institutional choices, it is the only social welfare programme that shifted from the state to the federal level.[19] The population targeted by Supplemental Security Income has remained the one that slips through the cracks of Social Security's two main components, the old age pension and the disability insurance, because of insufficient past contributions. Although financed separately, the programme was integrated into Social Security and, accordingly, is managed by the Social Security Administration.

In fact, the vast bulk of the SSI caseload is made up of non-elderly disabled. Among them, a majority are indigents suffering from a mental impairment, such as retardation.[20] However, the eligibility requirements to qualify for the benefit are very tight. The income threshold to be considered needy amounts to only 75% of the official poverty line – which equates to the maximum amount of the grant. Furthermore, the applicant must be either aged 65 or older, or disabled. The definition of disability used to determine eligibility for Supplemental Security Income is the same to the one used in Disability Insurance. It means that to be granted the benefits, one has to succeed in proving an inability to perform any substantial gainful activity for at last one year due to medical reasons. Supplemental Security Income is therefore *de facto* reserved, with regard to the non-elderly, to persons who are both very poor and medically completely unable to work. Moreover, disabled persons whose incapacity was caused by alcoholism or drug addiction have been excluded from the benefits since the drastic overhaul of the social assistance schemes in 1996 (see *infra*, IV).

As to the benefit amounts, they are, as mentioned, far below the official poverty line. But they are inflation-indexed, which is not the case for all means-tested cash transfers. Most states supplement the federal grant, but according to requirements and to an extent highly variable from state to state. About a third of the Supplemental Security Income caseload receives some state supplements.[21]

---

[19] K. Finegold, "The United States: Federalism and its Counter-Factuals", in H. Obinger, S. Leibfried and F. Castles (eds.), *Federalism and the Welfare State. New World and European Experiences*, Cambridge, Cambridge University Press, 2005, pp. 168-169.

[20] *Green Book, op. cit.*, pp. III-21 and III-24.

[21] *Ibid.*, p. III-21.

IV. Temporary Assistance for Needy Families: "Reformed" Social Assistance to Families with Children

At present, the question that arises is: what benefit is accessible to all the jobless poor who are not totally disabled? Historically, the solution that was adopted by all Member States of the European Union, except Italy and Greece – but including the Eastern countries – was the setting up of a universal minimum income.[22] Besides some schemes targeted specifically at the disabled and the elderly, what is generically called social assistance provides a minimum income for the very poor who are unable to get any other benefit and are available for work.

There is no such thing in the U.S., at least not at the federal level. In 1972, the U.S. Congress rejected the Nixon administration's Family Assistance Plan, which is, to date, the only serious attempt to enact a federal programme that would have provided financial support to all low-income families.[23] Congress only agreed to pass legislation creating Supplemental Security Income, because, and this is telling of policymakers' preoccupations, providing cash assistance to individuals not expected to work – the aged and the severely disabled – seemed unlikely to have much of an effect on their participation in the labour market, contrary to a universal income floor. Nonetheless, some forms of general public assistance do exist, but they have always been quite limited, in their scope as well as in their level of generosity. More precisely, the United States has two distinct kinds of benefits for the very poor. Both have been significantly downsized over the past two decades.

The first benefit is what is colloquially known as "welfare". In the American context, welfare refers only to one specific programme, and not, as is generally the case elsewhere, to the whole system of social protection. In the U.S., it is roughly a synonym for public assistance to poor families with children. Before it was drastically "reformed" in the mid-1990s, welfare consisted in a programme named AFDC – Aid to Families with Dependent Children. Created by the 1935 Social Security Act, it provided some cash assistance to poor families living under a certain income threshold. In fact, the Social Security Act put in place a dual model: while universal social insurance schemes, such as old age

---

[22] For an overview, see C. Saraceno, "Concepts and Practices of Social Citizenship in Europe: The Case of Poverty and Income Support for the Poor", in J. Alber and N. Gilbert (eds.), *United in Diversity? Comparing Social Models in Europe and America*, Oxford, Oxford University Press, 2010, pp. 162-168.

[23] On this largely unknown episode of the U.S. social welfare history, see B. Steensland, "Cultural Categories and the American Welfare State: The Case of Guaranteed Income Policy", *American Journal of Sociology*, Vol. 111, No. 5, 2006, pp. 1273-1326.

pensions, were established at the federal level, targeted means-tested benefits for the poor, such as AFDC, were assigned to the states, under federal supervision. The choice of decentralisation for social assistance programmes was necessary to obtain the vote of the Southern Democrats. They largely controlled the South at that time and were the political voice of the powerful plantation owners, who strongly opposed policies that could potentially enable their African American labour force to leave the cotton fields.[24]

Given these preoccupations, Aid to Families with Dependent Children was initially designed for widows who, it was considered, should not be expected to work, so that they could take care of their families. However, in the early 1960s, protest and litigation actions organised by welfare rights activists led to the removal of various legal and administrative barriers to enrolment, as well as to more federal control of the programme. As a result, the AFDC caseload began to rise quickly and to expand to a new population: poor unwed single mothers.[25] In the space of a few years, the vast majority of recipients became single heads of household, and among them, African Americans were clearly overrepresented. AFDC began to play the role of unemployment insurance and a safety net for poor young mothers of colour. But from the 1980s, the continuous increase of recipients coupled with the recurrent exposure in the media of the disastrous living conditions in the black ghettos went hand in hand with an assault by the conservatives on the so-called "welfare queens" – an expression abundantly used by Ronald Reagan. Beneficiaries were constantly depicted as abusing the generosity of the welfare state and corrupting family values as well as the work ethic by their deviant way of life. This political and discursive process of delegitimisation of welfare proved to be very efficient,[26] to the extent that by the early 1990s, AFDC was "the most disliked public program in America".[27]

---

[24] See K. Finegold, "The United States: Federalism and its Counter-Factuals", *op. cit.*, pp. 162-163. For the same reason, agricultural and domestic workers, who were overwhelmingly black, remained excluded from Social Security until the 1950s.

[25] On the history of welfare, see generally the synthesis of K. Gustafson, *Cheating Welfare. Public Assistance and the Criminalization of Poverty*, New York, New York University Press, 2011, pp. 17-50.

[26] On this process, see, for a detailed account, F.F. Piven and R. Cloward, "Welfare State Politics in the United States", in Z. Ferge and J. Kolberg (eds.), *Social Policy in a Changing Europe*, Frankfurt-Boulder (CO), Campus Verlag-Westview Press, 1992, pp. 57-75; J. Peck, "Workfare: A Geopolitical Etymology", *Environment and Planning, D, Society and Space*, Vol. 16, No. 2, 1998, pp. 133-161.

[27] M. Katz, *The Price of Citizenship. Redefining the American Welfare State* (2001), updated edition, Philadelphia, University of Pennsylvania Press, 2008, p. 1.

In 1996, after the Republicans took full control of Congress, AFDC was finally, with president Clinton's support, abolished and replaced by TANF. The meaning of the abbreviation speaks for itself: TANF means Temporary Assistance for Needy Families. This sweeping reform is probably the most discussed and disputed reform in the history of social welfare in the U.S. – although the major overhaul of the health care system enacted under Obama in 2010 is an increasingly serious challenger. It was enacted by a law tellingly entitled the Personal Responsibility and Work Opportunity Reconciliation Act.[28] In short, the main change consisted in transforming the former federal entitlement into a block grant, i.e. a fixed amount of money devolved to the states, which received wide discretion over the design and the administration of the programme. At the same time, federal law imposed a maximum lifetime limit of five years on the receipt of benefits, as well as stringent work requirements.

In order for a state to get federal funding, at least half of its caseload must be engaged in work activities, usually for thirty hours a week, in return for the aid. Through a mechanism known as the "caseload reduction credit", this 50% work participation target is reduced by one percentage for each percentage point by which a state reduces its caseload below its level in 2005. In other words, states are strongly financially incentivised to make families leave the welfare rolls. And at any rate, the aid cannot be received in excess of five years over the course of an adult lifetime, except if it is funded entirely by state money. States are also free, in the opposite direction, to set up shorter time limits, which about one-third of them do. The motto behind the reform was the need to break the so-called "culture of dependency" that would have developed among recipients of AFDC. States took advantage of the huge margin of flexibility they were given to implement the reform in very different ways. But overall, most of them defined the work activities that count to meet the federal target quite restrictively, often excluding or limiting vocational training and prioritising instead immediate placement into employment, work experience and community services.[29] Analysis of field-level implementation reveals the magnitude of the culture change

---

[28] A summary of the major provisions of the law, including those relating to the promotion of marriage and the reduction of what American conservatives call "illegitimate", i.e. nonmarital, births, can be found in the appendix "The Welfare Law that Reshaped American Social Policy" of R. Haskins, *Work over Welfare. The Inside Story of the 1996 Welfare Reform Law*, Washington DC, Brookings Institution Press, 2006, pp. 364-376.

[29] For a thorough examination of how each of the 50 states defined "work" in its respective regulations, see N. Zatz, "Welfare to What?", *Hastings Law Journal*, Vol. 57, No. 5, 2006, pp. 1131-1188.

that took place in welfare offices, whose primary mission has become to change the applicants' and recipients' behaviour by hammering home the message "get a job quickly".[30]

What concrete effects has the welfare reform had so far?[31] The most prominent one is that the caseload has literally plunged. Only five years after the Personal Responsibility and Work Opportunity Reconciliation Act was passed, the number of family recipients had fallen by around 60%, from over 5 million cases to about 2 million – a level not seen since the 1960s.[32] Nobody amongst the supporters or detractors of the reform had anticipated such a massive drop. As a consequence, it was hailed a success by most policymakers and in public opinion, and even a "triumph" by intellectuals such as Lawrence Mead, the spiritual father of neo-paternalism in social policy.[33] At least, the issue of poverty has, since the adoption of the reform, largely disappeared from the political discourse and agenda in the United States.

Nevertheless, the apparent success indicated by the decline in the rolls is seriously counterbalanced by two worrying findings. The first flip side of the coin is that a growing group of poor single mothers now live totally "off the books". They are no longer on welfare, because they have exhausted their benefits or were sanctioned for non-compliance with the work requirements. Yet, they are not working either, usually because they face significant barriers to employment: health issues, mental troubles, residential instability, a very low level of education, addictions, domestic violence, etc. Under the new post-entitlement regime, these poor "disconnected" single mothers, and their children, are completely left to fend for themselves.[34] The depiction that can be found in ethnographic literature of the survival strategies that "no-work,

---

[30] T. Gais et al., "Implementation of the Personal Responsibility Act of 1996", in R. Blank and R. Haskins (eds.), *The New World of Welfare*, Washington DC, Brookings Institution Press, 2001, pp. 35-69.

[31] For a review of the abundant literature devoted to this question, see R. Blank, "What We Know, What We Don't Know, and What We Need to Know about Welfare Reform", in J. Ziliak (ed.), *Welfare Reform and its Long-Term Consequences for America's Poor*, New York, Cambridge University Press, 2009, pp. 22-58.

[32] *Green Book, op. cit.*, pp. VII-26 and VII-27.

[33] L. Mead, "Why Welfare Reform Succeeded", *Journal of Policy Analysis and Management*, Vol. 26, No. 2, 2007, pp. 370 and 373. Lawrence Mead is a professor of politics at New York University and the author of two highly influential books: *Beyond Entitlement. The Social Obligations of Citizenship* (1986) and *The New Politics of Poverty. The Nonworking Poor in America* (1992).

[34] On the extent of the problem, see R. Blank and B. Kovak, "The Growing Problem of Disconnected Single Mothers", in C. Heinrich and J.K. Scholz (eds.), *Making the Work-Based Safety Net Work Better. Forward-Looking Policies to Help Low-Income Families*, New York, Russell Sage, 2009, pp. 227-258.

no-welfare" households are compelled to put into place is, to say the least, quite startling.[35]

Secondly, TANF is by definition completely impervious to the evolutions of the economic situation, since the federal funding operates by means of a frozen block grant, which is not even inflation-indexed. Except for individuals not able to take a job, this seemed to pose no major problem in the second half of the 1990s and the beginning of the 2000s, when strong growth allowed many adult recipients to move towards work, leading to the aforementioned major decline in the welfare rolls. But the start of the Great Recession in 2007 has brought to light the structural inability of a block grant programme to play the role of a reliable minimum safety net. Despite the skyrocketing unemployment rate, the TANF caseload has remained at the same historically low level. This status quo does not mean that there are less (very) poor American families than before the reform. Rather, it masks the fact that more impoverished households than ever before are totally deprived of minimal assistance. Confronted with an upsurge in poverty and unemployment, and with a federal grant that has lost almost 30% of its real value since 1996, states are indeed tightening their eligibility requirements, reducing time limits and harshly cutting into the level of the benefits. This level is now equivalent to less than half of the official poverty line in all states.[36]

In total, it is striking to see how the 1996 welfare reform reinforced the duty to work for poor American jobless heads of households. Access to benefits has been made much narrower, giving many claimants no other solution but to get along on the labour market, while those who manage to obtain the benefits are required to participate in mandatory work programmes.[37]

V. General Assistance: The Endangered Social Assistance to Childless Adults

While TANF is directed at families, General Assistance is targeted at childless adults. It is – or, as we shall see, it used to be – the safety net of

---

[35] See for instance the inquiry led into Chicago's African American ghetto by S. Venkatesh, *Off the Books. The Underground Economy of the Urban Poor*, Cambridge (MA), Harvard University Press, 2006.

[36] L. Schott and L. Pavetti, "Many States Cutting TANF Benefits Harshly Despite High Unemployment and Unprecedented Need", Washington DC, Centre on Budget and Policy Priorities, 2011, 8 pp.

[37] In this respect, it must be noted that, with the exception of the International Covenant on Civil and Political Rights, the United States is not part to any of the international human rights instruments prohibiting forced labour and protecting the right to freely chosen work that are studied by Elise Dermine in her two contributions to this volume.

very last resort, the safety net for the poorest of the poor. Its specificity, and the reason why it is, quite surprisingly, almost never covered in the literature on social welfare in the U.S., is that it is not subject to any federal oversight. In other words, it is entirely up to the states to decide to run it or not, and to fund it or not. For the same reason, if such a programme is set up, it can either be operated on a uniform basis state-wide, or, as in California, be mandated state-wide with important local variations.

The overall evolution undergone by general assistance programmes in the last twenty years is particularly striking. No later than in the mid-1990s, forty states had some form of General Assistance, while the ten others – almost all located in the South – had no programme at all.[38] In 2011, only thirty states still had a general assistance scheme. And among the remaining programmes, the vast majority had been very severely cut back.[39] The most widespread evolution, which began at the same time as the push for welfare reform, consisted in excluding the people who were judged able-bodied from benefits and, thus, in limiting benefits for those considered unemployable – i.e. those who have some degree of physical or mental disability but do not qualify for SSI. These benefits are not only now much more limited in scope; they have also become extremely modest in their amount. In most states, they are now below one quarter of the poverty line. For instance, general assistance in Los Angeles amounts to $221 a month, not inflation-indexed. For individuals deemed employable, this benefit is furthermore limited to nine months per year, to avoid recipients becoming "dependent".[40]

But several states have opted for a much more radical "solution". Some have completely eliminated their General Assistance, such as the state of Illinois, which purely and simply terminated its programme in summer 2011, leaving 10,000 recipients in Chicago without any income

---

[38] For a review, see S. Anderson, A. Halter and B. Gryzlak, "Changing Safety Net of Last Resort: Downsizing General Assistance for Employable Adults", *Social Work*, Vol. 47, No. 3, 2002, pp. 249-258.

[39] For a synopsis, see L. Schott and C. Cho, "General Assistance Programs: Safety Net Weakening Despite Increased Need", Washington DC, Centre on Budget and Policy Priorities, 2011, 19 pp. Information on general assistance programmes is scarce since, after the passage of welfare reform, and in the wake of the devolution movement, the federal Department of Health and Human Services stopped collecting and centralising the data that states used to report annually.

[40] The present author was able to spend an afternoon in one of the LA county offices. The scene did not leave indifferent: overcrowded with homeless, many of whom clearly had serious mental health issues, the facility was equipped with firearms detectors and displayed prominently the faces and identities of former recipients sentenced for cheating, while caseworkers were separated from their clients by a thick glass window and communicated with them through a microphone.

overnight.[41] This happened in the midst of a massive economic crisis, with unemployment remaining persistently high. Nonetheless, the issue has not elicited audible political protest, nor has it even been subject to coverage in the major media.

In short, General Assistance is clearly an endangered species. Its silent dismantling represents one more drawback in the social protection of the needy unemployed.

VI. The Earned Income Tax Credit: Financial Support to Low-income Working Households

Finally, one last programme needs to be addressed in this concise overview of the American case: the Earned Income Tax Credit, best known as EITC. EITC is a tax credit conditional upon the exercise of a job. Although it is somewhat unfamiliar to Continental eyes, it is important to take it into account, because it plays a major role in stimulating the work efforts of individuals living on the margins of the labour market.

The Earned Income Tax Credit is a refundable credit against federal income tax designed to supplement low wages. It is said to be refundable in the sense that if the credit exceeds tax liability, the extra amount is paid as a cash transfer. As a consequence, workers making less than the threshold triggering federal income tax liability get money from the Department of the Treasury instead of having to pay contributions. EITC therefore operates as a direct earnings subsidy for low-income working households. The programme was initiated as an experimental measure in 1975, before becoming permanent three years later.[42] Entirely designed, managed and funded by the federal government, the programme both supports low income and rewards work: the more you work, as an employee or self-employed, the higher the refunded tax credit. Interestingly, it is this linkage between financial help and economic activity that convinced Congress to enact EITC, while it had defeated the more radical Family Assistance Plan a few years earlier. It is also this linkage that explains why EITC has, since its creation, often enjoyed a broad bipartisan backing.

Initially very modest in size, the programme has been greatly expanded over time, particularly in the 1990s under Clinton. It is indeed important to specify that Clinton, while advocating a significant downsizing of welfare, also pushed to increase financial support to the working poor.

---

[41] L. Schott and C. Cho, "General Assistance Programs", *op. cit.*, p. 9.
[42] On EITC's genesis and its subsequent evolutions, see J. Hotz and J.K. Scholz, "The Earned Income Tax Credit", in R. Moffit (ed.), *Means-Tested Transfer Programs in the United States*, Chicago, University of Chicago Press, 2003, pp. 143-147.

It is the cornerstone value of work that simultaneously justified a major dismantling of the entitlement accessible to the non-working poor and an expansion in government transfers to low-wage workers.[43] Combined with important increases in child-care subsidies and a flourishing economy, the growth of EITC helped many "welfare mothers" to leave the rolls during the second half of the 1990s. EITC has now become the largest cash means-tested anti-poverty programme. It is a bigger source of income support than the classic social assistance benefits such as TANF and SSI.

The subsidy amount is determined by the household level of income, which must be below a certain threshold, and by the household composition.[44] The rate at which the refunded credit grows increases with the number of children. Modest for childless workers, this rate reaches 35% for families with one child, goes up to 40% for families with two children, and, since the passage of an important stimulus bill in 2009, peaks at 45% for families with three children or more. This means that, for large families, the government adds up to 45 cents to each dollar earned through work. Thanks to this massive subsidy of poor parents' work, the Earned Income Tax Credit lifts several million Americans above the official poverty line every year. Thus, it significantly boosts the disposable income of low-wage working families. It is estimated that EITC can be credited with reducing the poverty rate by 10%, which makes it the most efficient of the cash means-tested programmes. Furthermore, EITC can, as SSI, be supplemented by states, which about half of them do.

However, if the programme is a major source of financial support for the working poor, it is needless to say that outlining this data does not aim at embellishing the situation of precarious American families. In particular, EITC offers no solution to people durably disconnected from the labour market – nor to their children.

Conclusion: Work First

To conclude, let us quickly take stock of this survey of the main American social welfare programmes that relate to the jobless and the working poor. Generally speaking, it is striking that these programmes are strongly fragmented. Instead of a real, European-style, "system" of social protection, one finds a superposition of schemes whose regulation, management and funding are split between different levels of power, resulting in significant gaps in the coverage against the principal social risks.

---

[43] N. Zatz, "Welfare to What?", *op. cit.*, p. 1131.
[44] The figures that follow are all excerpted from B. Meyer, "The Effects of the Earned Income Tax Credit and Recent Reforms", *Tax Policy and the Economy*, Vol. 24, 2010, pp. 153-180.

As regards the different categories of the population, it can be said, in sum, that individuals who cannot work because of a disability benefit from a certain income support. The legal definition of disability is, however, particularly restrictive, so that applicants who are not able to prove total medical incapacity to hold a job are indirectly required to work. The U.S. social welfare policies also express some concern for poor single mothers and their children: they are provided with some public assistance. The drastic 1996 welfare reform has, nevertheless, made cash benefits subject to stricter work requirements and stringent time limits, so as to push beneficiaries off the rolls. Finally, working-age adults deemed able-bodied, especially if they are childless, are treated as the least deserving of all. No matter the difficulties they face, they are, to a large extent, held solely responsible for their situation. Access to unemployment benefits is quite restricted, while General Assistance, which used to be the ultimate safety net, is on the verge of being completely dismantled. As a consequence, working-age adults considered employable have in practice no choice but to ensure their financial autonomy exclusively through work. They are supported in this way by the Earned Income Tax Credit, which somewhat mitigates the lack of a universal minimum income by supplementing low earnings. But the benefit of this tax tool is, again, conditional upon employment, which appears as the real gateway to the whole system.

Overall, the global picture that emerges is one of a social protection system very strongly "work-conditioned", to use Rebecca Blank's illuminating expression.[45] Strict eligibility requirements and low benefit levels force entitlement claimants to seek or to actually perform work, when they do not explicitly act as a deterrent, while at the same time low-income workers are financially aided to reach self-sufficiency. Evolutions in the last twenty years have strongly increased the legal and moral duty to work, whereas this duty has always been very deeply rooted in the American culture. Given the comparatively limited scope of redistributive policies and their fragmentation, it is hardly surprising that the United States is characterised by the persistence of a particularly high rate of relative poverty. No less than one out of four Americans lives on less than 60% of the national median income,[46] which is the usual indicator of poverty risk. By contrast, the at-risk-of-poverty rate is 16% on average in the European Union.[47]

---

[45] R. Blank, "The New American Model of Work-Conditioned Public Support", in J. Alber and N. Gilbert (eds.), *United in Diversity?, op. cit.*, p. 194.

[46] G. Notten and C. de Neubourg, "Monitoring Absolute and Relative Poverty: 'Not Enough' is not the Same as 'Much Less'", *Review of Income and Wealth*, Vol. 57, No. 2, 2011, p. 255.

[47] A. Atkinson *et al.*, "Income Poverty and Income Inequality", in A. Atkinson and E. Marlier (eds.), *Income and Living Conditions in Europe*, Luxembourg, Publications Office of the European Union, 2010, p. 119.

Some authors have hailed the fact that the U.S. set of public programmes designed to support income security "improve[s] the standard of living for Americans (...) in ways compatible with flexible and competitive labour markets".[48] Supposing that ensuring this "compatibility" should really be the primary concern of policymakers, one can wonder at what price this goal has been achieved. For our part, it seems hard not to consider American activation policies frankly harsh on vulnerable people. But since it is always somewhat sensitive to make value judgements about a country that is not one's own, the last word will be left to the American sociologist David Brady. In his book *Rich Democracies, Poor People*, Brady writes, "the United States may be the best place to live if you are rich, but it may be the worst affluent democracy to live in if you are poor".[49]

---

[48] B. Quade, C.J. O'Leary and O. Dupper, "Activation from Income Support in the U.S.", *op. cit.*, p. 407.

[49] D. Brady, *Rich Democracies, Poor People. How Politics Explain Poverty*, New York-Oxford, Oxford University Press, 2009, p. 178.

Activation Policies for the Unemployed in France: "Social Debt" or "Poor Laws"?

Diane ROMAN

Unemployment is dramatically on the increase in France: in June 2013, there were 3,246,000 people unemployed and the level of unemployment is close to reaching its historical peak of 1997. Even though the French welfare state is said to be generous, only 2.2 million job seekers receive unemployment benefits (*Allocation d'aide au retour à l'emploi*). Entitlement to these benefits relies on past contributions to the social security system, and the rules relating to this contributory requirement are extremely complex. The benefit level amounts to between 57% and 75% of the jobseeker's last gross salary and a minimum amount is guaranteed (approximately 868 € a month). Unemployment benefits are paid for a maximum of two years.

Along with the contributory unemployment system, some means-tested transfers have been implemented for decades. The latest and probably most significant one for the field of activation policies is the *Revenu de solidarité active* (RSA), which is an earned income supplement, created in 2008. The RSA is an allowance designed to replace several former means-tested benefits (primarily the *Revenu minimum d'insertion* [RMI]). It aims to secure a minimum income for people, regardless of whether or not they work. The amount of RSA is 485 € for a single person and, for instance, 1,015 € per month for a couple with two children (household allowance not taken into account). These benefits are far below the official at-risk-of-poverty line (in France, 964 € for a single person, 2,400 € for a family with two children). Meanwhile, despite the fact that 13.5% of its population live below the poverty line, the poverty rate of France is amongst the lowest throughout Europe (21.8% in Spain, 16.2% in the United Kingdom, 10.5% in Norway according to Eurostat). In the opinion of many politicians and analysts, this is the result of a strong welfare state, pursuing fair wealth redistribution policies.[1]

However, the rise in joblessness stresses the current difficulty that the French social security system, and more generally the French welfare

---

[1] See, for instance, N. Duvoux, *Le nouvel âge de la solidarité. Pauvreté, précarité et politiques publiques*, Paris, Le Seuil (La vie des idées), 2012.

state, is having to deal with: how to face poverty and to secure a sufficient and sustainable minimum income to guarantee human life above the poverty line?

Since the French Revolution, the traditional answer has been to clearly distinguish between those who are able to work and those who are not (children, pregnant woman, old people, people with disabilities). For the latter, a wide range of welfare programmes have been gradually designed; for the former, a principle has been repeatedly stated: the duty of the people "able to work" to live by their own labour takes precedence over the collective duty to provide them with social assistance. In this context, the issue of "employability" has become key. As has been pointed out, "employability" is not a mere technical concept, i.e. a measure of an individual's capacity for employment (degree of schooling, skills and personal qualifications). Employability is also a social construct, characterising "the outcome of strategies of various interveners as well of the change of the institution of employment, the family and social assistance [...]. Employability thus concerns the condition of those men and women who society believes have a duty to be employed".[2] Consequently, if cash relief is subsidiary to the financial resources individuals are supposed to obtain from paid employment or from their family, and if employability is a social statement about the capacity of individuals to earn their own livelihood through paid work, the core issue is to define the eligibility criteria for social assistance. This kind of logic implies selection of the beneficiaries, in order to separate "the wheat from the chaff".

In recent years, this issue has taken a new form, reflecting a departure from the traditional solutions. The core idea is now less to distinguish between those who are physically able to work and those who are not: it is more to incentivise the unemployed to go back to the job market and to avoid the so-called "unemployment trap". Thus, the question of employability has turned from "Who are the able-bodied poor?" to "What kind of incentives should be used, in order to reward which behaviour?" It is in this overall context that the current debate on the activation of social policies has taken shape. As one author points out, "activation refers to the notion of empowering the unemployed: the means to act on individual variables (compensation, behaviour, occupational and geographical mobility) to suit the needs of the labour market".[3] The

---

[2] S. Morel, *The insertion Model or the Workfare Model? The transformation of Social Assistance within Quebec and Canada*, report, Ottawa, Status of Women Canada, 2002, p. 4.

[3] L. Lavitry, "Activation French Policies: Dilemmas of the Employment Counselors and their Clients Coping with Unemployment Traps", contribution to the XVII ISA World Congress of Sociology, July 2010, Gothenburg, Sweden.

term "activation", initially applied to expenditures, nowadays relates to the activation of the beneficiaries themselves and the different kinds of incentives used to increase employment. In Europe, most countries have adopted an activation-based intervention paradigm, resulting in major reforms of the European social welfare systems.[4] Even though the way the worldwide spread of activation policies has been implemented varies from country to country,[5] turning "old fashioned" welfare states into "active" welfare states has been seen in many Western countries as a way to solve the problem of massive unemployment. France is not unique in this respect. The growing issue of unemployment over the last thirty years has been a strong incentive to take into account other national experiences. At the end of the 1990s, comparative studies have for instance focused on the Danish social programmes. During the last few years, German experiences have also been seen as a model to follow.[6] This interest in foreign national experiences has led to the implementation of social welfare reforms: during the last twenty years, active labour market policies have been elaborated to help unemployed people return to work. From this perspective, job placement services and labour market programmes such as training and job creation have been implemented. As some authors have pointed out, "with respect to activation, France certainly is not to be classified as a laggard".[7]

However, a French specificity must be stressed: orientation towards activation is related in some aspects to a liberal vision (intensification of the logic incentive/penalty) but it is also animated by the concept of "social solidarity", which is enshrined in the French vision of the welfare state. Within this framework, as a matter of significant importance, the trend towards activation has so far not led to the implementation of programmes like those that are called "workfare programs" in the United States.[8] There is still in the French context a strong reluctance

---

[4] A. Serrano Pascual and L. Magnusson (eds.), *Reshaping Welfare States and Activation Regimes in Europe*, Brussels, P.I.E. Peter Lang (Work & Society), 2007; P. Vielle, P. Pochet and I. Cassiers (eds.), *L'État social actif. Vers un changement de paradigme?*, Brussels, P.I.E. Peter Lang (Travail & société), 2005.

[5] W. Eichhorst, O. Kaufmann and R. Konle-Seidl (eds.), *Bringing the Jobless into Work? Experiences with Activation Schemes in Europe and the U.S.*, Berlin, Springer, 2008.

[6] M. Heinrich and R. Juanico, Rapport d'information déposé au nom du comité d'évaluation et de contrôle des politiques publiques sur l'évaluation de la performance des politiques sociales en Europe, Assemblée nationale, Paris, December 2011, p. 15.

[7] J.C. Barbier and W. Ludwig-Mayerhofer, "The Many Worlds of Activation", *European Societies*, Vol. 6, No. 4, 2004, pp. 423-436.

[8] See S. Morel, *Les logiques de la réciprocité. Les transformations de la relation d'assistance aux États-Unis et en France*, Paris, Presses universitaires de France (Le lien social), 2000. See also the contribution of Daniel Dumont in this volume.

towards this idea, which is seen to be punitive.[9] As some authors have underlined, "while Britain's classically liberal individualism is held to have legitimised the pursuit of an 'active society', in France the embeddedness of Republican conceptions of solidarity are understood to have made much of the current international reform agenda appear as anathema".[10]

Despite this firm foothold of the notion of solidarity in French political culture, one can nevertheless notice a real change since the accession to power of the UMP, the French conservative party, from 2002 to 2012. A notable shift in the political discourse has increasingly argued that French social welfare policies are wasteful and that only the "deserving poor" should be entitled to social benefits. As a matter of fact, one member of the former conservative government, under Nicolas Sarkozy's presidency, even dared to say that there is a French problem stemming from the "cancer of aid-policies".[11] Newspapers and magazines regularly focus on social benefit recipients, who are stigmatised as scroungers or cheaters,[12] and above all, in the political discourse, a strong emphasis is being made on the need to tackle social security fraud. Hence, recent social welfare reform policies have focused on activation and incentive programmes as a sustainable way to distinguish between the "deserving" and "non-deserving" poor. These activation policies are nowadays related to a particular theme, which has become a kind of new motor in the French political field and the social arena: the articulation of "rights and duties".

This change in political discourse and social policies needs to be scrutinised. Is it a radical move, trying to import workfare programmes that might be somehow reminiscent of the British "Poor laws", and which could be seen as a threat to the French welfare state? Or is it trying to imagine a new social policy, aimed at conciliating the deeply embedded

---

[9] See, for instance, L. Wacquant, *Punishing the Poor. The Neoliberal Government of Social Insecurity*, Duke, Duke University Press, 2009; E. Chelles, *Gouverner les pauvres. Politiques sociales et administration du mérite*, Rennes, Presses universitaires de Rennes (Res Publica), 2012.

[10] J. Clasen and D. Clegg, "Unemployment Protection and Labour Market Reform in France and Great Britain in the 1990s: Solidarity Versus Activation?", *Journal of Social Policy*, Vol. 32, No. 3, 2003, pp. 361-381.

[11] Laurent Wauquiez declared: "Cette question de la différence entre le travail et l'assistanat est aujourd'hui l'un des vrais cancers de la société française, parce que ça n'encourage pas les gens à reprendre un travail, parce que ça décourage ceux qui travaillent" (May 8, 2011).

[12] See, for instance, *Le Figaro magazine*, "Enquête sur la France des assistés: ces allocs qui découragent le travail", June 6, 2011; *Le Point*, "La France assistée: les scandales du 'modèle français'. Les profiteurs d'allocations. Comment sortir du piège", April 12, 2007.

idea of solidarity with the current trend for incentive policies? This article will focus on the French historical legal framework (I.) and the recent changes that have resulted in a variety of new statute laws (II.). In doing so, it will highlight that there is so far no evidence of a major change in French social policies. Instead there is proof of the resilience of the French social welfare system to adapt to new political, economic and social issues.

I. The French Idea of Social Debt: The Historical Hesitation between Human Rights and Mutual Duty

The French welfare state has a long history. Its roots date back to the French Revolution, even though the main principles were established at the beginning of the 20th century. In this context, the sedimentary construction of the social security system reflects an uncertainty in choosing a clear and specific model: not without certain ambiguities, social protection has been designed at the same time as a human right (A.) and as a counterpart to individual obligations and duties (B.).

A. *Social Protection as a Human Right*

Many French constitutional and legislative bills have conceived social welfare as a human right, sometimes of constitutional value.

During the French Revolution, assistance to the needy was identified by the revolutionaries as a "sacred debt": the idea that society owes assistance to the individual underpinned the French concept of fraternity.[13] Although it did not appear in the 1789 Declaration, which did not recognise any kind of social rights, it was highlighted in the first republican Constitution. The *Déclaration des droits de l'homme et du citoyen* (Declaration of the Rights of Man and Citizen) of 1793, in its article 21, indeed stated that "public relief is a sacred debt. Society owes maintenance to unfortunate citizens, either by procuring them work or by providing the means of existence for those who are unable to work". Along with the Constitution of the Second Republic, proclaimed in November 1848, social assistance was defined in the French constitutional framework as a social debt. Article VIII of its preamble stated "it is the duty of the Republic [...], by fraternal assistance, to provide the means of existence to necessitous citizens, either by procuring them employment, within the limits of its resources, or by giving relief to those who are unable to work and who have no relatives to help them".

---

[13] M. Borgetto, *La notion de fraternité en droit public*, Paris, Librairie générale de droit et de jurisprudence, 1993; M. Gauchet, *La révolution des droits de l'homme*, Paris, Gallimard, 1989.

Thereafter, the idea of assistance as a human right has been strongly asserted throughout the 20th century, along with the global affirmation of human rights. After the Liberation, at the end of the Second World War, the new Constitution declared some social rights in its preamble: "[The Nation] shall guarantee to all, notably to children, mothers and elderly workers, protection of their health, material security, rest and leisure. All people who, by virtue of their age, physical or mental condition, or economic situation, are incapable of working, shall have the right to receive suitable means of existence from society". This preamble still has constitutional value. This constitutional obligation to provide financial assistance to those deemed socially vulnerable has been implemented by the creation of the social security system and the establishment of unemployment insurance in the years following the end of the war.[14]

Fifty years later, the 1998 Social Exclusion Act referred to the same idea by addressing the fight against poverty and social exclusion as a general goal to provide effective access to human rights.[15] Article 1 of the 1998 Act, also referred to as article L. 115-1 of the Welfare and Family Code, states that "measures to combat exclusion are a national necessity based on respect for the equal dignity of all human beings and must be accorded priority in every sphere of national policy. Efforts to combat exclusion are aimed at guaranteeing throughout the territory effective access to all fundamental rights in the areas of employment, housing, health protection, justice, education, training and culture, family and child protection".

Meanwhile, a universal minimum income (the RMI) was created in 1988. The RMI – which, as explained above, was replaced in 2008 by the Active Solidarity Income (RSA) – enabled every person, whether or not they were able to work, to have a minimum income. The adequacy of these two minimum incomes has never been seen in terms of what is needed to live a decent life, but in terms of what is seen as a "fair" compensation for people not involved in the labour force. From the beginning of the RMI, the fear of the "inactivity trap" has not acted as a deterrent: the low level of both incomes was designed as a "safety net" meant to protect people against extreme poverty and not as an incentive for people not to work.

This logic of social rights as human rights has led to a new approach for welfare programmes. It has allowed the building of a "welfare state

---

[14] Unemployment insurance in France was first established in December 1958 by a collective agreement concluded by trade unions and employer associations.

[15] Loi No. 98-657 du 29 juillet 1998 d'orientation relative à la lutte contre les exclusions.

under the rule of law" (*État de droit social*)[16] and reveals a sharp change of direction. The old social insurance system, based on employees' and employers' contributions (Bismarckian model),[17] has been remodelled: social rights are henceforth fundamental rights, and some authors could even refer to the current implementation of a freedom from need based on citizenship.[18] Some universal social rights have indeed been set up. This has been the case, for instance, with the introduction of medical insurance in the 27th July 1999 Universal Health Coverage Act. The *couverture maladie universelle* guarantees access to health care through a national health insurance system to every citizen or documented foreign resident. In addition to basic health coverage, people with low incomes are entitled to free coverage without any compulsory payroll contribution. Other examples can be given, such as the 2007 Enforceable Right to Housing Act[19] or the national case law providing asylum seekers access to decent living conditions.[20]

B. Social Protection as a Mutual Duty

There remains, nevertheless, some ambiguity at the core of the French social system. While the protection of the needy appears in some respect as a human right, other historical texts defined assistance to the poor differently. The general idea was that assistance is at the confluence of a twofold duty: emphasis was placed on the "good poor", deserving support, as opposed to the "undeserving poor", namely beggars and vagrants.[21] This idea, strongly supported during the key periods of French history (mainly the French Revolution and the Third Republic) (1.), still has some legal consequences (2.).

---

[16] D. Roman, "La justiciabilité des droits sociaux ou les enjeux de l'édification d'un État de droit social", *Revue des droits de l'homme* (online journal), No. 1, 2012, available at <http://revdh.org>.

[17] For a historical perspective, see R. Castel, *Les métamorphoses de la question sociale. Une chronique du salariat*, Paris, Fayard, 1995 (translated into English in 2002: *From Manual Workers to Wage Laborers. Transformation of the Social Question*, New Brunswick, Transaction Publishers, 2002); F. Ewald, *L'Etat providence*, Paris, Grasset, 1986.

[18] J.P. Chauchard, "Les nécessaires mutations de l'État-providence: du risque social à l'émergence d'un droit-besoin", *Droit social*, 2012, No. 2, p. 135.

[19] Loi No. 2007-290 du 5 mars 2007 instituant le droit au logement opposable.

[20] "Demandeurs d'asile: le droit à des conditions matérielles d'accueil décentes", *Plein droit*, No. 84, 2010, p. I-VIII.

[21] For a historical survey, see B. Geremek, *Poverty. A history*, Oxford, Wiley-Blackwell, 1994; *Id.*, *La potence et la pitié*, Paris, Grasset, 1987; P. Sassier, *Du bon usage des pauvres. Histoire d'un thème politique: XVIe-XXe siècle*, Paris, Fayard, 1990.

1. The Historical Affirmation of a Mutual Duty

During the French Revolution, several proclamations focused on the mutual agreement that underlined social welfare: the public obligation to provide aid echoed the individual obligation to work. In other words, providing help to genuinely needy persons was for a long time considered the fulfilment of a double duty: that of the able-bodied individual to work and that of the society to assist him/her if (s)he was unable to do so. This confluence of two duties was at the core of a famous parliamentary report, written by the Duke of La Rochefoucault-Liancourt in the early 1790s. "If those who live have the right to tell society: 'give me something to live', then society also has the right to answer: 'give me your workforce'".[22] Nevertheless, the French liberal ideology did not imply any kind of "workhouses" for those who were physically able to work. The state's duties were thought to be fulfilled by stimulating the economy and abolishing the obstacles preventing people to work. Admittedly, during the Second Republic (1848-1852), some experiences of mandatory work (*Ateliers généraux*) were randomly implemented, with inconclusive results.[23] Meanwhile, the poor who did not comply with the obligation to work could not receive any kind of help, except if they were not physically able to work (due to maternity, disability, illness or age). In addition, some very tough criminal penalties were adopted in order to punish vagrancy.[24]

During the Third Republic (1875-1940), the idea of a reciprocity of duties was underpinned by the influential doctrine of Solidarity (the *Solidarisme*).[25] At the turn of the 19th century, a very influential reform movement – les *solidaristes*, led by Léon Bourgeois, who became a member of the government – promoted the idea of a common interaction between all members of society. The doctrine of solidarism imagined a new reciprocity of rights and duties, where the latter came first. The core idea was that work is an individual obligation, and solidarity a collective one. Influential solidarist lawyers, such as Léon Duguit, insisted that this social interdependency is at the basis of the rule of law and implies some

---

[22] "Si celui qui existe a le droit de dire à la société: 'Faites-moi vivre', la société a également le droit de lui répondre: 'Donne-moi ton travail'". For a historical analysis, M. Borgetto, *La notion de fraternité en droit public, op. cit.*; D. Roman, *Le droit public face à la pauvreté*, Paris, Librairie générale de droit et de jurisprudence, 2002, pp. 170-180.

[23] M. Borgetto, *La notion de fraternité en droit public, op. cit.*; F. Dreyfus, *L'assistance sous la Seconde république*, Paris, E. Cornely, 1907. See also the contribution of Fernand Tanghe in this volume.

[24] J. Bart, "La Révolution française, le manque d'ouvrage et le devoir de travailler", in A. Supiot (ed.), *Les sans emploi et la loi*, Paris, Calligramme, 1988, p. 18.

[25] M.C. Blais, *La solidarité. Histoire d'une idée*, Paris, Gallimard, 2007.

legal effects. The State has the legal commitment to provide education and assistance to the poor, while individuals are required to work and to participate in the development of society. As Léon Duguit wrote, "in the solidarist conception, people have no rights, they only have social duties".[26] On the one hand, the unemployed have the legal obligation to work; if they do not, they become useless and ostracised by society.[27] On the other hand, and as a consequence, the State has the same obligation to give employment to those who are able to work. This is the reason why the issue of unemployment is so crucial. Duguit concluded: "it is a strict commitment for the government to provide some solutions".[28]

At this time, members of parliament insisted on the superposition of individual and collective duties. As one bill stated, "the same moral law that obliges society to assist the poor in his/her sufferance and needs, obliges with an equal force the able-bodied poor to work, to contribute and to save money, which are the only way to create means of assistance. True social harmony is the result of the achievement of a double duty and not of the coexistence of a right and a duty".[29]

This strong historical link between individual and collective duties can also explain the current French constitutional framework dealing with the right to work.

2. Right and Duty to Work: An Asymmetric Relationship

The current French Constitution claims that "each person has the duty to work and the right to employment" (preamble to the Constitution of 27 October 1946). Thus, the idea of reciprocal rights and duties is stated at the highest level of French law. Nevertheless, the two ideas expressed

---

[26] L. Duguit, *Traité de droit constitutionnel*, 3rd edition, Vol. 3, Paris, Boccard, 1930, pp. 643-644.

[27] "Il n'est pas permis à un être humain, en âge de travailler, et ayant la force physique nécessaire, de rester inactif. En le faisant, il manque au premier devoir que lui impose sa qualité d'homme social. S'il ne travaille pas, s'il ne produit pas, il est un être inutile que la société tôt ou tard rejettera de son sein […]. Chacun doit travailler, suivant ses forces et ses aptitudes, et l'État peut et doit intervenir pour contraindre, directement ou indirectement, les récalcitrants" (*Ibid.*, pp. 644-645).

[28] "Puisque les individus ont, dans l'intérêt même de la société, le devoir de travailler, il faut que la force sociale qui appartient à l'État intervienne pour procurer du travail à chaque individu en état de travailler. Il n'est pas admissible que celui qui veut travailler et qui, en le voulant, ne fait que remplir le devoir social qui lui incombe, puisse ne pas trouver de travail. Voila pourquoi la question du chômage est si grave et pourquoi c'est pour tous les gouvernements une obligation stricte de lui donner une solution" (*Ibid.*).

[29] Députés Roussel et Morvan, Proposition de loi ayant pour objet l'organisation de l'assistance médicale dans les campagnes et dans les localités dépourvues d'un service public de secours médicaux pour les indigents, Assemblée nationale, *J.O. Doc. Parl.*, July 9, 1912, annexe No. 1281.

in the preamble have been interpreted differently, so that the idea of an asymmetric relationship can be sustained: the constitutional right to work has been interpreted as a poorly consistent right, whereas the duty to work has been significantly implemented by law.

The right to work is weakly monitored by the Constitutional Council (*Conseil constitutionnel*). On the one hand, case law recognises its constitutional value, as the Constitutional Council stated in 2006: the right to work imposes on the legislature the commitment to "lay down rules to ensure the right of everyone to get a job while ensuring the largest possible exercise of this right and, where applicable, endeavouring to remedy the precariousness of employment".[30] But, on the other hand, the legislator's obligations are undermined by the *Conseil constitutionnel*. The case law insists on the legislative margin of appreciation. As the *Conseil constitutionnel* states, "the constitutional requirement deriving from the provisions referred to above implies implementing a policy of national solidarity in favour of retired workers. Parliament is however free to choose such concrete means of implementation as it shall see fit in order to comply with this requirement".[31] The *Conseil constitutionnel* does not consider itself to have the jurisdiction to review the substantive content of legislative enactments in the fight against unemployment, and it has refused to decide whether a liberal, non-interventionist policy or a social interventionist policy is required by the Constitution. In a way, the French case law is somewhat reminiscent of the American version. As the U.S. Supreme Court states, "the intractable economic, social and even philosophical problems presented by public welfare assistance programs are not the business of this Court".[32] Such a jurisdictional self-restraint can also be found in the administrative case law.[33] In a nutshell, the legislative obligation has played a reduced role. As a matter of fact, the right to work neither implies the right to keep one's job nor the prohibition of lay-off plans on economic grounds.[34]

If the constitutional right to work is weakly implemented, the constitutional duty to work, on the contrary, is strongly implemented. For decades, academics have underlined that the constitutional duty to work could only be interpreted as a moral value or at least had only a limited

---

[30] Conseil constitutionnel, décision No. 2006-535 DC, March 30, 2006, Loi pour l'égalité des chances.
[31] Conseil constitutionnel, décision No. 2010-617 DC, November 9, 2010, Loi portant réforme des retraites.
[32] Supreme Court, Dandridge v. Williams, 397 US 471 (1970), 487.
[33] For example Court administrative d'appel de Nancy, June 30, 2006, No. 06NT00655.
[34] Conseil constitutionnel, décision No. 2006-545 DC, December 28, 2006, Loi pour le développement de la participation et de l'actionnariat salarié.

scope,[35] insofar as France abolished slavery and forced or compulsory labour a long time ago.[36] Nevertheless, this statement needs to be specified, as the duty to work has always been set as a legal obligation, at least in a financial dimension: for a long time, vagrancy and mendicancy were criminally sanctioned.[37] This is no longer the case (since 1992),[38] but the unemployed still have the legal obligation to actively seek work. In 1979, after the first economic crisis, the job-search obligation and mobility requirements attached to unemployment benefits were strengthened.[39] Actually, the duty to work has a twofold financial role. First, in order to get unemployment benefits, the unemployed person must have previously paid social security contributions. The involuntary characteristic of a job loss is the standard prerequisite for receiving unemployment benefits, bar a few exceptions. Secondly, unemployment benefits and minimum income schemes cover people of working age but generally require that the person is actively seeking work. According to article L. 5421-3 of the Labour Code (*Code du travail*), criteria for monitoring the job search imply "positive acts and repeated genuine and serious job seeking" and reasonable job offers cannot be withheld without good reason (see below). In this regard, the Constitutional Council states that the right to unemployment benefits cannot be removed because it is a subsidiary to the right to work. However, the law may subordinate such entitlement to the acceptance by the jobseeker of a job or training offer.[40]

To sum up, the French system is characterised by its complexity, due to a mixture of traditional solutions based on different and even contradictory logics. The main logic is focused on an articulation of rights

---

[35] See for instance M. Borgetto, "L'alinéa 5 du Préambule de la Constitution de 1946", in G. Conac, X. Prétot and G. Teboul (eds.), *Le préambule de la Constitution de 1946. Histoire, analyse et commentaires*, Paris, Dalloz, 2001, pp. 133-134.

[36] See for instance J. Savatier, "Liberté du travail", *Répertoire de droit du travail*, Paris, Dalloz, 2005, § 96: "Le préambule constitutionnel de 1946 pose que 'chacun a le devoir de travailler'. Mais cela ne constitue qu'une obligation morale, et non juridique. C'est au contraire une liberté fondamentale de l'homme de ne pas être astreint contre sa volonté à un travail sous l'autorité d'autrui".

[37] See D. Roman, "Les sans-abri et l'ordre public", *Revue de droit sanitaire et social*, 2007, No. 6, pp. 952-964. For a general overview of homelessness in France, see J. Damon, *La question SDF. Critique d'une action publique*, Paris, Presses universitaires de France (Le lien social), 2012.

[38] Loi No. 92-683 du 22 juillet 1992 portant réforme des dispositions générales du code pénal.

[39] Y. Rousseau and B. Wallon, "Du droit pour un chômeur de refuser un emploi", *Droit social*, 1990, No. 1, pp. 27-28; C. Daniel and C. Tuchszicher, *L'Etat face aux chômeurs. L'indemnisation du chômage de 1884 à nos jours*, Paris, Flammarion, 1999.

[40] Conseil constitutionnel, décision No. 94-657 DC, January 25, 1995, Loi portant différentes dispositions d'ordre social.

and duties for all stakeholders: public authorities and social services as well as the unemployed and individual households. It is in this context that activation policies have been introduced.

II. The Current Articulation of Social Activation Policies: Conditionality and Individual Support

Activation policies for the unemployed, which were launched in France in the 2000s, have been present in academic debate since the 1990s.[41]

These policies modified the former ones launched in the late 1970s, which were focused on "insertion". As one author underlines, "with hindsight, programmes introduced from 1975 onwards under the banner of insertion can be seen as precursors to activation reforms later implemented elsewhere, especially in Spain and Italy. Yet, when they were introduced for the disabled and the young unskilled, their justification was to 'activate' these groups in a very specific sense: exactly as the opposite of a punishment or as the only way out from presumed 'dependency', work was here promoted as a positive channel for integration into society and accessing full political citizenship [...]. In the initial solidaristic insertion philosophy, 'social integration' was never meant primarily in terms of constraining people to take jobs on the market".[42] As a matter of fact, the RMI's scheme never included any strict obligation to work: the recipient was only supposed to sign an individualised contract with social services and to engage in a series of activities among which orientation towards the labour market was only an option.[43] The RMI was a tool dedicated to securing the right to a minimum income, and the emphasis was made on "social insertion" rather than on "professional activation".

The real change in the social policies toward activation came later. It was strongly linked to the political conservative discourse that appeared

---

[41] For a general overview, see J.C. Barbier, "The French Activation Strategy in a European Comparative perspective", in A. Serrano Pascual and L. Magnusson (eds.), *Reshaping Welfare States and Activation Regimes in Europe, op. cit.*, pp. 145-172; *Id.*, "The French Strategy against Unemployment: Innovative but Inconsistent", in W. Eichhorst, O. Kaufmann and R. Konle-Seidl (eds.), *Bringing the Jobless into Work?, op. cit.*, pp. 69-120.

[42] J.C. Barbier, "The French Social Protection System in the Throes of Reform (1975-2007)", *Documents de travail du Centre d'économie de la Sorbonne*, No. 2007/48, p. 6.

[43] See R. Lafore, "Les trois défis du RMI. A propos de la loi du 1er décembre 1988", *Actualité juridique – Droit administratif*, 1989, No. 10, pp. 563-585. The 1988 law included an obligation to get involved in the actions required by social or professional insertion without any legally complying character.

in the 2000s, urging the government to fight the – supposedly important – fraud and abuse in the welfare policies.[44] Welfare was accused of being wasteful, and even seen as a threat to the "wage society", and the unemployed were easily stigmatised as unscrupulous scroungers. As a result, the emphasis was put on individual responsibility and autonomy. Activation policies were seen as an answer to the situation of unemployment and, more generally, to a kind of moral and ethical crisis affecting the welfare state. These activation policies had mainly the jobless in mind although other policies of individual accountability existed, especially in the field of migration, school attendance and access to care. But it should be noted, however, that there has been no global French activation policy, unlike the "Work First" programme in the Netherlands or the German *Fordern und Fördern*. Only specific and non-coordinated policies were launched. Despite this fragmentation, some overall strategy can be noticed. Their common goal is both to rely on individual responsibility and flexibility to fit into the labour market and to act on individual variables (compensation, behaviour, occupational and geographical mobility) to suit its needs (A.). Meanwhile, emphasis is also put on the social support, participation and involvement of the jobless (B.).

A. Conditionality for Social Protection and Individual Responsibility

The first characteristic of the French activation policies is the strong emphasis put on the individual responsibility of the unemployed. As a corollary, social benefits are nowadays strongly dependent on individual acts and behaviours.[45] As a result, the granting of benefits is more precarious and uncertain: the poor have to "deserve" the allowance they ask for. In the right-wing political discourse, this emphasis on merit and responsibility is a common way to blame people for their situation. In the 2000s, different laws were passed to implement the common idea of the necessity to remind the unemployed of their duties. Three laws should be scrutinised in particular:

- 2006-339 Act on the return to work and the rights and duties of social assistance recipients (*loi No. 2006-339 du 23 mars 2006 relative au retour à l'emploi et sur les droits et les devoirs des bénéficiaires de minima sociaux*)

---

[44] P. Warin (ed.), *L'envers de la fraude sociale. Le scandale du non-recours*, Paris, La Documentation française, 2012.

[45] C. Willmann, "Politiques de l'emploi, prestations sociales: existe-t-il un modèle vertueux? A propos de la 'conditionnalité' des revenus de remplacement et autres minima sociaux", *Droit social*, 2012, No. 1, pp. 79-86.

- 2008-758 Act on the rights and duties of the jobseekers (*loi No. 2008-758 du 1er août 2008 relative aux droits et aux devoirs des demandeurs d'emploi*)
- 2008-1249 Act generalising the RSA and reforming inclusion policies) (*loi No. 2008-1249 du 1er décembre 2008 généralisant le revenu de solidarité active et réformant les politiques d'insertion*)

These three laws pursue the same goal: increasing control over the jobless in order to reinforce the "rights and duties" approach both in the unemployment insurance programmes (1.) and the social assistance policies (2.).

1. The Increasing Control over Jobseekers: "An Offer You Can't Refuse"

In 2005, a Law for Social Cohesion launched the reform of the public employment service.[46] This change was finally completed by the merger in January 2009 of the different unemployment insurance agencies and the creation of a new structure called *Pôle Emploi*. Title 1 of the Social Cohesion Act called for "mobilisation for employment" and had as its aim a "systematic departure from the logic of assistance". The official presentation of the bill stated that, "the unemployment allowance is a compensation, it must become an investment, a tool for the return to work, a reconstruction step". In this activation scheme, unemployment benefit ceases to be the consequence of previous payroll contributions: the logic of counterparts has been enhanced. The main idea of the 2005 Social Cohesion Act was to do away with the "welfare state approach" by changing the definition of job search.

These incentive schemes for the resumption of employment were completed, three years later, by the previously mentioned 2008 law on the rights and duties of the unemployed. Since then, article L. 5411-6 of the Labour Code details the obligations of jobseekers. Henceforth, to be considered unemployed within the French law meaning, one must:

- be available for work as soon as the occasion presents itself;
- participate and cooperate in the development and maintenance of one's individual job-seeking plan (*projet personnalisé d'accès à l'emploi* [PPAE]). This engagement takes the form of a contract that the unemployed concludes with *Pôle Emploi*;
- be actively and repeatedly searching for work;
- accept the "reasonable offers of employment" that could be proposed.

---

[46] Loi No. 2005-32 du 18 janvier 2005 de programmation pour la cohésion sociale.

This Act has restricted the number of job offers the unemployed can refuse and has introduced penalties for non-acceptance of geographic mobility and wage reduction. The principle is that benefits are cancelled or suspended if the jobseeker refuses "two reasonable offers of employment" that are compatible with his/her skills and are located within a 30 km radius from his home. Sanctions become more severe with the duration of unemployment. The general idea is that the more time passes, the more the pressure grows on the jobseekers.

Meanwhile, administrative practices have also become much stricter, because the modalities of sanctions imposed by the job counsellors have been reviewed in a more coercive way. A 2005 decree made these sanctions easier and meant that they could be triggered after a shorter period of time.[47] Amongst them, the toughest are removal from the unemployment list and suspension of unemployment benefits. Situations leading to these penalties are strictly defined by statute. Striking off the unemployment list is an administrative sanction and must be (in theory) legally pronounced, not arbitrary and appropriate. Under the statute, these sanctions can be imposed if the jobseeker refuses to sign a PPAE, or if (s)he refuses a reasonable job offer. Besides, article L. 5412-1 of the Labour Code provides that the penalty can be imposed on a jobseeker who "refuses, without any good reason, to appear after being summoned by *Pôle Emploi*". However, in practice, administrative regulations have interpreted as an unjustified refusal the mere non-appearance following a summons or a simple unanswered phone call from *Pôle Emploi*. A recent report by the *Pôle Emploi*'s ombudsman mentioned that some unanswered phone calls but also summons that were never received due to an address change as well as emails from *Pôle Emploi* ending up in the recipient's spam email box have led to them being struck off the unemployment list.[48] The severity of the sanction and its effects (loss of benefits) stand in stark contrast with the practice, which is highly arbitrary and disproportionate.

2. The Reinforced Rights and Duties Approach:
The Case of the revenu de solidarité active *(RSA)*

The Law of December 1st, 2008, introduced deep changes in the field of social assistance and employment policy, which may be classified as "active" measures. The government's aim was to simplify existing programmes and to fight poverty. The new system, the RSA, replaced

---

[47] Décret No. 2005-915 du 2 août 2005 relatif au suivi de la recherche d'emploi.
[48] Médiateur national de Pôle Emploi, *Gestion de la liste des demandeurs d'emploi. Les radiations*, report, January 2013.

several existing programmes (the RMI, the single parent allowance [*API*] and the back-to-work bonus). Its main goals were to enhance activation policies, by providing a return to an active status for unemployed persons who depend on social assistance, a decrease of hiring barriers and then, ideally, the resumption of a steady job.

Article L. 115-2 of the Family and Welfare Code henceforth provides that "the social and professional insertion of the people living in a vulnerable situation contributes to the national necessity of combating poverty and social exclusion. The RSA provides households that lack any form of resources with a minimum income and supplements the earned income of recipients whose income is insufficient to enable them to escape poverty or who are at the bottom of the wage ladder. The beneficiary has a right to a social and professional support in order to facilitate his sustainable insertion in employment".

The allowance that is paid to jobless beneficiaries has been maintained at a very low level (the same level as the former RMI, increased for single parents according to the criteria established by the former API).

The implementation of the RSA was also supposed to encourage the resumption of employment. The benefit is not allocated on the basis of employment status (employed or unemployed). In other words, it is also available to "working poor" with very low incomes. The goal was to prevent situations where the recipient earns a certain amount of money by finding a part-time job, and then proportionately loses a part of their benefits. In other words, the RSA was designed to guarantee higher incomes and to propose a financial incentive so that people who "work more, earn more", according to Nicolas Sarkozy's motto during the 2007 presidential campaign. Some additional benefits can also be paid for costs related to the return to work (such as transportation and child care). Thus, this programme seeks to promote the return to active employment: former president Nicolas Sarkozy's administration wanted to make sure that paid work would be more attractive than social assistance.

At the same time, one of the key ideas of the RSA is that it is conditional and requires some kind of counterpart: beneficiaries have enhanced obligations to seek employment. Article L. 262-28 of the Family and Welfare Code provides that RSA beneficiaries have the obligation to take the necessary steps to create their own activity or actions needed for better social and professional inclusion. People earning less than 500 € a month are a specific case, according to article D. 262-65 of the Family and Welfare Code. After a social and professional balance sheet, they enter the scope of a "rights and duties" scheme: poor people are required to follow an "inclusion path" (*parcours d'insertion*), by signing a contract. This contract can be a PPAE with *Pôle Emploi*. In this case, RSA is suspended after the refusal of reasonable job offers, except in cases of particular personal obstacles (especially child care). For people far from the labour market, a specific "social and professional inclusion contract", which is called a "mutual commitment contract" (*contrat d'engagement réciproque*), can be signed. Recipients can be penalised for failing to abide by their "inclusion contract" or refusing "reasonable job offers" that match their profile. Enforcement procedures and penalties that can be inflicted by the local authorities (cancellation of the RSA) were recently amended in order to be more fair and equitable. This is supposed to respect the adversarial principle and be gradual and proportionate.[49]

Moreover, regardless of the subsidies provided by *Pôle Emploi* or the RSA, optional support can be allowed by local authorities. Some of them require pro-active and positive behaviour from the unemployed. Pursuant to the administrative case law, a city hall is entitled to impose hours of community service in order to benefit from this optional help.[50]

The recent statutory changes, concerning the increasing control over jobseekers and the implementation of the RSA, lead to one main conclusion: that the priority given to individual duties has somehow changed the nature of the French social welfare system. The new trends characterising current social policies reinforce the imposition of individual duties where before there were rights. The replacement of the former RMI with the RSA is an obvious example. The goal of the former was to ensure the insertion of its recipients. Its purpose was to frame a dual right, combining the right to a minimum income and the right to insertion, in a logic of social debt.[51] The emphasis was more on the responsibility of society for the exclusion of the individual and on the right to insertion. Insertion was therefore an objective and not a condition.[52] On the contrary, the logic of the RSA stresses the individual duty of the poor to contribute to society by personally engaging in deserving behaviour.[53] In the RSA's scheme, individual rights have been covered over with individual duties.

---

[49] Décret No. 2012-294 du 1er mars 2012 relatif aux procédures d'orientation, de suspension et de radiation applicables aux bénéficiaires du revenu de solidarité active; articles R. 262-40 and R. 262-68 of the Welfare and Family Code.

[50] Conseil d'État, June 29, 2001, *Mons-en-Barœul*, No. 193716.

[51] R. Lafore, "La pauvreté saisie par le droit", in R. Castel and J.F. Lae (eds.), *Le revenu minimum d'insertion, une dette sociale*, Paris, L'Harmattan, 1992, p. 76.

[52] P. Vanlerenberghe, *RMI, le pari de l'insertion*, Rapport de la Commission nationale d'évaluation du RMI, Paris, La Documentation Française, 1992, p. 112.

[53] S. Morel, *The Insertion Model or the Workfare Model?*, *op. cit.*, p. 9.

B. Social Support and Autonomy, the New Motto of Activation Policies

The recent and general shift in these activation policies is based on an individual-focused approach. When pushed to its extreme, it can trigger human tragedies. Indeed, the emphasis on stigmatising scroungers has severe consequences: various academic studies have demonstrated that the "climate of fear" whipped up by official and media stories surrounding benefit fraud delays or stops people in need from obtaining help. Hardening attitudes towards people suspected of being scroungers and cheaters discourages poor people from applying for basic benefits. A phenomenon called non-take up (failure to exercise one's rights) is highlighted, especially with regard to the RSA.[54] At the same time, recent examples remind us that behind the statistics and bureaucratic policies, there are real people, living and suffering. Reports have pointed to the burnout of social services' employees, due to lack of funding and staff shortages.[55] And the reduction in social policies together with the economic crisis may lead to social desperation. Since 2012, at least four unemployed people have committed suicide by self-immolation inside social services buildings...

As a consequence, and in order to rebalance the liberal vision of activation, reconciliation with the concept of social solidarity has appeared to be necessary. As a correction of the liberal understanding (intensification of the logic incentive/penalty, of which the RSA is a good illustration), new fulfilments for social services animated by the concept of social solidarity are being developed. Two main ideas can here be highlighted: social support (1.) and autonomy (2.).

1. Social Support for the Unemployed

The idea of social support (*accompagnement*) for long-term unemployed people is an emerging and recent one, which has spread in several domains.[56] The essence of these activation policies is to improve assistance for jobseekers, in the framework of a strengthened follow-up. Generally speaking, social support for long-term unemployed people has a twofold objective. First, facilitating the return to work, in a context

---

[54] P. Warin, "Non-Demand for Social Rights: A New Challenge for Social Action in France", *Journal of Poverty and Social Justice*, Vol. 20, No. 1, 2012, pp. 41-53.

[55] *Le Monde*, "La souffrance au travail des salariés de Pôle Emploi", October 19, 2009; Economic, Social and Environmental Council, *Pôle Emploi et la réforme du service public de l'emploi: bilan et recommandations*, report, 2011.

[56] See M. Borgetto (ed.), "L'accompagnement entre droit et pratique", *Revue de droit sanitaire et social*, 2012, No. 6, p. 973.

of social crisis, unemployment and insecurity. Second, enabling people experiencing social exclusion to regain or maintain their independence.

Many statutes refer to the idea of *accompagnement*. For instance, one can mention the *projet personnalisé d'accès à l'emploi*, which allows for "individually tailored employment support measures" (article L. 5411-6-1 of the Labour Code). Another example is provided by the Social Reintegration Centres policy. These centres offer care for homeless persons and families to help them regain their independence through social guidance and assistance with employment and housing "with the aim of helping them to access and regain social autonomy" (article L. 345-1 of the Welfare and Family Code). One can also refer to article L. 5131-3 of the Labour Code, which provides that "people aged between 16 and 25 who are in difficulty and face a risk of professional exclusion are entitled to state support for the purpose of access to professional life" or to article L. 262-27 of the Welfare and Family Code, which provides that "the beneficiary of the RSA is entitled to social and professional support according to his needs provided by one single advisor".

The idea of assistance involving the provision of professional and social guidance according to the needs of the recipient and organised by one single advisor is also at the core of the new tripartite agreement between the State, *Pôle Emploi* and the *UNEDIC* (the national institution that oversees the payment of unemployment benefits). This 2012-2014 agreement distinguishes between different follow-ups that job seekers can benefit from according to their "employability".[57] For people far from the labour market, it features intensive support with insistence on individualised meetings and intermediate support, and is called "guided support" (*accompagnement guidé*). For the recently unemployed, a simple follow-up and assistance with job searching is provided, mostly via remote and online coaching (email, chat and phone conversation).

As the concept of social support (or professional coaching) is becoming larger and tends to now cover a wider category of the population, it can be ubiquitous, without being clearly outlined.[58] However, two characteristic ideas define it: information and training.

On the one hand, statutes emphasise information: social services shall ensure that the vacancy information is of a sufficiently high quality to allow jobseekers to search and make an informed decision about applying for a job, and that employers receive applications from the most appropriate applicants. Case law has recently made clear that

---

[57] Convention pluriannuelle tripartite entre l'État, l'UNEDIC et Pôle Emploi, 2012-2014.
[58] A. Fretel, "La notion d'accompagnement dans les dispositifs de la politique d'emploi: entre centralité et indétermination", *Revue française de socio-économie*, No. 11, 2013, p. 55.

this is a legal commitment. Whether it comes from *Pôle Emploi*[59] or from the social assistance agencies (*Caisses d'allocations familiales*),[60] insufficient information can raise their legal liability.

On the other hand, support through training is another form of activation policy. It takes the form of specific employment contracts, the so-called *contrats aidés*. The purpose of these contracts is to integrate jobseekers through economic activity and, in the long term, to help them find traditional, steady jobs. The *contrats aidés* have simultaneously a social and professional vocation.[61] They can be permanent or fixed-term contracts, are subsidised by the State and exempt employers from payroll taxes. The most important are the "single inclusion contracts" (*contrats uniques d'insertion* [CUI]), which combine training and financial support to help long-term unemployed workers. CUIs are divided into two categories: a specific type of contract, the CUI-CIE (*contrat d'initiative à l'emploi*), has been created for the market sector and another, the CUI-CAE (*contrat d'accompagnement dans l'emploi*), for jobs in the public and non-profit sectors. These types of contracts are designed to provide professional support to the long-term unemployed. For example, one can mention article L. 5134-20 of the Labour Code: "the *contrat d'accompagnement dans l'emploi* aims to facilitate the professional inclusion of unemployed people facing specific social and professional difficulties in accessing employment. In this respect, it provides professional support".

However, these policies have not achieved the success expected of them: the number of these contracts remains very low. This discouraging outcome has not prevented politicians from legitimising and promoting these types of programmes, even though they have actually had a number of major negative effects. In some ways, they have indeed contributed to the increasing precariousness of the job market.[62] Furthermore, another difficulty of these "social support" policies remains the lack of funding for social services: a recent study shows that only 50% of RSA beneficiaries have a single advisor and less than half of them have signed an inclusion contract, even though these are legal obligations.[63]

---

[59] Cour de cassation (soc.), February 8, 2012, No. 10-30892.

[60] Cour de cassation (soc.), October 12, 1995, Bulletin, V, No. 269, p. 195; Cour de cassation (civ.), May 25, 2004, No. 02-30997.

[61] D. Baugard, "L'accompagnement dans l'emploi", *Revue de droit sanitaire et social*, 2012, No. 6, p. 994.

[62] R. Castel, "De l'indigence à l'exclusion, la désaffiliation. Précarité du travail et vulnérabilité relationnelle", in J. Donzelot (ed.), *Face à l'exclusion. Le modèle français*, Paris, Éditions Esprit, 1991, pp. 137-168.

[63] Minister of Labour, DREES-DARES, "L'accompagnement des bénéficiaires du revenu de solidarité active (rsa)", *DARES Analyses*, No. 8, February 2013.

2. Enforcing the Autonomy of the Unemployed, a Work in Progress

As one author points out, the mechanisms used to motivate the poor have changed in France. They are more than just an economic incentive that binds reward and behaviour together. They are less than a coercive approach where work is mandatory to receive financial relief. This third way consists in a paradoxical injunction: governing the poor to govern themselves.[64] Reinforcing the autonomy of the poor has become the new motto.[65] To achieve this – paradoxical – outcome, two key tools have been used over the last decade: the recourse to individual contracts and the improvement of participation.

The former is a major innovation in the recent activation policies. It lies in the development of mutual commitment contracts between benefit recipients and social services.[66] "Contractualisation" has become one of the key tools of activation policies. Nevertheless, it remains a symbolic tool, given that unemployment and welfare recipients are public services users and their situation is regulated by a statutory framework. In spite of this, contracts have become increasingly present in the social field, as a tool for participation and involvement of the different actors. However, this increased use of contracts in the social field remains problematic: it heavily relies on the assumption of the liberal and conventional idea that the parties entering into a contract are equal and free. Equal because both parties (here the recipient and the public service) have obligations; free because each party can supposedly determine the content and scope of the contract in an individualised manner.

Yet, the hollowness of the liberal contractual model becomes apparent when one considers the objective and concrete inequality between the recipient and the public service involved.[67] This may explain the recently imposed measures attempting to rebalance the parties' obligations. Some decisions concerning the provision of information that were described earlier fall into this category. Others need to be mentioned here as well.

A recent case, which emerged in 2012, is a particularly interesting example.[68] The applicant was an unemployed worker registered at *Pôle*

---

[64] E. Chelles, *Gouverner les pauvres, op. cit.*

[65] See N. Duvoux, *L'autonomie des assistés. Sociologie des politiques d'insertion*, Paris, Presses universitaires de France (Le lien social), 2009.

[66] For a general and comparative perspective, see J. Handler, "Social Citizenship and Workfare in the US and Western Europe: From Status to Contract", *Journal of European Social Policy*, Vol. 13, No. 3, 2003, pp. 229-243.

[67] See D. Tabuteau, "Topologie des politiques sociales, 2ᵉ partie", *Droit social*, 2012, No. 7-8, p. 661.

[68] Conseil d'État, October 4, 2012, *Pôle Emploi*, No. 362948.

Emploi. He argued that he had not been receiving any support from the agency nor any job offers or qualified training, in breach of the legal duties of the agency. Particularly, he met his counsellor only three times in three years and never received any job offers. Under the provisions of the Labour Code, *Pôle Emploi* has many responsibilities, amongst which is meeting job seekers on a regular basis, to share information about job offers, and to provide advice and training. But, due to a lack of funding, the agency in question had regularly failed to meet its legal obligations. The applicant claimed that these deficiencies had caused a violation of his right to work and did not comply with the principle of equality of all citizens in their relationship with the public service of unemployment. The applicant filed for an injunction, asking for remedies and summoning the agency to take several measures. The applicant won the case when it went to trial,[69] but the judgement was reversed on appeal by the *Conseil d'État*, the administrative supreme court, on procedural grounds (lack of emergency). Nevertheless, this case remains very interesting insofar as it recognised the rights of unemployed workers to be accompanied and helped by *Pôle Emploi*. At the same time, the first judgement (which was reversed) underlined the legal obligations of the employment agency and ordered some remedies: meetings on a regular basis, providing employment opportunities and skills trainings. This case can be read as a black mark on the individual and liberal vision of activation policies, which are usually focused on the duties of jobseekers themselves and their responsibility to actively seek work. Here, with this judgement, for the very first time, the court focused on the responsibilities of the public service to provide assistance to the unemployed. Other cases are still pending and new rulings are expected.

The second key tool, used to achieve the goal of reinforcing the autonomy of the unemployed, is participation. The idea of the active participation of beneficiaries to the delimitation and the application of welfare policies has recently met with great success.[70] Once more, this idea goes beyond the scope of activation policies.[71] But it takes on a specific meaning and force in the framework of activation policies. Associating people may be a way to empower them and to make them more active. This involvement is all the more important when we consider that French

---

[69] Tribunal administratif de Paris, September 11, 2012, ordonnance No. 1216080/9.
[70] See D. Berg-Schlosser, "Poverty and Democracy: Chances and Conflicts", in A. Sciurba (ed.), *Redefining and Combating Poverty. Human Rights, Democracy and Common Goods in Today's Europe*, Strasbourg, Council of Europe Publishing (Trends in Social cohesion), 2013, p. 217.
[71] See, for example, the 2002-2 Act involving the participation of people in social residential accommodations and creating "social life councils" (Loi No. 2002-2 du 2 janvier 2002 rénovant l'action sociale et médico-sociale).

trade unions traditionally have difficulties in representing unemployed people and precarious workers. This first appeared during the winter of 1997, when a "jobless rebellion" launched a high-profile action. One of the demands made by many of the associations of unemployed people, was to be able to "speak in the name of the jobless" within the agencies responsible for managing their situation. Following numerous debates, the 1998 Social Exclusion Act allowed associations of jobseekers to take part in new local liaison committees attached to the agencies for the training and placement of unemployed people (article L. 5411-9 of the Labour Code). However, the law did not provide for the representation of unemployed people within the unemployment insurance fund (UNEDIC). And fifteen years later, these liaison committees are not very effective: they still face difficulties in existing and playing an active role.

Similarly, the 2008 act that created the RSA provided the association of recipients with access to the implementation and the assessment of the scheme. Article L. 115-2 of the Family and Welfare Code states that "the definition, the conduct and the evaluation of the RSA policy are achieved according to terms and conditions that ensure an effective participation of the interested persons". For instance, RSA recipients must be part of the multidisciplinary teams that assist the president of the *département*, which is the territorial unit in charge of the allocation of the RSA. This is a way to allow RSA recipients to participate in the decisions concerning reorientation or suspension of the allowances. Again, although this participation is a legal requirement, it is not yet fully implemented. A recent study has invited the local authorities (*conseils généraux*) to go further down this path.[72]

Conclusion

So, to borrow the title of Robert Castel's latest book, what is the future of solidarity?[73]

The 2000s have put the French system of social protection under tension. As one author points out, "France is clearly not in the 'golden age' of social protection. But we are hardly witnessing the 'neo-liberal' debacle which some repeatedly predict, any more than a blanket convergence towards privatisation, the targeting of the poor, workfare and so on. Our analysis of trends in France does not show any significant realisation of such 'Anglo-American style' developments (other than a rhetorical one).

---

[72] See the report published by the French Minister of Solidarity and Social Cohesion, "Participation des personnes bénéficiaires du revenu de solidarité active au dispositif: Guide de recommandations", March 2012.

[73] R. Castel and N. Duvoux (eds.), *L'avenir de la solidarité*, Paris, Presses universitaires de France (La vie des idées), 2013.

The French social protection system has certainly undergone so many spectacular adaptations over the past thirty years that it would seem to be 'new'. But these changes in no way amount to a break-up of the system".[74] Even though these evolutions are not indicators of a system breakdown, they are nevertheless signs of change.

Indeed, it is obviously difficult to reconcile the different logics that currently exist in the domain of social policies: an individualistic logic that tries to stress an individual's responsibility and that sometimes leads to guilt and stigmatisation for its beneficiaries, and a collective logic that harks back to the French concept of solidarity and introduces new instruments such as social support, contract and participation. This reconciliation may nevertheless take place in a democratic framework of self-empowerment and social autonomy. However, this French solidarity model needs to come to terms with the financial crisis, de-industrialisation and the impact of an ageing population, which all affect social institutions, leaving them without the sufficient financial means to implement their policies. Therefore, many prominent ideas surrounding activation policies remain at the level of hollow political discourses. Putting the blame on the individual jobseekers seems to be easier... The time has therefore come to remind ourselves that, in the economy of rights and duties, both sides, including the state and corporations, have to face up to their responsibilities.

---

[74] J.C. Barbier, "The French Social Protection System in the Throes of Reform", *op. cit.*, p. 3.

III. Activation Policies for the Unemployed and the Human Right to Work

Activation Policies for the Unemployed and the International Human Rights Case Law on the Prohibition of Forced Labour

Elise DERMINE

Introduction

Since the early 1990s, Western Welfare States have entered into a spiral of reforms aimed at promoting the return to employment of social benefits recipients. In this perspective, the work-related obligations imposed on the recipients of unemployment and social assistance benefits have been reinforced. The scope of the availability for work condition has been expanded: in some countries, the traditional concept of "suitable" employment has been progressively weakened;[1] in others, the right to refuse non-suitable employment has even been replaced by the obligation to accept any "reasonable" offer of employment or any "generally accepted" employment.[2] In parallel, the granting of benefits is

---

[1] In the late 1990s, Norway and Germany suppressed the possibility for unemployment benefits recipients to refuse, during an initial period of unemployment, an offer of employment that does not correspond to their previous profession or their qualifications. In 2011, Belgium limited the protection period of the professional status and strengthened the requirements concerning the distance between residence and workplace. Since a reform of the employment insurance system carried out in 2012, the definition of suitable employment in Canada has varied, depending on the category of unemployed that the worker belongs to. The regulation distinguishes long-tenured workers who have only rarely had recourse to employment insurance benefits, occasional claimants and frequent claimants, such as seasonal workers. In the aftermath of their dismissal, frequent recipients must accept any employment considered as "similar" to the job they normally perform, and after six weeks of unemployment, they must extend their employment search to any work "they are qualified to perform".

[2] In reforming its unemployment insurance system in 2002, Denmark suppressed the distinction between "suitable" employment (corresponding to the abilities, qualification, experience and period in service of the jobseeker in its previous work) and "reasonable" employment (outside the activity sector of the jobseeker). Jobseekers have no longer the right to refuse non-suitable employment during the first three months of unemployment within the last six months. The Danish regulation now requires that jobseekers generally accept any offer of employment. In France, any reference to the notion of suitable employment was removed in 2008 and jobseekers must now accept any reasonable offer of employment. On the French case, see the contribution of Diane Roman in this book.

now being linked to increased obligations to actively seek work, or even to mandatory participation in work-related activities.[3]

It is traditionally considered that, when a State sets up a social protection system, the conditions for the granting of social benefits, including the work-related conditions, are not likely to be at odds with the prohibition of forced labour. The prohibition of forced labour would not be a relevant concept under which to assess the relationship between the recipients of social benefits and their public authorities. This idea was precisely expressed in the draft outline of the International Bill on Human Rights, submitted by the United Nations Division on Human Rights to the Drafting Committee: "Slavery and compulsory labour are inconsistent with the dignity of man and therefore prohibited by this Bill of Rights. But a man may be required to perform his just share of any public service that is equally incumbent upon all, and his right to a livelihood is conditioned by his duty to work".[4] In Western Welfare States, the entitlement to social benefits has always been conditioned by a duty to work. As expressed by Jon Elster, this duty to work seems necessary "to foreclose the free-rider option" in order to guarantee the model's sustainability or at least for reasons of fairness.[5]

In the current context of the activation of social benefits recipients, must this idea be abandoned? Are measures strengthening the duty to work of the unemployed not, in certain circumstances, likely to violate the prohibition of forced labour? Some lawyers have begun to raise this question in front of national courts.[6] If some authors are

---

[3] Several schemes condition the granting of unemployment or social assistance benefits to unpaid work performances in the private, public or non-profit sector. For example, one can refer to the *Work Experience Program* carried out in New York (1996) or the *Wisconsin Works (W-2)* programme in Wisconsin (1996), two emblematic workfare devices in the United States, to *Work for the Dole* in Australia (1997), to the *Work First* programme in the Netherlands (2011) and, finally, to the *Mandatory Work Activity Programme* (2011) and the *Community Action Programme* (2012) for the "very long-term" unemployed in the United Kingdom. On workfare schemes in the United States, see the contribution of Daniel Dumont.

[4] The Division of Human Rights of the Secretariat, Draft Outline of an International Bill of Rights, in *Report of the Drafting Committee on an International Bill of Human Rights*, Annex 1 July 1947 (E/CN.4/21), p. 11. See also M. Nowak, *U.N. Covenant on Civil and Political Rights. CCPR Commentary*, 2nd revised edition, Kehl, N.P. Engel Publisher, 2005, p. 202, § 19 and, *infra*, the traditional case law of the European Court of Human Right (II., *B.*).

[5] J. Elster, "Is There (or Should There Be) a Right to Work?", in A. Gutman (ed.), *Democracy and the Welfare State*, Princeton, Princeton University Press, 1988, p. 57.

[6] Mainly in the Netherlands and in the United Kingdom. See, for example, Rechtbank Arnhem, Uitspraak LJN BF 7284, 8 October 2008 (No. AWB 07/5115), www.jwwb. jure.nl; Centrale Raad van Beroep, 8 February 2010 (N) 08/5996 WWB – 08/5998 WWB, 09/2408 WWB, 09/5858 WWB, 09/5859 WWB, 09/5861 WWB, Nederlands

conscious of this issue, the question has thus far been tackled in very few in-depth doctrinal analyses.[7] In this context, we propose to undertake a critical review of international case law's evolution on this issue. More specifically, we will analyse the case law related to Article 8, § 3 of the International Covenant on Civil and Political Rights (1966) (ICCPR) and Article 4, § 2 and 3 of the European Convention on Human Rights (1950) (ECHR), which enshrine the prohibition of forced labour.[8]

In the first section, the material scope of application of these provisions will be clarified. The defining criteria of forced labour and possible exceptions to the scope of application of its prohibition will be identified. The drafters and interpreters of these provisions have often referred to Convention No. 29 of the International Labour Organization (1930) (ILO) concerning forced labour. Therefore, we will also pay special attention to its scope of application (I.).

In the second section, we will proceed to a review of the few cases that have given rise to a conformity assessment of the work-related obligations imposed on social benefits recipients with regard to the prohibition of

---

Juristenblad, 2010, liv. 8, p. 507; High Court of Justice, Queen's Bench Division, Administrative Court, 6 August 2012 (No. CO/260/2012 and CO/1087/2012), www.judiciary.gov.uk; Court of Appeal (Civil Division) on appeal from Queen's Bench Division Administrative Court, 12 April 2013 (No. B3/2012/2138/2141), www.judiciary.gov.uk.

[7] The question has been raised by Pascale Vielle in an international seminar on the trends of labour law reforms in Europe (P. Vielle, "La légitimité des mesures de droit social en temps de crise", in M.C. Escande Varniol, S. Laulom, E. Mazuyer and P. Vielle (eds.), *Quel droit social dans une Europe en crise?*, Brussels, Larcier (Europe(s)), 2012, p. 373). Earlier, G. J. Vonk argued in a very inspiring article that workfare policies may contravene the prohibition of forced labour (G. J. Vonk, "Hunger as a policy instrument?", in O. Hospes and B. van der Meulen (eds.), *Fed up with the right to food? The Netherlands' policies and practices regarding the human right to adequate food*, Wageningen, Wageningen Academic Publishers, 2009, pp. 79-90).

[8] The prohibition of forced labour is also considered a component of the right to freely chosen work as proclaimed in the international covenants on economic, social and cultural rights. We analyse the case law of the bodies supervising the application of those texts in the next chapter, entitled "Activation Policies for the Unemployed and the International Human Rights Case law on the Right to Freely Chosen Work". In so doing, we do not intend to question the relevance of the traditional classification of human rights in successive generations. Rather, splitting our analysis in two separate articles seems appropriate in order to reveal how this issue may be differently addressed by the bodies, depending on whether they apply texts dedicated to civil and political rights or to economic, social and cultural rights. Whether prohibition of forced labour is rooted in one type of legal text or the other may indeed influence its interpretation and its application to activation measures for social benefits recipients. *Prima facie*, we may expect the bodies controlling the application of texts on civil and political rights to be more reluctant to interfere in States' social policies and construe the prohibition of forced labour as disconnected from the idea that social protection should support freedom of work.

forced labour. We will verify whether the case law has considered, in line with the traditional thesis, that such measures cannot as a matter of principle violate the prohibition of forced labour, either because they would not enter into the definition of forced labour or because they would be excluded from the scope of application of the provisions establishing its prohibition (II.). This exercise will lead us to conclude that, even though they have so far never found a breach of the prohibition of forced labour, the international bodies supervising the application of covenants on civil and political rights admit that the work-related obligations imposed on social benefit recipients in the context of activation may, under certain circumstances, infringe the prohibition of forced labour.

I. The Material Scope of Application of the Provisions on the Prohibition of Forced Labour

This section aims at clarifying the material scope of application of the different international provisions on prohibition of forced labour. We will successively look at the Forced Labour Convention No. 29 of the ILO (*A.*), Article 8, § 3 of the ICCPR (*B.*), and Article 4, § 3 and 4 of ECHR (*C.*).

A. *The Prohibition of Forced Labour in Convention No. 29 of the International Labour Organization*

The Forced Labour Convention No. 29 of the ILO (1930) commits States' parties to suppress the use of forced or compulsory labour in all its forms within the shortest possible period. This Convention is part of the eight Fundamental Conventions of the ILO and one of the most ratified (by 177 countries as of 1st of November 2013). Although Convention No. 29 was drafted in the historical context of slavery under colonial administration, it is recognised to be of general applicability, which means that it concerns all new forms of forced labour.[9]

In this part, the defining criteria of forced labour within the meaning of the Convention No. 29 of the ILO will be explained (1.). A description of the measures excluded from the scope of application of the Convention will follow (2.). We will base our analysis on the text of the Convention and its interpretation by ILO bodies, such as the International Labour Conference (ILC), the Governing Body, tripartite committees set up by the Governing Body, the Committee of Experts

---

[9] Another convention of the ILO also addresses the issue of forced labour: the Abolition Forced Labour Convention No. 105 (1957). It complements Convention No. 29, by more particularly aiming at abolishing new forms of forced labour imposed for political or ideological reasons during and after World War II.

on the Application of Conventions and Recommendations (CEACR) and the Conference Committee on the Application of Standards.[10]

1. The Definition of Forced Labour

Forced or compulsory labour is defined by Article 2, § 1 of the Forced Labour Convention as a work or service that is exacted from any person under the menace of any penalty and for which the said person has not offered himself voluntarily.

The Convention gives a common definition to "forced labour" and "compulsory labour". Furthermore, the bodies supervising the application of the conventions draw no distinction between the two concepts.

The Convention, by only referring to a work or a service, does not apply to vocational training.[11] Admittedly, the principle of compulsory education, as established by several international instruments, aims at ensuring the full exercise of the right to education.[12] According to the CEACR, "by analogy with and considered as an extension to

---

[10] As a short reminder, the ILC is the tripartite assembly of the ILO that establishes and adopts international labour standards. Also composed of governments' members, employers and workers, the Governing Body is the executive body of the ILO. In the framework of its representation procedure, a three-member tripartite committee may be set up to examine the representation presented by an industrial association of employers or workers against a member State and its government's response. The committee is charged with submitting a report with recommendations to the Governing Body, which is entitled to publish both the representation and the response. Concerning the regular monitoring of ILO Conventions, the CEACR examines each State's report on their application of the ratified conventions. Composed of jurists appointed by the Governing Body for three-year terms, it is charged with providing an impartial and technical evaluation of a State's application of international labour standards. Following the examination, it makes observations on and direct requests to each State and publishes an annual report. On this basis, the Conference Committee on the Application of Standards, a tripartite body of the ILC, draws the attention of the ILC, in its general report, to the most serious cases of difficulty encountered with the States as regarding the application of ratified standards.

[11] I.L.O., C.E.A.C.R., *Eradication of Forced Labour*, General Survey, 2007, p. 19, § 36; I.L.O., C.E.A.C.R., *Abolishing Forced Labour*, General Survey, 1979, § 20; I.L.O., C.E.A.C.R., *Forced Labour*, General Survey, 1968, § 26. In contrast, the right to freely chosen work established in the texts dedicated to economic, social and cultural rights protects, to a certain extent, the free choice of vocational training. Concerning this issue, see the following chapter, E. Dermine, "Activation Policies for the Unemployed and the International Human Rights Case Law on the Right to Freely Chosen Work".

[12] Universal Declaration of Human Rights, Art. 26; I.C.E.S.C.R., Arts. 13 and 14. See also the ILO standards concerning the prescription of a school-leaving age, such as Art. 15, § 2, of the Social Policy (Basic Aims and Standards) Convention, 1962 (No. 117), and Art. 19, § 2, of the Social Policy (Non-Metropolitan Territories) Convention, 1947 (No. 82).

compulsory general education",[13] a compulsory scheme of vocational training cannot be considered a mandatory work or service within the meaning of Convention No. 29.[14] Vocational training often implies a certain amount of practical work, and one should assess, on a case-by-case basis, if a training programme solely constitutes vocational training, or if it imposes a work or a service that could be considered forced or mandatory labour.[15]

Regarding the criterion of the menace of any penalty, it was made clear, while the draft convention was being examined by the ILC, that this penalty was not necessarily meant to take the form of a criminal penalty. It may also consist in a loss of rights, advantages or privileges.[16] The threat may be physical or psychological; it could also be financial.[17] It can be the fact of public or private agents. This criterion must be understood in a very broad sense.[18]

The criterion of the absence of consent must be established in the person of the worker while the criterion of the menace of a penalty is related to the perpetrator of forced labour. The CEACR notes that "where consent to work or service was already given 'under the menace of a penalty', the two criteria overlap: there is no 'voluntary offer' under threat".[19] The CEACR further considers that external constraints or

---

[13] I.L.O., C.E.A.C.R., *General Survey on the Fundamental Conventions Concerning Rights at Work in light of the ILO Declaration on Social Justice for a Fair Globalization*, 2012, p. 111, § 269. See also, I.L.O., C.E.A.C.R., *Eradication of Forced Labour, op. cit.*, p. 19, § 36; I.L.O., C.E.A.C.R., *Forced Labour, op. cit.*, § 26; I.L.O., C.E.A.C.R., *Abolishing Forced Labour, op. cit.*, § 20.

[14] Regarding the distinction between work and vocational training, the CEACR refers in particular to the Special Youth Scheme Recommendation No. 136 (1970), which indicates that schemes of education and training involving obligatory enrolment of unemployed young people are fully complying with the conventions on forced labour, but do require the prior consent for any scheme involving an obligation to serve (art. 7, § 1 and 2, *a)* and *b)*).

[15] I.L.O., C.E.A.C.R., *Eradication of Forced Labour, op. cit.*, p. 19, § 36. See also I.L.O., C.E.A.C.R., *Abolishing forced labour, op. cit.*, § 20; I.L.O., C.E.A.C.R., *Forced Labour, op. cit.*, § 26.

[16] I.L.O., *Record of Proceedings*, I.L.C., 14th session, Geneva, 1930, p. 691. See also I.L.O., C.E.A.C.R., *Eradication of Forced Labour, op. cit.*, § 37; I.L.O., C.E.A.C.R., *Forced Labour, op. cit.*, § 27; I.L.O., C.E.A.C.R., *Abolishing Forced Labour, op. cit.*, § 21.

[17] I.L.O., Report of the Director-General of the I.L.O., *A Global Alliance Against Forced Labour*, Global Report under the Follow-up to the ILO Declaration on Fundamental Principles and Rights at Work, Report I (B), I.L.C., 93rd session, 2005, pp. 5-6, § 14.

[18] I.L.O., C.E.A.C.R., *General Survey on the Fundamental Conventions concerning Rights at Work in light of the ILO Declaration on Social Justice for a Fair Globalization, op. cit.*, p. 111, § 270.

[19] I.L.O., C.E.A.C.R., *Eradication of Forced Labour, op. cit.*, p. 20, § 38. On this overlap, see also M. Kern and C. Sottas, "Freedom of Workers: The Abolition of Forced

indirect coercion on formal consent may result in an invalidly expressed consent, the interested party having thus not been able to "offer himself voluntarily". Such constraints or coercion may result from an act of the public authorities. In this respect, the CEACR clarifies that "the State is not accountable for all external constraints or indirect coercion existing in practice: for example, the need to work in order to earn one's living could become relevant only in conjunction with other factors for which it is answerable".[20]

In summary, forced labour implies that the work relationship is characterised by "exercise of coercion" and "denial of freedom".[21] The notion of forced labour is thus defined by "the nature of the relationship between a person and an 'employer'", and not by the conditions of work.[22] But admittedly harsh conditions of work may denature a work relationship into forced labour.[23] Forced labour is the "antithesis of decent work"[24] and "there is a broad spectrum of working conditions and practices, ranging from extreme exploitation including forced labour at one end, to decent work and the full application of labour standards at the other. Within that part of the spectrum in which forced labour conditions may be found, the line dividing forced labour in the strict legal sense of the term from extremely poor working conditions can at times be very difficult to distinguish".[25]

One shall finally note that, by opting for a general definition of forced labour in its Convention No. 29, the ILO has demonstrated its willingness to embrace evolutive phenomenons.[26] In its general surveys dedicated

---

or Compulsory Labour", in J.-C. Javillier (ed.), *International Labour Standards. A Global Approach*, 75th Anniversary of the CEACR, Geneva, ILO Publications, 2002, p. 57.

[20] I.L.O., C.E.A.C.R., *Eradication of Forced Labour, op. cit.*, p. 21, § 39. On this matter, see M. Kern et C. Sottas, "Abolition du travail forcé ou obligatoire", in B.I.T., *Droits fondamentaux au travail et normes internationales du travail*, Geneva, Publications du Bureau International du travail, 2004, p. 39.

[21] I.L.O., Report of the Director-General of the I.L.O., *Stopping Forced Labour*, Global Report under the Follow-up to the ILO Declaration on Fundamental Principles and Rights at Work, Report I, I.L.C., 89th session, 2001, p. 7, § 2.

[22] I.L.O., Report of the Director-General of the I.L.O., *A Global Alliance Against Forced Labour, op. cit.*, p. 6, § 16.

[23] *Ibid.*, p. 70, § 295.

[24] I.L.O., C.E.A.C.R., *General Survey on the Fundamental Conventions concerning Rights at Work in light of the ILO Declaration on Social Justice for a Fair Globalization, op. cit.*, p. 104, § 255.

[25] I.L.O., Report of the Director-General of the I.L.O., *A Global Alliance Against Forced Labour, op. cit.*, p. 9, § 31.

[26] I.L.O., C.E.A.C.R., *General Survey on the Fundamental Conventions concerning Rights at Work in light of the ILO Declaration on Social Justice for a Fair Globalization*,

to forced labour,[27] the CEACR has insisted on the diverse nature that forced labour has been and still is able to display over time[28] and, as a consequence, on the dynamic construction of the phenomenon it has to favour.[29] In its general surveys on forced labour, the CEACR thus reviews the new national legislation and practice likely to be questioned regarding the conventions on forced labour.[30]

2. Exceptions to the Scope of Application of the Convention

While the draft convention was discussed, a strong majority of countries expressed their opposition to accepting such a wide definition of forced labour without any exceptions to its scope of application.[31] That is why the first paragraph of Article 2, which defines forced labour, is followed by a second paragraph listing measures that should "nevertheless" not be included in the notion of forced labour. The second paragraph therefore aims at excluding from the scope of the Convention certain specific forms of labour that "would otherwise have fallen under the general definition of forced or compulsory labour".[32]

Article 2, § 2 specifies that:

> Nevertheless, for the purposes of this Convention, the term forced or compulsory labour shall not include:
>
> (a) any work or service exacted in virtue of compulsory military service laws for work of a purely military character;

---

op. cit., p. 112, § 272; I.L.O., C.E.A.C.R., *Forced Labour*, Report I, I.L.C., 14th session, Geneva, 1930, pp. 129-131.

[27] I.L.O., C.E.A.C.R., *Eradication of Forced Labour, op. cit.*; I.L.O., C.E.A.C.R., *Abolishing Forced Labour, op. cit.*; I.L.O., C.E.A.C.R., *Forced Labour, op. cit.*

[28] Through this broad definition, ILO supervisory bodies were abled "to address traditional practices of forced labour, such as vestiges of slavery and slave-like practices, and various forms of debt bondage, as well as new forms of forced labour that have emerged in recent decades, as human trafficking" (I.L.O., C.E.A.C.R., *General Survey on the Fundamental Conventions concerning Rights at Work in light of the ILO Declaration on Social Justice for a Fair Globalization, op. cit.*, p. 112, § 272).

[29] I.L.O., C.E.A.C.R., *Eradication of Forced Labour, op. cit.*, p. 111, § 193.

[30] *Ibid.*, p. xii.

[31] L. Thomann, *Steps to Compliance with International Labour Standards. The International Labour Organization (ILO) and the Abolition of Forced Labour*, Wiesbaden, VS Verlag für Sozialwissenschaften, 2012, p. 192, referring to Bülck (H. Bülck, *Die Zwangsarbeit im Friedensvölkerrecht: Untersuchung öber die Möglichkeit und Grenzen allgemeiner Menschenrechte*, Göttingen, Vandenhoeck & Ruprecht, 1953, p. 59).

[32] I.L.O., C.E.A.C.R., *Eradication of forced labour, op. cit.*, p. 22, § 42. See also M. Kern et C. Sottas, "Abolition du travail forcé ou obligatoire", *op. cit.*, p. 41; N. Valticos, *Droit international du travail*, 2nd Edition Paris, Dalloz, 1983, p. 274.

(b) any work or service which forms part of the normal civic obligations of the citizens of a fully self-governing country;

(c) any work or service exacted from any person as a consequence of a conviction in a court of law, provided that the said work or service is carried out under the supervision and control of a public authority and that the said person is not hired to or placed at the disposal of private individuals, companies or associations;

(d) any work or service exacted in cases of emergency, that is to say, in the event of war [...]

(e) minor communal services (...).[33]

We have seen that forced labour may be imposed by the State as well as by private actors.[34] However, it is notable that the exceptions to its scope of application exclusively target cases of works or services imposed by the State.

The CEACR points out that "the exceptions are subject to the observance of certain conditions, which define their limits". States having recourse to these forms of compulsory work need to demonstrate their respect of the conditions set out in the Convention.[35] The list of exceptions can thus be qualified as exhaustive.[36] To complement this established interpretation, the tripartite Committee set up by the Governing Body ruled however in 2008 that the so-called "duty lawyer roster system" in Chile, although it did not fit within the limits of one of the five exceptions to the scope of application of the Convention, could however equate to one of them, if it was contained within reasonable limits of proportionality.[37]

---

[33] We will not elaborate on this last exception since it has been reproduced neither in the ICCPR, nor in the ECHR. The drafters of those texts have indeed considered that the distinction between minor communal services for the territories under colonial administration and the civic obligations applying to the sovereign States was no longer acceptable (U.N., Secretary General, *Comments of the Draft Covenants*, Art. 4 of the ICCPR, Geneva, 1955 (A/2929), § 25; Eur. Com. HR, *Preparatory works for Art. 4 of the Convention*, Strasbourg, Council of Europe, 15 November 1962 (DH(62)10), p. 15).

[34] L. Thomann, *Steps to Compliance with International Labour Standards. The International Labour Organization (ILO) and the Abolition of Forced Labour*, op. cit., p. 191.

[35] I.L.O., C.E.A.C.R., *General Survey on the Fundamental Conventions concerning Rights at Work in light of the ILO Declaration on Social Justice for a Fair Globalization*, op. cit., p. 112, § 273; I.L.O., C.E.A.C.R., *Eradication of Forced Labour*, op. cit., p. 22, § 42.

[36] See also L. Thomann, *Steps to Compliance with International Labour Standards. The International Labour Organization (ILO) and the Abolition of Forced Labour*, op. cit., p. 192.

[37] I.L.O., *Report of the Committee set up to examine the representation alleging non-observance by Chile of the Forced Labour Convention, 1930 (No. 29), submitted under*

Beforehand, the Committee had stated that the system of assignment fell within the general definition of forced labour set out in Article 2, § 1 of Convention No. 29. One could not consider that lawyers had voluntarily accepted the system of assignments, although they had chosen, freely and well-informed, the profession of lawyer. In its view, "the lawyers have indeed no choice but to accept the general system governing their profession with all its legal requirements, which include the duty lawyer roster system".[38]

The Committee considered afterwards that the obligation imposed on appointed lawyers, by pursuing a general interest objective, i.e. access to justice, could be closely linked to the specific exceptions to forced labour listed in Article 2, § 2. Indeed, among the five exceptions to the prohibition of forced labour, four of them are based on general interest considerations. Each one of those exceptions is, however, subject to compliance with precise conditions aimed at guaranteeing that the imposed work or service does not constitute a disproportionate burden for the interested party regarding the pursued general interest objective. The Committee has taken the view that, as in the case of the exceptions explicitly provided for, the duty lawyer roster system had to comply with the principle of proportionality in order to be excluded from the scope of application of the Convention. It concluded that, in some cases, the load and the frequency of the tasks assigned in the framework of this obligation had a serious impact on the normal exercise of the profession of lawyer, which was in breach with the prohibition of forced labour.[39]

Nevertheless, how the Committee could equate such a measure with the Convention's exceptions seems difficult to reconcile with Article 2, § 2, considering that the exceptions, precisely defined by the States, are, in essence, of strict interpretation (and considering that the list is supposedly exhaustive). One may, however, understand the Committee's embarrassment in this matter, as it was facing a case involving work imposed by the State in the name of a general interest objective, even

---

    article 24 of the ILO Constitution by the Colegio de Abogados de Chile A.G., Geneva, 11 November 2008, § 35-38.

[38]   I.L.O., *Report of the Committee set up to examine the representation alleging non-observance by Chile of the Forced Labour Convention, 1930 (No. 29), submitted under article 24 of the ILO Constitution by the Colegio de Abogados de Chile A.G.*, Geneva, 11 November 2008, § 32.

[39]   In the *Van der Mussele* case (Eur. Ct HR, *Van der Mussele v. Belgium*, 23 November 1983 (app. No. 8919/80)), the ECHR was also brought to assess the compliance of a duty lawyer roster system with the prohibition of forced labour. Comparing the respective approaches of the Committee of the ILO Governing Body and of the European Court of Human Rights appears, as will be seen below, enlightening to understand how the notion of forced labour is conceived by those two bodies (see *infra*, B., 1 and 2).

though it was not included in the list of exceptions. It is even more understandable because organised systems of legal aid did not exist when the Convention was adopted, and as we know, the ILO is willing to develop a dynamic and evolutive approach to the forms of forced labour.

Concerning in particular the general exception to normal civic obligations, there is no ample case law. The CEACR has ruled that mandatory membership to a jury or the duty to assist a person in danger constitutes normal civic obligations.[40] It considers that the exception should be understood in a very restrictive way.[41] Besides, when investigating the complaint concerning the duty lawyer roster system in Chile, the tripartite Committee provided for the fact that the obligation on lawyers to provide legal defence for the most deprived people could not constitute a normal civic obligation, considering that it is only imposed on a certain category of persons and that it did not affect all citizens equally.[42] According to this ILO body, normal civic obligations are thus submitted to a condition of generality.

B. The Prohibition of Forced Labour in the International Covenant on Civil and Political Rights

Article 8 of the ICCPR establishes the prohibition of slavery, servitude and forced or compulsory labour.[43] Slavery and servitude are banned under the first and second paragraphs. The principle of the prohibition of forced or compulsory labour is contained in point a) of the third paragraph (1.). The points b) and c) of the same paragraph state an

---

[40] I.L.O., C.E.A.C.R., *General Survey on the Fundamental Conventions concerning Rights at Work in light of the ILO Declaration on Social Justice for a Fair Globalization*, op. cit., p. 113, § 277; I.L.O., C.E.A.C.R., *Eradication of Forced Labour*, op. cit., § 44; I.L.O., C.E.A.C.R., *Abolishing Forced Labour*, op. cit., § 34; I.L.O., C.E.A.C.R., *Forced Labour*, op. cit., § 37.

[41] I.L.O., C.E.A.C.R., *General Survey on the Fundamental Conventions concerning Rights at Work in light of the ILO Declaration on Social Justice for a Fair Globalization*, op. cit., p. 113, § 277.

[42] I.L.O., *Report of the committee set up to examine the representation alleging non-observance by Chile of the Forced Labour Convention, 1930 (No. 29), submitted under article 24 of the ILO Constitution by the Colegio de Abogados de Chile A.G.*, Geneva, 11 November 2008, § 35-38.

[43] Distinction between slavery, servitude and forced labour is about the gravity of the denial of freedom. Slavery occurs when a person literally "owns" another. Servitude involves that a person exercises a form of domination on another. For further details on the distinction between these concepts, see F. Martin, "Article 8", in. E. Decaux (ed.), *Le Pacte international relatif aux droits civils et politiques. Commentaire article par article*, Paris, Economica, 2011, pp. 227-233 and S. Joseph, J. Schultz and M. Castan, *The International Covenant on Civil and Political Rights. Cases, Materials and Commentary*, 2nd edition, Oxford, Oxford University Press, 2005, p. 295, 10.02.

exception to the scope of application of this prohibition as well as exclusions from the notion of forced labour (2.).

We will essentially base our analysis on the *travaux préparatoires* since the Human Rights Committee of the United Nations (HRC) has not adopted a General Comment on Article 8. Besides, very few cases permit an enlightening of its conception of the prohibition of forced labour.

1. The Definition of Forced Labour

Article 8, § 3, a) of the ICCPR provides that "no one shall be required to perform forced or compulsory labour". It does not contain any positive definition of the notion of forced labour. The definition adopted by the ILO has not been integrated into the text, since it did not seem fully satisfying to the drafters of the Covenant, regarding the way it was articulated with its exceptions.[44] The drafters of the Covenant were however willing to rely on the ILO definition of forced labour to construe Article 8, § 3, a) of the ICCPR.[45] As has been seen, forced labour consists in a work or a service performed against the will of a person under the menace of a penalty or any comparable sanction. This definition remains open-ended and must allow for an evolutive approach to the forms of forced labour. In that vein, the United Nations Human Rights Council set up a working group on the contemporary forms of slavery in 2007,[46] designed to identify and to combat the new faces of slavery but also of forced or compulsory labour.

2. The Exception to the Scope of Application of the Prohibition of Forced Labour and the Exclusions from this Notion

The prohibition of forced labour is accompanied by derogations and limitations established in points b) and c) of Article 8, § 3 of the ICCPR:

> (b) Paragraph 3 (a) shall not be held to preclude, in countries where imprisonment with hard labour may be imposed as a punishment for a crime, the performance of hard labour in pursuance of a sentence to such punishment by a competent court;
>
> (c) For the purpose of this paragraph the term "forced or compulsory labour" shall not include:

---

[44] M. Bossuyt, *Guide to the "Travaux Préparatoires" of the International Covenant on Civil and Political Rights*, Dordrecht, Martinus Nijhoff Publishers, 1987, p. 169.

[45] S. Joseph, J. Schultz and M. Castan, *The International Covenant on Civil and Political Rights. Cases, Materials and Commentary, op. cit.*, p. 295, 10.03; M. Nowak, *UN Covenant on Civil and Political Rights. CCPR Commentary*, 2nd revised edition, Kehl, N.P. Engel Publisher, 2005, p. 201, § 15.

[46] U.N., Council of Human Rights, *Resolution 6/14*, 21st session, 28th of Sept. 2007.

(i) Any work or service, not referred to in subparagraph (b), normally required of a person who is under detention in consequence of a lawful order of a court, or of a person during conditional release from such detention;

(ii) Any service of a military character and, in countries where conscientious objection is recognized, any national service required by law of conscientious objectors;

(iii) Any service exacted in cases of emergency or calamity threatening the life or well-being of the community;

(iv) Any work or service which forms part of normal civil obligations.

The case referred to in point b) is a form of forced labour in the sense of the Covenant, but is nevertheless considered admissible. It is an exception to the scope of application of the prohibition of forced labour. On the contrary, the cases covered by point c) do not constitute forced or compulsory labour within the meaning of the Covenant.[47] According to Nowak,[48] this formal distinction has no bearing on the application of the law. However, in the absence of any positive definition of forced labour, since the cases referred to in point c) are not to be considered forced or compulsory labour, Article 8, § 3, c) could be interpreted delineating the notion of forced labour by negative construction and could thus provide guidance for the interpretation of the notion of forced labour as stated in Article 8, § 3, a). As we will see in the next part, Article 4, § 3 of the ECHR, which also states forms of work that cannot be considered forced labour, has in this way been considered by the European Court of Human Rights as an aid to interpret the notion of mandatory work.[49] In our view, the distinction between the exception to the scope of application of the prohibition of forced labour and the exclusions of the notion of forced labour could thus be fundamental for the application of the Covenant. This question has not so far been addressed by the HRC.

---

[47] S. Joseph, J. Schultz and M. Castan, *The International Covenant on Civil and Political Rights. Cases, Materials and Commentary*, op. cit., p. 295; F. Martin, "Article 8", op. cit., p. 229; M. Nowak, *UN Covenant on Civil and Political Rights. CCPR Commentary*, op. cit., p. 203, § 21. See also Ludovic Hennebel who does not make this distinction and considers that points b) and c) of Article 8, § 3 both establish exceptions to the prohibition of forced labour (L. Hennebel, *La jurisprudence du Comité des droits de l'homme des Nations-Unies. Le Pacte international relatif aux droits civils et politiques et son mécanisme de protection individuelle*, Brussels, Bruylant (Droit et Justice), 2007, p. 146, § 166).

[48] M. Nowak, *UN Covenant on Civil and Political Rights. CCPR Commentary*, op. cit., p. 203, § 21. The other authors mentioned in the previous note do not discuss this question.

[49] See *infra*, C.

Finally, the reference to normal civic obligations directly derives from Convention No. 29 and can thus be given the same definition.

C. The Prohibition of Forced Labour in the European Convention on Human Rights

Article 4 of the ECHR establishes the prohibition of slavery, servitude and forced labour.[50] Slavery and servitude are banned under the first paragraph. Forced or compulsory labour is prohibited under the second (1.). Then, in the third paragraph, the forms of work or service that cannot be considered to be forced or compulsory labour are laid out (2.).[51]

1. The ILO Definition of Forced Labour as a Starting Point for the Interpretation of Article 4 of the ECHR

As Article 8 of the ICCPR, Article 4 of the ECHR does not contain any positive definition of forced or compulsory labour. In the *Van der Mussele v. Belgium* case, the European Court of Human Rights (hereafter the Court) referred to the definition given by the ILO. In this case, it was asked to assess the conformity of the obligation imposed on pupil avocats, *in casu* Mr Van der Mussele, to defend indigent persons, with regard to the prohibition of forced labour. Having noted that no guidance could be found in the various documents of the Council of Europe, the Court held that the drafters of the ECHR had clearly drawn on Convention No. 29 of the ILO on forced labour. The Court observed "the striking similarity,

---

[50] The Convention bodies have clarified distinctions between these three notions. The concept of slavery ought to be interpreted narrowly. It requires that a person exercises a genuine right of ownership over another and reduces her to the status of an object (Eur. Ct HR, *Siliadin v. France*, 26 July 2005 (app. No. 73316/01), § 122). The concept of servitude is an "aggravated" forced labour. The fundamental distinction with forced labour lies in "the victim's feeling that their condition is permanent and that the situation is unlikely to change" (Eur. Ct HR, *C.N. et V. v. France*, 11 October 2012 (app. No. 67724/09), § 91).

[51] For general commentaries of Article 4 of ECHR, see F. Kurz, "Lutte contre le travail forcé, l'exploitation économique et la traite des êtres humains: des concepts légaux à l'application judiciaire", *Chroniques de droit social*, 2008, pp. 317-330; Z. Leventhal, "Focus on Article 4 of the ECGR", *Judicial Review*, Vol. 10, 2005, pp. 237-243; V. Mantouvalou, "The Prohibition of Slavery, Servitude, Forced and Compulsory Labour", in F. Dorssemont, K. Lörcher and I. Schömann (eds.), *The European Convention on Human Rights and the Employment Relation*, Oxford-Portland, Hart Publishing, 2013, pp. 143-158; J. Moerman, "Article 4 EVRM: een kritische analyse van het verbod op slavernij en dwangarbeid", *Chroniques de droit social*, 2010, pp. 509-522; A. Mowbray, *Cases and Materials on the European Convention on Human Rights*, 2nd edition, Oxford, Oxford University Press, 2007, pp. 229-239; C. Ovey and R. White, *The European Convention on Human Rights*, 4th edition, Oxford, Oxford University Press, 2006, pp. 110-121.

which is not accidental, between paragraph 3 of Article 4 of the European Convention and paragraph 2 of Article 2 of Convention No. 29".[52] After observing that Convention No. 29 binds nearly all member States of the Council of Europe, it ruled that the definition of forced labour enshrined in the first paragraph of Article 2 of Convention No. 29 provides a "starting-point for the interpretation of Article 4 of the European Convention".[53] Subscribing to a dynamic approach to human rights, the Court then recalled that the Convention is a living document that must be read "in the light of the notions currently prevailing in democratic States".[54]

In its ruling on *Siliadin v. France* in 2005,[55] the Court also referred to the ILO definition of forced labour.[56] Likewise, it made clear that the Convention is "a living instrument that must be interpreted in the light of present-day conditions, and that the increasingly high standard being required in the area of the protection of human rights and fundamental liberties correspondingly and inevitably requires greater firmness in assessing breaches of the fundamental values of democratic societies".[57]

Unlike the bodies of the ILO, the Court distinguishes between forced and compulsory labour. In its view, forced labour implies physical or mental constraint,[58] while compulsory labour refers to a work "exacted [...] under the menace of a penalty" and "for which one has not offered himself voluntarily".[59] This definition corresponds to that of Convention No. 29 of the ILO.

In the *Van der Mussele* case, the Court had recourse to the criterion of the menace of a penalty to define forced labour. By contrast, the European Commission of Human Rights generally established forced or compulsory labour to be on the basis of the satisfaction of two conditions – the lack of willingness and the "unjust" or "oppressive" character of the obligation to carry out the work – without referring to

---

[52] Eur. Ct HR, *Van der Mussele v. Belgium*, 23 November 1983 (app. No. 8919/80), § 32.
[53] *Ibid.*, § 32.
[54] *Ibid.*, referring to the *Guzzardi* case (Eur. Ct HR, *Guzzardi v. Italy*, 6 November 1980 (app. No. 7367/76), § 95).
[55] Eur. Ct HR, *Siliadin v. France*, § 115-116.
[56] On the interplay between Article 4, § 3 of the ECHR and ILO Forced Labour Convention No. 29 and its merits, see V. Mantouvalou, "The Prohibition of Slavery, Servitude, Forced and Compulsory Labour", *op. cit.*, pp. 154-157. See also V. Mantouvalou, "Labour Rights in the European Convention on Human Rights: An Intellectual Justification for an Integrated Approach to Interpretation", *Human Rights Law Review*, Vol. 13, No. 3, 2013, pp. 529-555.
[57] Eur. Ct HR, *Siliadin v. France*, § 121.
[58] Eur. Ct HR, *Van der Mussele v. Belgium*, § 34.
[59] *Ibid.*

the ILO criterion of the menace of a penalty.[60] We will nevertheless see in the second section that, without referring to the ILO definition of forced labour, the European Commission of HR as an exception has used the criterion of the menace of a penalty from 1976 in cases of work-related obligations imposed on unemployment benefits recipients.

Following the case law of the ILO, the Court considered, in the *Van der Mussele* case, that the menace did not necessarily have to take the form of a criminal sanction, but could also consist in a loss of status. According to the Court, the risk of having the *Council of the Order* strike his name off the roll of pupils or reject his application for entry on the register of lawyers could constitute a menace of a penalty.[61]

The existence of a menace having been established, the Court then turned to the second element contained in the definition of compulsory labour: that the interested person must perform it against his will. The Court found that Mr Van der Mussele "had consented in advance to the situation he complained of".[62] He had indeed chosen to enter the profession of lawyer, well aware of the fact that his status would require him to sometimes defend clients free of charge and without reimbursement of his expenses. Nevertheless, the Court considered that the fact that he had to comply with that requirement in order to enter the bar needed to be taken into account. The Court therefore considered that his prior consent, formally expressed, was not sufficient to conclude that he had offered himself voluntarily. Obviously, the Court followed the ILO supervisory bodies, which had already emphasised that the expression of a formal consent did not permit to necessarily conclude that its author has offered himself voluntarily.[63]

Having established "the relative weight to be attached to the argument regarding the applicant's prior consent",[64] the Court did however not conclude that Mr Van der Mussele had taken part in the duty lawyer roster system against his will.[65] It decided that, in order to assess his lack

---

[60] Eur. Com. HR, *Iversen v. Norway*, 17 December 1963, Decision on the admissibility (app. No. 1468/62); see also Eur. Com. HR, *Ackerl and others Limberger v. Austria*, 9 September 1998, Decision on the admissibility (app. No. 09/97).

[61] Eur. Ct HR, *Van der Mussele v. Belgium*, § 35.

[62] *Ibid.*, § 36.

[63] See *supra*, A. 1.

[64] Eur. Ct HR, *Van der Mussele v. Belgium*, § 37.

[65] One will remember that regarding the system of assignments in Chile, the tripartite Committee of the Governing Body of the ILO had on the contrary decided in 2008 that lawyers could not be considered as having voluntarily offered themselves since they had no choice but to accept this system in order to enter the profession (I.L.O., *Report of the committee set up to examine the representation alleging non-observance by Chile of the Forced Labour Convention, 1930 (No. 29), submitted under article*

of will, elements other than his formal consent needed to be taken into account. These elements were identified by the Court from a review of the concerns underpinning Article 4 of the ECHR, and more particularly its third paragraph enouncing exclusions from the notion of forced labour. We will detail those factual elements in the next paragraph.

2. Exclusions from the Notion of Forced Labour Providing Guidance for the Construction of Article 4 of the ECHR

The third paragraph of Article 4 of the ECHR provides that:

"3. For the purpose of this Article the term "forced or compulsory labour" shall not include:

(a) any work required to be done in the ordinary course of detention imposed according to the provisions of Article 5 of this Convention or during conditional release from such detention;

(b) any service of a military character or, in case of conscientious objectors in countries where they are recognised, service exacted instead of compulsory military service;

(c) any service exacted in case of an emergency or calamity threatening the life or well-being of the community;

(d) any work or service which forms part of normal civil obligations".

In its *Van der Mussele* ruling, the Court made it clear that the third paragraph of Article 4 was not intended to "limit" the scope of the prohibition of forced labour, but to "delimit" the notion of forced labour.[66] By listing measures that do not constitute forced labour, paragraph 3 contributes to shedding light on the construction of the concept of forced labour, as enunciated in the second paragraph. Paragraph 2 and 3 thus forms a whole, allowing the contours of the notion of forced labour to be marked out. The Court's interpretation relied on the text of the third paragraph, which lists the works and services that "the term 'forced or compulsory labour' shall not include".

In the Court's view, from the different forms of labour listed in the third paragraph, the common ideas of general interest, social solidarity and normality emerge. From these common features, the Court specified the factual elements other than formal consent that would

---

24 of the ILO Constitution by the Colegio de Abogados de Chile A.G., Geneva, 11 November 2008, § 32. See *supra*, A. 2.).

[66] This case law has been confirmed since then. See in particular, Eur. Ct HR, *Karlheinz Schmidt v. Germany*, 18 July 1994 (app. No. 13580/88), § 22; Eur. Ct HR, *Spöttl v. Austria*, 15 May 1996, Decision on the admissibility (app. No. 22956/93), § 2; Eur. Ct HR, *Kovalova v. Czech Republic*, 30 November 2004, Decision on the admissibility (app. No. 57319/00), § 1.3.

allow it to determine if the burden imposed on the trainee attorneys was disproportionate and implied that no one could have imagined that it was accepted voluntarily. In this perspective, the Court stressed the following points:

- the services to be rendered are of a similar nature as the usual and normal tasks of a lawyer and do not imply a restriction of his freedom in the conduct of the case;
- the lawyers can find compensation through the advantages attaching to the profession, such as the exclusive right of audience and of representation;
- the concerned lawyer will personally benefit from his work, in terms of experience or notoriety;
- the obligation is based on an idea of general interest and social solidarity, since it aims at guaranteeing the right of access to justice for all;
- the system leaves the lawyer enough time to perform his paid work.[67]

Concerning the absence of remuneration for the services provided, the Court recalled that remunerated work may also qualify as forced or compulsory labour. It also added that the lack of remuneration and of reimbursement of expenses did constitute an element to be taken into account in the assessment of the proportionate character of the measure.[68]

In this case, the Court found that the prejudice was not excessive, considering, in particular, the advantages granted and the time dedicated to those cases compared to the paying ones. The Court concluded that, in the presence of a priorly expressed consent, "only a considerable and unreasonable imbalance between the aim pursued – to qualify as a lawyer – and the obligations undertaken in order to achieve that aim would alone be capable of warranting the conclusion that the services exacted by Mr Van der Mussele in relation to legal aid were compulsory despite his consent".[69]

This conclusion having been reached, the Court did not have to judge if the obligation imposed on pupil avocats to provide legal aid could qualify as a "normal civic obligation" while only affecting a specific category of citizens. On this matter, the European Commission of HR ruled that the requirement for holders of shooting rights to participate

---

[67] Eur. Ct HR, *Van der Mussele v. Belgium*, § 39.
[68] *Ibid.*, § 40.
[69] *Ibid.*

in the gassing of fox-holes as part of a campaign against an epidemic amounted to a normal civic obligation,[70] as well as the obligation for employers to withhold tax on wages and other contributions from their employees.[71] Unlike the ILO tripartite Committee in the Chilean case, the European Commission thus considered that normal civic obligations could apply to specific categories of persons.

It must be noted that the test of proportionality applied by the Court in the *Van der Mussele* case did not formally act as an autonomous criterion for the definition of compulsory labour, which would eventually override the criteria of the lack of will. The Court considered it as a complementing criterion permitting them to determine, through a balancing test between the general interest and the burden carried by the individual, if prior consent had been validly expressed. The Court in this way stated that the service required of Mr Van der Mussele could fall within the prohibition of compulsory labour "if the service imposed a burden which was so excessive or disproportionate to the advantages attached to the future exercise of that profession, that the service *could not be treated as having been voluntarily accepted beforehand*". In its discourse, the Court thus applied the two defining criteria of forced labour enounced in the Forced Labour Convention No. 29 of the ILO – i.e. the menace of a penalty and the lack of will.

Nevertheless, we may observe that all the factual elements identified by the Court to deduce the lack of will were largely disconnected from this criterion, which tends to indicate that the proportionate character of the imposed work *de facto* supplanted the criteria of the lack of will. The factual elements taken into consideration for the test of proportionality were in reality largely borrowed from the European Commission of HR case law concerning the "unjust" or "oppressive" character of the obligation to carry out work.[72] As a matter of fact, in the *Reitmayr v. Austria* case, subsequent to the *Van der Mussele* case, the European Commission merged both criteria and had recourse to the test of proportionality to assess if the obligation for the public medical service to carry out examinations on some patients without payment was unjust or oppressive.[73]

---

[70] Eur. Com. HR, *S. v. Germany*, 4 October 1984, Decision on the admissibility (app. No. 9686/82).

[71] Eur. Com. HR, *Four Companies v. Austria*, 27 September 1976, Decision on the admissibility (app. No. 7427/76).

[72] See for example the *X. v. The Federal Republic of Germany* case also concerning the obligation for attorneys to provide legal aid (1 April 1974 (app. No. 4653/70)).

[73] Eur. Com. HR, *Reitmayr v. Austria*, 28 June 1995, Decision on the admissibility (app. No. 23866/94).

In our view, it would be more satisfying to explicitly construe the proportionality criterion as an autonomous criterion overriding the lack of will criterion, in situations where the work is allegedly imposed in the name of a general interest objective. Our point of view relies on the fact that the proportionality criterion has arisen from a combined reading of the measures excluded from the notion of forced work in § 3, which all embrace situations where work is imposed by the State in the name of a general interest objective.

Moreover, construing the test of proportionality as a complementing criterion to assess the validity of the consent, leads, in our view, to questionable outcomes. By definition, the test of proportionality only applies when the work is requested by a State pursuing a general interest objective, since it consists in balancing the burden imposed on the individual with the general interest. This criterion is thus not relevant in situations where the work is imposed by a private agent pursuing a personal goal, e.g. in the cases of trafficking in persons for the purpose of labour exploitation. Besides, we have showed that construing the test of proportionality as a complementing criterion does not tighten the definition of forced labour. On the contrary, it broadens it by allowing a more flexible construction of the lack of will criterion, the application of the test of proportionality permitting a possible invalidation of the expressed consent. As a result, establishing a violation of the prohibition of forced labour would be easier in the case of work imposed by the State pursuing a general interest objective, than in that of an individual acting for private purposes. Logically, the definition of forced labour should on the contrary be narrowed when the imposed work serves a general interest objective. It is in fact in this perspective that the drafters of the Convention have drawn up the list of exclusions of the notion of forced labour. In these cases, a certain level of coercion is admitted, since work is imposed on the basis of general interest considerations.

The interpretation of Article 2, § 2 of Convention No. 29 of the ILO differs from that of Article 4, § 3 of the ECHR. According to ILO case law, the measures listed in Article 2, § 2 fall within the definition of forced labour set out in the first paragraph but are nevertheless specifically excluded from its scope. This list of exceptions is exhaustive and of strict interpretation. Unlike Article 4, § 3 of the ECHR, Article 2, § 2 takes no conceptual part in defining forced labour. It seemed therefore unlikely that ILO case law would discover in the measures listed in Article 2, § 2 a complementing or autonomous criterion for the definition of forced labour, which would be applicable to all hypotheses of work imposed by a State pursuing a general interest objective. Facing such a case, we have seen hereinabove that a tripartite Committee of the ILO Governing Body did however consider – exactly like the European Court – that a common requirement of proportionality could emerge from those measures. It therefore had recourse to the test of proportionality, not in order to assess if the duty lawyer roster system could be related to the exceptions to forced labour listed in Article 2, § 2 of Convention No. 29. On the basis of criteria largely similar to those selected by the Court in the *Van der Mussele case*, it found that, in the case it was dealing with, the load and the frequency of the tasks assigned in the framework of the obligation could affect the normal exercise of the profession of lawyer and did thus constitute forced labour.[74]

* * *

At the end of this section, some relevant elements regarding activation measures for the unemployed may be pointed of the general international case law on the prohibition of forced labour.

Throughout international case law, the menace of a penalty and the lack of will are the general defining criteria of forced labour. Through these large criteria, international bodies are willing to develop an evolutive approach of the notion of forced labour and to apprehend all new phenomenons that could amount to it. Concerning the criterion of the menace of a penalty, we will particularly underline that international bodies consider that the penalty can consist in the loss of a right or an advantage. As for the lack of will criterion, their evaluation goes beyond formally expressed consent. Indirect coercion may for example invalidate the expressed consent.

Beyond these general criteria, we have noticed that the question of proportionality emerges whether in the case law on ILO Forced Labour Convention or in the case law of the ECHR, when the work is imposed by a State on individuals under general interest considerations. This criterion is in fact rooted in a separate paragraph following the general prohibition of forced labour, listing in both instruments very similar forms of work imposed on individuals by States in the name of a general interest objective, such as compulsory military service, work in detention or normal civic obligations. Theses paragraphs have nevertheless a different status in each instrument, which leads to different difficulties and ways of handling the question of proportionality.

In the ILO Forced Labour Convention, the forms of work listed in Article 2, § 2 fall under the general definition of forced labour but are

---

[74] I.L.O., *Report of the committee set up to examine the representation alleging non-observance by Chile of the Forced Labour Convention, 1930 (No. 29), submitted under article 24 of the ILO Constitution by the Colegio de Abogados de Chile A.G.*, Geneva, 11 November 2008, § 38.

exempted from Convention No. 29. As an exception to the scope of the general definition of forced labour, this paragraph should be of strict interpretation. We have, though, observed that ILO tripartite Committee has had recourse to interpretations by analogy and have subsequently judged that forms of work imposed under general interest considerations may equate with the Convention's exceptions if the charge imposed on the individual is proportionate.

The European Court faces different problems. According to her, Article 4, § 3 participates in delineating the notion of forced labour. It has thus considered the proportionate character of the work as a defining criterion of forced labour, arising from paragraph 3. Probably willing to develop an interpretation that is consistent with the ILO definition of forced labour, the Court has formally considered the test of proportionality as a secondary test to assess the reality of the expressed consent. Admitting that the test of proportionality has a prevailing role in defining forced labour when work is imposed under general interest considerations, may however, be justified on the fact that Article 4, § 3 contributes to defining the notion of forced labour, unlike Article 2, § 2 of the ILO Convention.

To conclude this first section, we will finally observe that normal civic obligations may be a very interesting concept in terms of the work-related obligations imposed on social benefits recipients. On this matter, the general international case law seems open as to whether normal civic obligations have to affect all citizens or if they may target specific categories of persons. Besides, few case law developments have been devoted to the abstract criterion of normality.

II. Activation Policies for the Unemployed in the International Case Law on Prohibition of Forced Labour

In this second section, an analysis will be delivered of all the cases in which the organs controlling the application of the ICCPR (*A*.) and the ECHR (*B*.) have had to look into the work-related obligations imposed on social benefits recipients from the angle of the prohibition of forced labour.[75] We will determine if jurisprudence considers this type of

---

[75] The ILO case law related to the conformity of activation measures regarding the prohibition of forced labour is not analysed here. This paper aims at emphasising the specific approach to the prohibition of forced labour in the case law applying texts dedicated to civil and political rights (ICCPR and ECHR). Yet, the ILO bodies have also, if not mainly, analysed activation measures through the prism of social rights, such as the right to freely chosen work or the right to social security. For that matter, ILO bodies consider that the prohibition of forced labour supports the right to freely

obligation as not meeting the definition of forced labour or as excluded from the scope of application of its prohibition. These particular cases will also be compared to the general case law on the material scope of application of the prohibition of forced labour, as analysed in the first section.

If the case law on the prohibition of forced labour is generally not abundant, this is equally the case for the particular question of the work-related obligations imposed on social benefits recipients. According to Bouziri and Martin, this is probably due to the precarious situation of its potential victims.[76] This tends to be confirmed by the fact that absolutely no cases concerning social assistance recipients have been brought before international bodies. These people generally face an even more precarious situation than unemployment benefits recipients.

A. The **Faure v. Australia** *Case and Article 8, § 3 of the ICCPR*

The Human Rights Committee (HRC) of the United Nations has only once been called upon to decide on the conformity of an activation measure regarding the prohibition of forced labour. This was in 2005, in the *Faure v. Australia* case.[77] We propose a critical analysis of this case, which has thus far at most only been mentioned in some commentaries on Article 8, § 3.[78]

In order to combat long-term unemployment amongst its youth, the Australian government set up the *Work for the Dole* scheme in the late 1990s, according to which the long-term jobless had to accept work of 12 to 15 hours a week, or face a penalty of having their unemployment benefits reduced or suspended for two months. This programme was part of the unemployment assistance system, for which no prior contribution was required, and the benefits of which were unlimited in time. This type of work programme has since spread to some European countries, such as the United Kingdom and the Netherlands, mainly in universal unemployment benefits systems and in social assistance systems.

---

chosen work. The ILO case law is therefore examined in the next chapter dedicated to the right to freely chosen work.

[76] N. Bouziri, *La protection des droits civils et politiques par l'ONU. L'œuvre du Comité des droits de l'homme*, Paris, L'Harmattan, 2003, pp. 303-304; F. Martin, "Article 8", *op. cit.*, p. 239.

[77] H.R. Committee, *Faure v. Australia*, communication No. 1036/2001, 23 November 2005 (CCPR/C/85/D/1036/2001).

[78] L. Hennebel, *La jurisprudence du Comité des droits de l'homme des Nations-Unies. Le Pacte international relatif aux droits civils et politiques et son mécanisme de protection individuelle*, *op. cit.*, pp. 147-148, § 168; F. Martin, "Article 8", *op. cit.*, pp. 236-237.

Mrs Faure, a young unemployed woman who had never worked, had her unemployment benefits suspended for two months, because of unexplained absences from the work she had been assigned in the framework of the *Work for the Dole* scheme. Mrs Faure lodged a complaint in the HRC, arguing that she had been compelled to perform forced or compulsory labour, in breach of Article 8, § 3, a) of the Covenant. Moreover, she claimed to not have any legal remedy to pursue her grievances, thus violating paragraph 2 and 3, a), b) and c) of Article 2 of the Covenant.

Concerning admissibility, the HRC found that the complainant's allegations based on Article 8, § 3, a) did fall within the scope of the Covenant and were sufficiently supported to be deemed admissible.[79] The HRC thus accepted the idea that an obligation to work imposed on unemployed persons as a condition for the granting of their benefits could, under certain circumstances, appear to be contrary to the prohibition of forced labour, enshrined in Article 8, § 3, a) of the Covenant.

In her separate opinion,[80] Mrs Ruth Wedgwood, an American Committee member, considered, by contrast, that the complaint of forced labour should have been dismissed as inadmissible, through lack of substantiation. She argued that the work-related obligations imposed on unemployment benefits recipients could clearly not equate to forced labour. She claimed that the analysed facts could absolutely not be compared with "horrific instances such as the forced labour required by colonial powers to build canals and roads". Her argument was based on an approach to the forms of forced labour that might be considered quite static. So far, we have indeed shown the shared will of international supervisory bodies to follow an evolutive interpretation of the phenomenon of forced labour.

Mrs Wegwood then referred to Nowak, according to which "the mere lapse of unemployment assistance when a person refuses to accept work not corresponding to his or her qualifications does not [...] represent a violation [of Article 8]; in this case, neither the intensity of the involuntariness nor that of the sanction reaches the degree required for forced or compulsory labour".[81] Nowak based his argument on the *X v. The Netherlands* case of the European Commission of Human Rights, delivered in 1976. In our view, such a statement cannot however be inferred from this case. As will be explained in our next point, in

---

[79] H.R. Committee, *Faure v. Australia*, § 6.3.
[80] *Ibid.*, Appendix, Individual opinion by Committee member Ms Ruth Wedgwood.
[81] M. Nowak, *UN Covenant on Civil and Political Rights. CCPR Commentary, op. cit.*, p. 202.

X v. The Netherlands the European Commission of Human Rights did come to a decision on the conformity of the availability for work condition, imposing on unemployment benefits recipients to accept any suitable job that would match their professional skills. Nothing relevant for the *Faure* case can emerge from the *X. v. The Netherlands* case, since the *Faure* case is about absences from a compulsory work programme imposed on unemployment benefits recipients, without any consideration of their professional skills.

Concerning a potential violation of Article 2 of the Covenant, the HRC recalled that States must provide legal remedies for any violation of the rights enshrined in the Covenant. This guarantee would be void if it was not available where a violation had not yet been established. Article 2 ensures the alleged victims with a legal protection if their complaints are sufficiently well founded as to be arguable under the Covenant. In this case, the Committee concluded that Article 2, read together with Article 8, had been breached, since the complainant did not benefit from an effective national remedy that would have allowed her to have her obligation to work controlled regarding the prohibition of forced labour.[82]

The HRC then investigated the alleged breach of the third paragraph of Article 8. The Committee had already recognised that the definition of forced or compulsory labour in the relevant ILO instruments may contribute to the construction of Article 8, § 3, a). It however made clear that it falls ultimately under its own responsibility to identify the prohibited practises. So, in its view:

"The term 'forced or compulsory labour' covers a range of conduct extending from, on the one hand, labour imposed on an individual by way of criminal sanction, notably in particularly coercive, exploitative or otherwise egregious conditions, through, on the other hand, to lesser forms of labour in circumstances where punishment as a comparable sanction is threatened if the labour directed is not performed".[83]

In this paragraph, reference is indirectly made to the ILO criterion of the menace of a penalty that does not need to take the form of a criminal sanction.

Surprisingly, without even analysing if the obligation to work fell into the definition of forced labour, the HRC then immediately specified the general requirements that needed to be met for a work or service to be considered as a normal civic obligation. In its view, "to so qualify as a normal civic obligation, the labour in question must, at a minimum, not be an exceptional measure; it must not possess a punitive purpose or

---

[82] H.R. Committee, *Faure v. Australia*, § 7.2.-7.4.
[83] *Ibid.*, § 7.5.

effect; and it must be provided for by law in order to serve a legitimate purpose under the Covenant".[84] The HRC does thus not seem to require the obligation to affect all citizens on an equal footing, as will be later required by the Committee of the ILO Governing Body in the Chilean case.[85]

At this stage, one would have expected the HRC to individually apply to the case each one of the criteria it had identified, in order to determine if the obligation to work in the framework of the *Work for the Dole* scheme did, or not, constitute a normal civic obligation, compatible with the prohibition of forced labour. This was, however, not the case. Instead, the HRC concluded its review in one sentence:

"In the light of these considerations, the Committee is of the view that the material before it, including the absence of a degrading or dehumanizing aspect of the specific labour performed, does not show that the labour in question comes within the scope of the proscriptions set out in article 8. It follows that no independent violation of article 8 of the Covenant has been made out".[86]

Given the brevity of the reasoning, it is hard to understand if the HRC based its conclusions on Article 8, § 3, a) or on the point c). In the beginning, the HRC seemed to want to determine if the obligation to work imposed on Mrs Faure could be qualified as a normal civic obligation, within the meaning of Article 8, § 3, c). Its conclusion is nonetheless very general, with the HRC having confined itself to merely finding that the work imposed on Mrs Faure did not constitute forced labour, as prohibited by Article 8, § 3, a).

In particular, the finding of the HRC is based on the fact that the required work could not be considered as degrading or dehumanising. This criterion appears far more restrictive than the normality criterion, generally required for the exception of normal civic obligations. It recalls the former case law of the European Commission of Human Rights, which had proposed the unfair or oppressive nature of the work as a defining criterion of forced labour.[87] The criterion favoured by the HRC implies, however, a much graver threshold. It echoes the threshold required to

---

[84] *Ibid.*
[85] It must be noted that in 2005, the tripartite Committee of the Governing Body of the ILO had not yet made clear that a condition of generality was required regarding the civic nature of the obligation (I.L.O., *Report of the committee set up to examine the representation alleging non-observance by Chile of the Forced Labour Convention, 1930 (No. 29), submitted under article 24 of the ILO Constitution by the Colegio de Abogados de Chile A.G.*, Geneva, 11 November 2008).
[86] H.R. Committee, *Faure v. Australia*, § 7.5.
[87] Eur. Com. HR, *Iversen v. Norway*; Eur. Com. HR, *Ackerl and others v. Austria*.

trigger the applicability of Article 3, which prohibits torture and inhuman or degrading punishment or other treatments. It is astonishing that the HRC did not apply the ILO defining criteria of forced labour, i.e. the menace of any penalty and the lack of will, used by the ECHR in the *Van der Mussele* case, to which the Australian government itself had even referred in its answer to the complaint's author.[88]

B. The X, Talmon and Schuitemaker v. The Netherlands Cases and Article 4, § 3 of the ECHR

The European Court and Commission of Human Rights have so far only had three opportunities to address the issue of work-related obligations imposed on unemployment benefits recipients, from the angle of the prohibition of forced labour: the *X v. The Netherlands* (1976),[89] the *Talmon v. The Netherlands* (1997)[90] and the *Schuitemaker v. The Netherlands* (2010)[91] cases. These three disputes concerned the suspension or the reduction of unemployment benefits, justified on the grounds of the complainants' refusal to take up employment on the labour market. Thus far, the Convention bodies had never had to assess the conformity of compulsory work schemes with Article 4, § 3 of the ECHR.

None of the abovementioned cases passed the admissibility test. The Convention bodies did not identify any problem regarding their material competence in deciding the cases submitted to them. In the three cases, the applications were declared inadmissible for being manifestly ill-founded. As a reminder, the Convention bodies consider that "any application will be considered 'manifestly ill-founded' if a preliminary examination of its substance does not disclose any appearance of a violation of the rights guaranteed by the Convention, with the result that it can be declared inadmissible at the outset without proceeding to a formal examination on the merits".[92] This implies that, even if the Court case law on the issue is not abundant, the organs of the Convention have considered the situation as sufficiently simple to conclude, regarding the existing jurisprudential elements, that there was no indication of violation of the Convention.

---

[88] H.R. Committee, *Faure v. Australia*, § 4.9.
[89] Eur. Comm. H. R., *X. v. The Netherlands*, 13 December 1976, Decision on the admissibility (app. No. 7602/76).
[90] Eur. Comm. H. R., *Talmon v. The Netherlands*, 26 December 1997, Decision on the admissibility (app. No. 30300/96).
[91] Eur. Ct HR, *Schuitemaker v. The Netherlands*, 4 May 2010, Decision on the admissibility (app. No. 15906/08).
[92] Council of Europe, *Practical Guide on Admissibility Criteria*, Strasbourg, Council of Europe Publishing, 2011, pp. 68-69.

The factual background of the *X. v. The Netherlands* case is as follows.[93] The applicant, a specialised construction worker, had refused an employment offer made by the municipal plantations service, for the reasons that it did not match his professional skills and that it was socially disreputable, those kinds of jobs being, in his view, mainly for disabled persons. Following this refusal, he was excluded from unemployment benefits for 25 weeks. Before the European Commission of HR, he argued that he had been summoned to perform forced or compulsory labour, banned by Article 4, § 2 of the Convention.

The Commission declared the application manifestly ill-founded after a very concise – and quite formalistic – reasoning:

> In pursuance of Dutch legislation relating to unemployment benefits, no one is forced, by whatever penalty, to accept a job offer made by competent public authorities. A refusal does not constitute an infringement of the law. The acceptance of a convenient employment is only a condition for granting unemployment benefits. The refusal is penalised by the temporary loss of these benefits, excluding any other measure. There can therefore be no question of forced or compulsory labour within the meaning of Article 4, § 2 of the Convention.[94]

It would indeed be inconsistent to consider that the loss of unemployment benefits for refusing suitable work constitutes forced labour, while, according to international standards, unemployment benefits can be refused, suppressed, suspended or reduced if the interested party fails to accept a suitable employment.[95] As a reminder, the notion of suitable employment essentially protects the professional status of the unemployed person who must have the right, during a first reasonable period of unemployment, to refuse an employment that does not correspond to her professional qualifications.[96]

Nevertheless, the unemployed individual in this case complained about having been excluded from unemployment benefits for refusing work that did not match his professional skills. One can thus deplore that the European Commission of HR confined its control to such a

---

[93] Eur. Comm. H. R., *X v. The Netherlands*, 13 December 1976, Decision on the admissibility (app. No. 7602/76).

[94] *Ibid.*, § 1.

[95] Article 21 of the ILO Convention No. 168 concerning Employment Promotion and Protection against Unemployment (1988).

[96] On the notion of suitable employment, see E. Dermine, "Suitable Employment and Job of Quality", in P. Vielle and S. Borelli (eds.), *Quality of Employment in Europe. Legal and Normative Perspective*, Brussels, PIE-Peter Lang (Work and Society), 2012, pp. 157-180.

formal regulation, without making sure that, concretely, the unemployed individual had not been compelled to accept a non-suitable employment.

Moreover, the Commission also applied the criterion of the menace of a penalty. As we can recall, the European Court of Human Rights had recourse for the first time to this criterion years later in the *Van der Mussele* case. Besides, it is exceptional that the Commission referred to this criterion, since following its consolidated case law forced labour was solely conditioned by the absence of will and its unjust or oppressive character. The Commission considered that this criterion was clearly not met. It seemed to base this finding on the fact that in this case, refusal of the suitable employment was not punished by a criminal penalty. In its view, it was normal that the refusal would be punished by the temporary loss of benefits, since this was one of the conditions for their granting. This reasoning seems now outdated, considering the subsequent case law of the Court on the notion of forced labour. The Court currently refers to the case law of the ILO bodies and thus now considers that the penalty should not necessarily take the form of criminal sanction, but may also consist in the loss of a right, advantage, privilege or status.[97]

The second case, *Talmon v. The Netherlands* was submitted to the European Commission of HR in 1997 and relates to a beneficiary of unemployment assistance, who considered that the only suitable employment for him was that of an independent scientific expert or a social critic.[98] In his view, he had serious and insurmountable conscientious objections to taking up any other employment. The Dutch administration decided to reduce his unemployment benefits, since he refused to comply with his obligation to seek suitable employment. Indeed, other employments than those of independent scientific expert and social critic did match his professional skillset.

Again on the basis of a very concise reasoning, quite similar to the one made in the previous case, the Commission concluded that there could be no question of forced or compulsory labour, within the meaning of Article 4, § 2 of the ECHR. In its view, the applicant did not seem to have been compelled to perform any kind of labour, and the refusal to seek any other form of employment than those of independent scientific expert did not appear to have made him liable to any other kind of measures than the reduction of his unemployment benefits. The Commission therefore considered that his application was manifestly ill-founded.

The Commission seems to have made a distinction between the constraint and the menace of a penalty. This distinction probably echoes

---

[97] Eur. Ct HR, *Van der Mussele v. Belgium*, 23 November 1983.
[98] Eur. Comm. H. R., *Talmon v. The Netherlands*, 26 December 1997, Decision on the admissibility (app. No. 30300/96).

that made by the Convention bodies between forced labour implying constraint and compulsory labour implying the menace of a penalty.[99]

Just as in the first case, the Commission did not consider that the reduction of unemployment benefits may constitute, in itself, the menace of a penalty. In between these two cases, the Court had however delivered its judgement in the *Van der Mussele case*, where it ruled, in accordance with the case law of the ILO bodies, that the menace of a penalty could consist in the loss of a right. In our view, compliance with this criterion should thus have been more carefully assessed, or at the very least, the Commission's reasoning should have been more widely developed.[100] The Commission would have then eventually examined the second criterion of the lack of will, which it has not yet applied to work-related obligations imposed on social benefits recipients.

As the work-related requirement is a condition for the granting of unemployment benefits and is only sanctioned by the loss of those benefits, it could not, in the European Commission of HR's view, be a question of forced labour. States would thus be completely free to choose the granting conditions to impose on the recipients of the benefits systems they set up. One shall however note that, at that time, the Commission could probably not imagine the multiple forms that work-related obligations imposed on unemployed persons would take a decade later.

In 2010, in the *Schuitemaker v. The Netherlands* case, the Convention bodies investigated for the first time a case where the availability for work condition had been expanded to all "generally accepted" employment.[101] In the surrounding context of activation, the Netherlands had indeed reformed their regulation on unemployment assistance, in order to force the unemployed to take up any generally accepted employment, and not only suitable employments. This new obligation had a much wider scope, since it included employments the unemployed had no experience or qualifications for and even no affinity with and only excluded employments that were generally not socially accepted. According to this reform, the unemployed could also refuse employments for which they had conscientious objections. Before the Court, the applicant argued that

---

[99] See *supra*, I., C. and, in particular, the *Van der Mussele* case commentary.
[100] In certain circumstance, ILO bodies have considered that the reduction or suspension of unemployment benefits for non-compliance with a work-related obligation constituted a menace of losing a right. On this case law, see the next chapter, E. Dermine, "Activation Policies for the Unemployed and the International Human Rights Case law on the Right to Freely Chosen Work".
[101] Eur. Ct HR, *Schuitemaker v. The Netherlands*, 4 May 2010, Decision on the admissibility (app. No. 15906/08).

this new requirement to accept any generally accepted employment, and not solely suitable employments, may compel her to perform forced or compulsory labour.

The applicant had not concretely had her benefits reduced following a refusal to take up employment. Following the case law of the Court, in the absence of an individual measure of implementation, individuals can only contend that a law violates their rights within the meaning of Article 34 of the Convention if they run the risk of being directly affected by this law.[102] On the basis of this case law, the applicant argued that this law applies to all recipients of benefits. The Court however ruled that it did not have to assess the applicant's status of victim, since its application was in any case manifestly ill-founded for other reasons.

The Court stated that, "it must in general be accepted that where a State has introduced a system of social security, it is fully entitled to lay down conditions that have to be met for a person to be eligible for benefits pursuant to that system".[103] Reading this assertion, the Court seems to be confirming the traditional position according to which work-related obligations imposed on unemployed persons in the framework of a social security system can in principle never violate the prohibition of forced labour, whatever the nature of the work relationship and the working conditions.

However, the Court further nuances this affirmation, in the next paragraph:

> In particular a condition to the effect that a person must make demonstrable efforts in order to obtain and take up generally accepted employment cannot be considered unreasonable in this respect. This is the more so given that Dutch legislation provides that recipients of benefits pursuant to the Work and Social Assistance Act are not required to seek and take up employment which is not generally socially accepted or in respect of which they have conscientious objections. Therefore, the condition at issue cannot be equated with compelling a person to perform forced or compulsory labour within the meaning of Article 4, § 2 of the Convention.[104]

Moreover, the Court could only rule on the abstract content of the law. If the applicant had had her unemployment benefits reduced following a refusal to take up employment, the Court may have reviewed the concrete elements of the case and determine if what was required from

---

[102] Eur. Ct HR, *Klass and others v. Germany*, 6 September 1978 (app. No. 5029/71), § 33; Eur. Ct HR, *Marckx v. Belgium*, 13 June 1979 (app. No. 6833/74), § 25-27.
[103] Eur. Ct HR, *Schuitemaker v. The Netherlands*, § 5.
[104] *Ibid.*

the applicant did reach the threshold of forced or compulsory labour, within the meaning of Article 4, § 2 of the Convention.[105]

In terms of principles, this was an important ruling, since it was the first time that the Court indirectly recognised that the measures aimed at activating unemployment benefits recipients could, under certain circumstances, constitute forced labour prohibited by the Convention.

Otherwise, the decision can be deemed somewhat disappointing. The Court did not refer to the defining criteria of forced labour that it had itself identified in the *Van der Mussele case* (menace of a penalty and offer against one's will). Knowing that the Court considers non-contributory social benefits to constitute "possessions" in the sense of Article 1 of the First Additional Protocol, the same as contributory benefits,[106] one may have expected the Court to rule, within this new jurisprudential framework, that the threat to suspend unemployment assistance benefits constituted a menace of depriving of a right, as the loss of unemployment insurance benefits.

The Court confines itself to applying a test of proportionality, considering that the obligation to seek and to take a generally accepted employment imposed by the law is not unreasonable, especially as the unemployed person has the opportunity to refuse any employment for which she may have a conscientious objection. Since the Court does not refer to the absence of will criterion, we do not know if the test of proportionality is used as an autonomous defining criterion of forced labour or if its use aims at implicitly assessing the existence of a real consent on the part of the applicant. Since the Court further states that it does not possess the concrete elements to conclude that the threshold of forced or compulsory labour has been reached, one may be tempted to think that the Court uses the unreasonable nature of the imposed work as an autonomous defining criteria of forced labour.

Conclusion

A certain duty to work has always been inherent to the social protection systems of the Western Welfare States. Traditionally, it was considered that this duty could not enter into conflict with the prohibition of forced labour.

Since the 1990s, the duty to work of unemployment benefits and social assistance recipients has been steadily reinforced: classical

---

[105] *Ibid.*, § 6.
[106] Eur. Ct HR, *Koua Poirrez v. France*, 30 September 2003 (app. No. 40892/98); Eur. Ct HR, *Stec and others v. United Kingdom*, 6 July 2005, Decision on the admissibility (app. No. 65731/01 and No. 65900/01).

availability for work conditions have been deepened and new work-related obligations have been introduced in legislations. In this context, one can ask if the classical thesis of complete impermeability between work-related obligations in social protection systems and the prohibition of forced labour is still topical. To shed an original light on this question, we have turned to the relevant international case law on this issue.

The first section of our study was dedicated to an overview of the general case law on the prohibition of forced labour. In view of this general case law, we could assume that the work-related obligations imposed on social benefits recipients should not be excluded by principle from the notion of forced labour or from the scope of application of the prohibition of forced labour and that they should, on the contrary, be assessed on a case-by-case basis. This assumption relies on three observations.

Firstly, the defining criteria of forced labour are large and open. The menace of a penalty can consist in the loss of rights or advantages. If the unemployed persons, as former workers, have contributed in order to later be eligible for unemployment insurance benefits, one could thus argue that the loss of unemployment benefits in cases of refusals to take up employment or training consist in a loss of a right. And given that the European Court of Human Rights considers non-contributory social benefits as constituting "possessions" in the sense of article 1 of the First Additional Protocol, one could think that the threat to suspend unemployment assistance or social assistance benefits also constitutes a menace of a loss of a right. As for the criterion of the absence of consent, international bodies do not limit it to formally expressed consent. They take into consideration external elements of coercion that could invalidate expressed consent. This criterion thus offers a margin of discussion to potential claimants. In the first section, we also have put into perspective the emergence of an ultimate defining criterion: the proportionate character of the burden imposed on the individual balanced with general interest considerations. This criterion requires as a matter of course a case-by-case analysis in order to determine if the activation measure has exceeded in practise the reasonable charge that may be imposed on social benefits recipients.

Secondly, work-related obligations imposed on social benefits recipients are not the subject of a specific exclusion from the scope of application of the prohibition of forced labour nor of an exclusion from the notion of forced labour itself. One may though wonder if they could be qualified as a normal civic obligation. The international case law has still not definitively judged if a normal civic obligation can affect a specific category of persons or if it must concern all citizens equally. The normality criterion should moreover give rise to a case-by-case analysis.

Finally, the will of international bodies to adopt an evolutive approach of the prohibition of forced labour in order to apprehend new forms of forced labour has appeared throughout the international case law overview.

Following the general overview of this promising case law, we examined in the second section a few cases in which the international case law assessed the conformity of work-related obligations imposed on social benefits recipients with regard to the prohibition of forced labour.

We have identified two cases brought before the European Commission of Human Rights in 1976 (*X. v. the Netherlands*) and 1997 (*Talmon v. the Netherlands*) concerning the classical availability for work condition in unemployment benefits systems and two other cases concerning the activation measures of unemployment benefits recipients, the first one brought before the HRC in 2005 (*Faure v. Australia*) and the second brought before the European Court of Human Rights in 2010 (*Schuitemaker v. the Netherlands*).

In the two first cases, the European Commission of Human Rights considered, in line with the traditional thesis, that work-related obligations imposed on social benefits recipients cannot conflict with the prohibition of forced labour. In short and authoritative reasonings, it asserted, without explaining its position regarding the defining criteria of forced labour, that States, as soon as they set up a social protection system, are free to choose the work-related obligations to be imposed on benefits recipients.

In the *Schuitemaker* case, the European Court of Human Rights moved away from the traditional principle of a complete impermeability between work-related obligations in social protection systems and the prohibition of forced labour. It assessed if the activation measure was *in casu* contrary to the prohibition of forced labour. By undertaking this examination, it implicitly admitted that some activation measures could raise concerns regarding the prohibition of forced labour. In the *Faure* case, the HRC also accepted to assess if the activation measures complied with the prohibition of forced labour. Given the state of the case law, we can thus affirm that supervisory organs of the international texts dedicated to civil and political rights today admit that work-related obligations imposed on unemployment benefits and social assistance recipients might, in certain circumstances, come to violate the prohibition of forced labour.

Notwithstanding, the case law opening remains very formal. In the *Schuitemaker* case as well as in the *Faure* case, the international bodies did not refer to the classic defining criteria of forced labour, i.e. menace of a penalty and absence of will, as these have been progressively defined by the general international case law on forced labour. The HRC required, in its *Faure* decision, that work should be inhuman and degrading in nature in order to be qualified as forced labour. This criterion involves such a high threshold that the possibility to interfere with the choices made by States remains minimal. In the *Schuitemaker* case, the European Court limited itself to declaring that it did not possess the concrete elements to consider that the work imposed on the unemployed was unreasonable. This criterion clearly echoes the test of proportionality, applied in the *Van der Mussele* case. Nonetheless, in its *Schuitemaker* ruling, the Court seems to have disconnected this criterion from any verification of the absence of will criterion.

On this particular question, we will recall that it is in our view fully legitimate to institute the test of proportionality as an autonomous criterion in cases where the work is imposed in the name of a general interest objective, since Article 4, § 3 of the ECHR, from which the idea of proportionality emerged, participates in defining the notion of forced labour. Within the framework of work-related obligations imposed on the unemployed, the burden imposed on the unemployed should thus be balanced with the collective objective of a labour market including the highest number of working people.

In conclusion, supervisory bodies of international covenants on civil and political rights have taken the first step by admitting that the activation measures of unemployment benefits recipients might contravene the prohibition of forced labour. We now hope that, departing from a formalistic approach, they will observe from case to case in what really consists the activation measure that is contested (content of the measure, its objective, its concrete effects, the accompanying sanctions) and confront it with the defining criteria of forced labour identified in their general case law. In order to give international case law the opportunity to develop in this way, pleaders would be advised to invoke the prohibition of forced labour in front of national courts, in support of claims against activation measures, and bring these cases up to international jurisdictional bodies.

International supervisory bodies and national courts may feel uncomfortable in concretising the abstract defining criteria of the prohibition of forced labour. On this matter, one must know that international bodies supervising the application of economic, social and cultural rights do protect the prohibition of forced labour under the right to freely chosen work. These bodies have already identified concrete elements to assess the existence of a menace of a penalty and the proportionate character of the work imposed on the benefits recipients. They have essentially derived these elements from the case law concerning the right to social security and international minimum standards on social protection.[107] We hope that the international supervisory bodies and national rights courts will rely on this substantial case law and benefit from the expertise of the international bodies supervising the application of social rights. The adoption of an "integrated approach to human rights"[108] is in this case all the more desirable since the prohibition of forced labour is both a civil right – protecting the individual freedom and the physical integrity – and a social right – supporting the freedom of work.

---

[107] On international case law concerning the right to freely chosen work and activation policies, see again the next chapter, E. Dermine, "Activation Policies for the Unemployed and the International Human Rights Case Law on the Right to Freely Chosen Work".

[108] On this concept, see V. Mantouvalou, "Labour Rights in the European Convention on Human Rights", *op. cit.*, pp. 529-555.

Activation Policies for the Unemployed and the International Human Rights Case Law on the Right to Freely Chosen Work

Elise DERMINE

Introduction

Since the early 1990s, Western Welfare States have tended towards strengthening the work-related obligations for their unemployment benefits and social assistance systems, in order to reduce social spending and promote the return to employment. The reforms imply a much wider understanding of the jobs that social benefits recipients have to accept, an increase in the intensity of obligations to actively look for work, as well as the development of training, work-related activities and work programmes.

With regards to human rights, these reforms are essentially questioned in the light of the right to social security or of the right to social assistance, since they are implemented in social protection systems. Considering unemployment benefits systems, it is generally argued that these reforms are likely to reduce the covered risk of involuntary job loss, in a way that contravenes the right to social security as it is framed in the international conventions.[1] Regarding the reforms taking place in social assistance systems, the sanctions attached to the obligations, i.e. either the reduction or the complete loss of the benefit, are questioned in the light of the right to social assistance, which guarantees an adequate means of subsistence to those in need.[2]

---

[1] For an overview of the international case law on this issue, see E. Dermine, "Suitable Employment and Job of Quality", in P. Vielle and S. Borelli (eds.), *Quality of Employment in Europe. Legal and Normative Perspectives*, Brussels, P.I.E.-Peter Lang (Work and Society), 2012, pp. 157-180.

[2] For example, see the case law of the European Committee of Social Rights on Article 13 of the European Social Charter (ESC) (right to social and medical assistance): E.C.S.R., *General Introduction to Conclusions XIV-1, Statement of Interpretation Concerning Article 13 of the ESC*, 30th of March 1998; E.C.S.R., *Conclusions 2006, on the Application of Article 13 of the ESC*, Estonia, 30th of June 2006; E.C.S.R., *Conclusions XVIII-1, on the Application of Article 13 of the ESC*, the Netherlands, 31st of October 2006.

But these reforms are also likely to affect social benefits recipients' freedom of work,[3] protected under the right to work. It is true that in certain situations, activation policies positively impact social benefits recipients' real opportunities to access employment (i.e. their effective freedom of work). However, by limiting the reasons for refusal to take up employment or training, or even by establishing work performance or training participation as a condition for receiving benefits, those same policies often also restrict the free choice of employment of those concerned (i.e. their formal freedom of work). This second aspect of the freedom of work is protected under the right to freely chosen work, which is a component of the right to work. Compared to the right to social security and to social assistance, the right to freely chosen work is largely unknown by pleaders. We have, however, a hunch that it will be particularly promising to evaluate activation policies for the unemployed since they are, as shown above, infused with freedom of work concerns.

In this chapter, we thus propose to examine whether evaluation criteria concerning activation policies for the unemployed may be inferred from the international human rights case law related to the right to freely chosen work. The case law review will include the case law of the International Labour Organization (ILO) bodies regarding ILO conventions that contribute to the realisation of the right to freely chosen work, the Committee on Economic, Social and Cultural Rights (CESCR) case law concerning Article 6, § 1 of the International Covenant on Economic, Social and Cultural Rights (adopted in 1966) (ICESCR) (right to work) and the European Committee of Social Rights (ECSR) case law concerning Article 1, § 2 of the European Social Charter (adopted in 1961, revised in 1996) (ESC) (right of the worker to earn his living in an occupation freely entered upon).

In the first section, we will specify the scope and the characteristics of the right to freely chosen work (I.). We will then examine, in a second section, cases in which the international jurisdictional bodies evaluated the conformity of activation measures for the unemployed with the right to freely chosen work (II.). Through this study, we will point out that the central evaluation criteria of activation measures used in the international case law on the right to freely chosen work are actually largely borrowed from the case law on the right to social security and correspond to international minimum norms on unemployment benefits. This will lead us to highlight the large, but still underexploited, potentialities of the right to freely chosen work to develop a systematic, global and effective monitoring of activation measures from the angle of the freedom of work.

---

[3] On the concept of "freedom of work", see the introduction to this volume.

I. The Right to Freely Chosen Work: Contours of an Unheralded Right

In the first part of this section, we will clarify the content of the right to work and point out that the right to freely chosen work corresponds with the negative side of the right to work. By doing so, we will bring to light the complexity of characterising the right to freely chosen work. This right clearly illustrates the conceptual limits of the classical distinction between first and second generation rights. While it is enshrined as a component of the right to work in texts dedicated to second generation rights, it indeed shares some of its basic features with first generation rights (*A.*).

In the second part of this section, we will show how the right to freely chosen work is articulated with the prohibition of forced labour, which has been studied in the previous chapter.[4] The prohibition of forced labour, enshrined in international covenants on civil and political rights, constitutes one of the main components of the right to freely chosen work. We will show that, comparatively, the right to freely chosen work has a much wider and more evolutive content (*B.*).

A. *The Right to Freely Chosen Work and the Right to Work*

In international human rights instruments, the right to freely chosen work is considered a component of the broader right to work. For instance, Article 23, § 1 of the Universal Declaration on Human Rights provides that "everyone has the right to work, to free choice of employment, to just and favourable conditions of work and to protection against unemployment". The ICESCR, in its Article 6, § 1, specifies that "the States Parties to the present Covenant recognise the right to work, which includes the right of everyone to the opportunity to gain his living

---

[4] As a reminder, we decided to separately analyse the prohibition of forced labour, enshrined in international covenants on civil and political rights, and the right to freely chosen work, proclaimed in texts dedicated to economic, social and cultural rights. With this structure, we wish to emphasise how the nature of the texts these two rights are enshrined in, may influence the protection of freedom of work they offer to the unemployed. International bodies supervising the application of texts dedicated to social rights have elaborated an extensive case law on the conformity of activation measures with the right to social security (see footnote 1). Moreover, we will see that the right to social security has been conceived, in those texts, as a right that supports the freedom of work. One may thus expect a certain permeability between the case law concerning the right to social security and the case law concerning the right to freely chosen work. By contrast, we have seen in the previous chapter that the bodies controlling the application of texts on civil and political rights are still very reluctant to interfere in States' social policies. If they now admit that activation policies may, in certain circumstances, infringe the prohibition of forced labour, they still conceive the prohibition of forced labour as disconnected from the idea that social security should support freedom of work.

by work which he freely chooses or accepts, and will take appropriate steps to safeguard this right". In order to ensure the effective exercise of the right to work, the States parties to the ESC, following its Article 1, § 2, commit to "protect effectively the right of the worker to earn his living in an occupation freely entered upon".

The right to freely chosen work corresponds to the negative side of the right to work. It implies obligations to respect and to protect, meaning that States must refrain from themselves hampering the free choice of employment, and must prevent others from doing so.[5]

The positive right to work, or right to work in the strict sense, is the other side of the right to work. It implies obligations to fulfil the right to work, by developing an appropriate employment policy, by ensuring access to free employment services, and by setting up training and guidance schemes, in order to reach as high an employment rate as possible. It aims at ensuring the unemployed not only a formal freedom of choice, but also an effective freedom of access to employment. The second paragraph of Article 6 of the ICESCR provides that "the steps to be taken by a State Party to the present Covenant to achieve the full realisation of this right shall include technical and vocational guidance and training programmes, policies and techniques to achieve steady economic, social and cultural development and full and productive employment under conditions safeguarding fundamental political and economic freedoms to the individual". In the same way, the ESC provides, in its first Article, that "with a view to ensuring the effective exercise of the right to work, the Contracting Parties undertake:

1. to accept as one of their primary aims and responsibilities the achievement and maintenance of as high and stable a level of employment as possible, with a view to the attainment of full employment;
2. to protect effectively the right of the worker to earn his living in an occupation freely entered upon;
3. to establish or maintain free employment services for all workers;
4. to provide or promote appropriate vocational guidance, training and rehabilitation".

The positive right to work is conceived by international case law as an aspirational principle. States do not have to immediately provide every

---

[5] J. Elster, "Is There (or Should There Be) a Right to Work?", in A. Gutman (ed.), *Democracy and the Welfare State*, Princeton, Princeton University Press, 1988, p. 56; R.L. Siegel, "The Right to Work: Core Minimum Obligations", in A. Chapman and S. Russell (eds.), *Core Obligations: Building a Framework for Economic, Social and Cultural Rights*, Antwerp, Intersentia, 2002, pp. 44 and 47.

individual with a job. They commit to gradually striving towards the full realisation of the right to work, using all the resources at their disposal.[6]

Historically, the right to social security, including protection against the risk of unemployment, has been proclaimed as a supplementary right for those having been deprived of their work against their will. This right further supports the right to freely chosen work, by allowing individuals to decently live on the fringes of the labour market as long as they do not find a suitable employment.[7] The right to social security is equally programmatic.[8] Let us note that the Universal Declaration on Human Rights originally established the linkage between the right to work in the larger sense and protection against unemployment by proclaiming them together in Article 23, § 1.

The positive right to work and the right to social security are generally considered hardly justiciable. Their implementation implies important economic and social choices from the legislator. It is thus uneasy for a court to establish their violation, since it has always been delicate for the judiciary to intervene in these choices.[9] By contrast, the right to freely chosen work is considered highly justiciable. The resulting obligations to respect and to protect are sufficiently precise for a judge to establish their violation.[10]

---

[6] N. Elkin and M. Su Thomas, "Le droit au travail", in J.-M. Thouvenin and A. Trebilcock (eds.), *Le droit international social. Droits économiques, sociaux et culturels*, Vol. 2, Brussels, Bruylant, 2013, pp. 916; J. Elster, "Is There (or Should There Be) a Right to Work?", *op. cit.*, p. 56; P. Harvey, "Human Rights and Economic Policy Discourse: Taking Economic and Social Rights Seriously", *Columbia Human Rights Law Review*, Vol. 33, No. 2, 2001-2002, p. 381; L. Samuel, *Droits sociaux fondamentaux. Jurisprudence de la Charte sociale européenne*, 2nd edition, Strasbourg, Council of Europe Publishing, 2002, p. 14; J. Sarkin and M. Koenig, "Developing the Right to Work: Intersecting and Dialoguing Human Rights and Economic Policy", *Human Rights Quarterly*, Vol. 33, No. 1, 2011, pp. 13-14 and 16; R.L. Siegel, "The Right to Work: Core Minimum Obligations", *op. cit.*, pp. 33-36 and 47.

[7] I.L.O., Committee of Experts on the Application of Conventions and Recommendations (C.E.A.C.R.), *Recurrent Discussion on Social Protection (Social Security) under the ILO Declaration on Social Justice for a Fair Globalization*, 100th session, 2011, § 228: the CEACR has emphasised that the core principle of the freely chosen work supports the social security model enshrined in international labour norms.

[8] C. Nivard, *La justiciabilité des droits sociaux. Etude de droit conventionnel européen*, Brussels, Bruylant, 2012, pp. 500-508.

[9] On the difficult enforcement of social rights, see *ibid.*, pp. 461-493. On the justiciability of the right to work more particularly, see E. Elster, "Is There (or Should There Be) a Right to Work?", *op. cit.*, p. 56; R.L. Siegel, "The Right to Work: Core Minimum Obligations", *op. cit.*, p. 47.

[10] C. Nivard, *La justiciabilité des droits sociaux, op. cit.*, pp. 39-407. See also E. Elster, "Is There (or Should There Be) a Right to Work?", *op. cit.*, p. 56; R.L. Siegel, "The Right to Work: Core Minimum Obligations", *op. cit.*, p. 47.

According to the international instruments, the positive right to work and the right to freely chosen work constitute two sides of the same right. As a consequence, the full realisation of the former cannot be pursued to the detriment of the latter. For example, ILO Employment Policy Convention No. 122 and Recommendation No. 169 (1964) clearly bind both aspects of the right to work. Following Convention No. 122, States must design and apply "an active policy designed to promote full, productive and freely chosen work". The ILO General-Director underlined the connection established in Convention No. 122 between these two facets of the right to work: "Under the Employment Policy Convention, 1964 (No. 122), Members are to formulate and apply an active policy aimed at promoting full, productive and freely chosen employment. By looking at the other side of the coin, from the perspective of freedom of labour, the instrument places emphasis on the positive labour market interventions and other measures that can help to eradicate coercive systems of work".[11] In its General Comment No. 18 on the Right to Work, the Committee on Economic, Social and Cultural Rights (CESCR) refers to ILO Convention No. 122 and notes that it "links the obligation of States parties to create the conditions for full employment with the obligation to ensure the absence of forced labour".[12] As for the ESC, it proclaims each side of the right to work in distinct paragraphs. In our view, the European Committee of Social Rights (ECSR) should beware of disconnecting both facets of the right to work, and should foster a cross-interpretation of the paragraphs.

In sum, the right to work in its broad sense is an aggregate right.[13] In fact, related literature often identifies a third and sometimes even a fourth component of the right to work. The third component, related to the quality of employment, is the right to fair remuneration and to adequate working conditions.[14] While focusing on the freedom of work

---

[11] I.L.O., Report of the Director-General, *Stopping Forced Labour. Global Report under the Follow-up to the ILO Declaration on Fundamental Principles and Rights at Work*, 2001, p. 122.

[12] C.E.S.C.R., *General Comment No. 18. Article 6 of the International Covenant on Economic, Social and Cultural Rights*, 35th session, 24th of Nov. 2005, E/C.12/GC/18, § 4.

[13] K. Drzewicki, "The Right to Work and Rights in Work", in A. Eide, C. Krause and A. Rosas (eds.), *Economics, Social and Cultural Rights: A Textbook*, Dordrecht, Martinus Nijhoff, 1995, p. 173; J. Sarkin and M. Koenig, "Developing the Right to Work: Intersecting and Dialoguing Human Rights and Economic Policy", *op. cit.*, p. 8; R.L. Siegel, "The Right to Work: Core Minimum Obligations", *op. cit.*, p. 23.

[14] G. Mundlak, "The Right to Work: Linking Human Rights and Employment Policy", *International Labour Review*, Vol. 146, No. 3-4, 2007, pp. 192-193; J. Sarkin et M. Koenig, "Developing the Right to Work: Intersecting and Dialoguing Human Rights and Economic Policy", *op. cit.*, pp. 9 and 10.

of the unemployed from the angle of the right to work, we will not be interested in this dimension of the right to work, unless indecent working conditions, an aspect linked to the right to adequate working conditions, reveals an absence of will to work, and thus a violation of the right to freely chosen work. We will come back to this later on.[15] Some authors consider the equal access to employment to be a fourth component of the right to work.[16] According to us, this issue falls under both the negative and positive aspects of the right to work at the same time, so that there is no need to create a fourth dimension of the right to work in order to address it. Following the international case law, non-discrimination in the access to the labour market is protected under the right to freely chosen work (see *infra*, *B.*). We furthermore consider that the pursuit of real equal opportunities of access to available jobs falls under the positive dimension of the right to work.

The content and the legal scope of the right to work can be summarised in a broad sense as follows.

Right to Work	
Right to freely chosen work	Positive right to work
Obligation to "protect" and to "respect"	+ supplementary right to social security
	Obligation to "fulfil"
High justiciability	Weak justiciability
Formal freedom	Effective freedom

As aforementioned, the right to freely chosen work thus appears to blur the line between first and second generations of human rights. It is formally established in international texts dedicated to second generation rights, i.e. economic, social and cultural rights. It is an aspect of the broader right to work, which is generally classified in second generation rights, without any further distinction. However, the right to freely chosen work obviously displays the central features of first generation rights: it aims to protect individual freedoms from interference from States and other individuals. For this purpose, it imposes very precise obligations on States to respect and to protect the free choice of employment and is consequently considered highly justiciable.

---

[15] See *infra*, *B*.
[16] P. Harvey, "Human Rights and Economic Policy Discourse: Taking Economic and Social Rights Seriously", *op. cit.*, p. 380; R.L. Siegel, "The Right to Work: Core Minimum Obligations", *op. cit.*, p. 33.

B. The Right to Freely Chosen Work and the Prohibition of Forced Labour

International case law has progressively highlighted the different components of the right to freely chosen work, that is, the negative dimension of the right to work.

In its General Comment No. 18 on the right to work, the CESCR has noted that the right to a freely chosen or accepted work implies not being forced in any manner to engage in an activity or to take up work, benefiting from a protection system guaranteeing that every worker has access to employment and will not be unfairly deprived from their work.[17]

In the framework of the reports procedure, the ECSR has identified three issues to address under Article 1, § 2 of the ESC, which protects the worker's right to earn his living in an occupation freely entered upon: the prohibition of any kind of discrimination in employment, the prohibition of forced or mandatory labour (prison work, coercion in connection with domestic work...) and the prohibition of any other practice that may infringe upon the right to earn his living in an occupation freely entered upon.[18]

The prohibition of forced labour, explicitly proclaimed in the international covenants dedicated to civil and political rights, is thus an aspect of the right to freely chosen work, enshrined in the international covenants on economic, social and cultural rights. The CESCR as well as the ECSR do refer to the ILO definition of forced labour: it is a work or service that is exacted from a person under the menace of any penalty and for which the said person has not offered himself voluntarily.[19]

The ILO Director-General considers that the essence of the distinction between the scope of the prohibition of forced labour and that of the other aspects of the right to freely chosen work lies in the extent of the coercion or of the denial of the freedom of choice in the work relationship. He indeed stated that:

---

[17] C.E.S.C.R., *General Comment No. 18. Article 6 of the International Covenant on Economic, Social and Cultural Rights*, 35th session, 24th of Nov. 2005, E/C.12/GC/18, § 6.

[18] E.C.S.R., *Conclusions XVI-I, Statement of Interpretation of Article 1, § 2 of the ESC*, 30th of May 2003; E.C.S.R., *Conclusions I, Statement of Interpretation of Article 1, § 2 of the ESC*, 31st of May 1969.

[19] C.E.S.C.R., *General Comment No. 18. Article 6 of the International Covenant on Economic, Social and Cultural Rights*, 35th session, 24th of Nov. 2005, E/C.12/GC/18, § 9; E.C.S.R., *Digest of the Case Law of the ESCR*, Strasbourg, Council of Europe, 1st of September 2008, p. 22. For further analysis of the defining elements of the notion of forced labour, see the previous chapter.

There is a continuum including (both) what can clearly be identified as forced labour and other forms of labour exploitation and abuse. It may be useful to consider a range of possible situations with, at one end, slavery and slavery-like practices and, at the other end, situations of freely chosen work. In between the two extremes, there are a variety of employment relationships in which the element of free choice by the worker begins at least to be mitigated or constrained, and can eventually be cast into doubt.[20]

Freely chosen work and forced labour are thus, in principle, defined by the nature of the work relationship existing between the individual and the "employer", and not by the working conditions they are subject to. According to the Director-General, indecent working conditions can however reveal, despite formally expressed consent from the individual, an infringement on the free choice of employment and, in the most serious cases, a situation of forced labour.[21]

Following the bodies supervising the application of the instruments dedicated to economic, social and cultural rights, the right to freely chosen work does not only distinguish itself from the prohibition of forced labour by offering protection against less serious restrictions on freedom in the work relationship. It also protects the workers' freedom regarding their access to the labour market. In that sense, the CESCR and the ECSR forbid any form of discrimination in access to employment, in the name of the right to freely chosen work. In its *QCEA v. Greece* decision (2000), the ECSR ruled that the civilian service imposed instead of military service in Greece, although it was not to be considered forced labour, did however constitute a disproportionate restriction on the right to freely chosen work by depriving the individual from accessing the labour market for an excessive duration.[22]

This ruling is particularly enlightening with regards to the distinction between the prohibition of forced labour and other aspects of the right to freely chosen work. In support of its claim, the applicant, a Greek trade union, had argued that the obligation to perform an alternative civilian service did constitute forced labour, prohibited by Article 1, § 2 of

---

[20] I.L.O., Report of the Director-General of the I.L.O., *The Cost of Coercion*, Global Report under the Follow-up to the ILO Declaration on Fundamental Principles and Rights at Work, Report I (B), I.L.C., 98th session, 2009, p. 9, § 43.

[21] I.L.O., Report of the Director-General of the I.L.O., *A Global Alliance Against Forced Labour*, Global Report under the Follow-up to the ILO Declaration on Fundamental Principles and Rights at Work, Report I (B), I.L.C., 93rd session, 2005, p. 9, § 31 and p. 70, § 295.

[22] E.C.S.R., Decision No. 8/2000, *Quaker Council for European Affairs (QCEA) v. Greece* (decision on the merits), 25th of April 2000, Complaint No. 8/1999.

the Charter. The ECSR's reasoning was a two-stage process. First, it recalled that the obligation to perform civilian service was expressly excluded from the notion of forced labour by Article 4, § 3, b) of the ECHR. Favouring a consistent interpretation of the texts, it considered that such an obligation could not, in the same way, constitute a form of forced labour within the meaning of Article 1, § 2 of the ESC.[23] Secondly, the ECSR ruled that alternative civilian service could however amount to a restriction on the freedom to earn one's living in an occupation freely entered upon, in contravention with Article 1, § 2 of the ESC.[24] In this case, civilian service lasted 18 months more than the corresponding military service. Conscientious objectors could even have to perform alternative civilian service for up to 39 months. The ECSR ruled that those 18 additional months, during which conscientious objectors were denied their right to earn their living in an occupation freely entered upon, did constitute an unreasonable duration, compared to that of military service. Consequently, the ESCR decided this excessive duration did amount to a disproportionate restriction on the right of the worker to earn his living in an occupation freely entered upon, contrary to Article 1, § 2 of the Charter.[25]

The impact of this ruling should be well understood. The ECSR did not consider that civilian service, though it could not be qualified as forced labour, constitutes non-freely chosen work. It specified that conscientious objectors performing alternative civilian service were not "workers" who earn their living in an occupation freely entered upon, within the meaning of Article 1, § 2. In this case, the ESCR did not distinguish forced labour from non-freely chosen work on the basis of the gravity of the coercion exerted on the individual. It noted that the conscientious objector could not have access to employment during his civilian service. It therefore found that the excessive duration of civilian service did amount to a disproportionate restriction on the worker's right to earn his living in an occupation freely entered upon. With the right to freely chosen work, the ESC does not thus only aim at protecting the individual's freedom in their work relationship, but also their freedom to enter the labour market, which is of course an essential prerequisite to exercising their free choice of employment.

---

[23] *Ibid.*, § 22.
[24] *Ibid.*, § 23.
[25] *Ibid.*, § 25.

The right to freely chosen work			
Freedom in the work relationship		Freedom in the access to employment	
Prohibition of forced labour	Prohibition of other practices that may affect freedom in the work relationship	Prohibition of any form of employment discrimination	Prohibition of other practices that may affect free access to the labour market

* * *

At this end of this section, some relevant elements regarding activation policies for the unemployed may be inferred from the above developments dedicated to the right to freely chosen work. This right is likely to offer a larger spectrum of protection to the freedom of work of the unemployed than the prohibition of forced labour established in the international texts dedicated to civil and political rights. It guarantees the prohibition of forced labour but also protects against less serious forms of coercion in the work relationship. Moreover, it prohibits all practises – including those external to the work relationship – that may restrict free access to the labour market. By contrast with the prohibition of forced labour, which can only concern, according to the ILO definition, activation measures that consist in imposing work, the right to freely chosen work has a wider scope and enables the evaluation of other activation measures, such as training or job search programmes: these kind of measures do not directly involve work but may restrict free access to employment for the unemployed.

Concerning the criteria used by the case law to evaluate if the restriction to the freedom of work is contrary to the right to a freely chosen work, we may note that the ECSR had recourse to a test of proportionality in the *QCEA v. Greece* case. In this respect, we will remember that this criterion also emerged in the case law concerning the prohibition of forced labour, when international bodies applying texts on civil and political rights had to evaluate activation measures imposed on individuals by States in the name of general interest considerations.[26]

II. Activation Policies for the Unemployed in the International Case Law on the Right to Freely Chosen Work

In this second section, we will go through the cases in which international bodies confronted activation measures to the right to freely chosen work. We will identify the specific criteria used by international case law to assess the conformity of these measures with the right to freely chosen work.

---

[26] See the previous chapter in this book.

The first part will provide an overview of the jurisprudential stance of the ILO bodies regarding Forced Labour Convention No. 29[27] and Employment Policy Convention No. 122. These conventions participate in protecting the right to freely chosen work and are thus particularly relevant for our study. Indeed, the Forced Labour Convention edicts the prohibition of forced labour, which is, as we have seen, a component of the right to freely chosen work. Besides, Employment Policy Convention No. 122 links the positive side of the right to work with the protection of the right to freely chosen work, since it commits States to implementing an active employment policy designed to promote full, productive and freely chosen work (*A.*).

The second part will be dedicated to the analysis of the benchmarks defined by the ECSR on the basis of the right to earn one's living in an occupation freely entered upon, as protected by Article 1, § 2 of the ESC (*B.*).

The CESCR case law on activation policies with regard to Article 6 of the ICESR proclaiming the right to work will not be addressed, considering its scarcity and imprecision.[28]

A. *Activation Policies for the Unemployed and ILO Conventions No. 29 on Forced Labour and No. 122 on Employment Policy*

The ILO bodies progressively set boundaries to two types of work-related obligations imposed on unemployment or social assistance benefits recipients, firstly concerning the obligation to participate in a work programme (1.) and then concerning the general availability for work condition (2.).[29]

---

[27] Case law on ILO Convention No. 29 is examined in this chapter, not in the previous one, for the reason that the prohibition of forced labour, proclaimed in the convention, takes place in the ILO's more general mission to promote social rights. Moreover, ILO bodies link the prohibition of forced labour to the right to freely chosen work, since they both support freedom of work. Finally, strong similarities exist between the way the ILO bodies approach activation measures from the angle of the prohibition of forced labour and the case law of the ECSR on the right to freely chosen work. As to the manner to approach activation measures under the prohibition of forced labour, ILO case law remains, by contrast, largely disconnected from the case law developed by international bodies supervising the application of the instruments dedicated to civil and political rights.

[28] On this embryonic case law, see B. Saul, D. Kinley and J. Mowbray, *The International Covenant on Economic, Social and Cultural Rights. Commentary, Cases, and Materials*, Oxford, Oxford University Press, 2014, pp. 343-344; and, in this book, the footnote 15 in the conclusions of Olivier De Schutter.

[29] For a short recall on the different ILO bodies, their compositions and functions, reference is made to footnote 10 of the previous chapter.

1. The Mandatory Participation to a Work Programme

During the 1980s, the Committee of Experts on the Application of Conventions and Recommendations (CEACR) examined two Chilean laws. The first one, adopted in 1974, conditioned the granting of non-contributory unemployment benefits to the completion of a minimal work programme. The second law, from 1981, assigned the contributory unemployment insurance recipients to community work.

These two Chilean reforms are not part, strictly speaking, of the phenomenon we are studying, i.e. the increasing activation of social benefits recipients in Western Welfare States since the early 1990s. Nevertheless, those cases must be taken into account, since they confronted the CEACR for the first time with the question of whether work-related obligations in social protection systems could be examined from the angle of the right to freely chosen work, and more specifically from the angle of the prohibition of forced labour. Afterwards, the CEACR regularly had to take positions on the activation measures adopted in Western Welfare States, and widely followed the jurisprudential principles established in these two cases.

Under the first Chilean law, workers assigned to the minimal work programme were enrolled on a full-time basis, earned only half the minimum wage and did not benefit from the social security system nor from paid vacation. The CEACR found that persons enrolled in this programme could not be considered as benefiting from a productive and freely chosen work, within the meaning of Employment Policy Convention No. 122.[30] Considering the representations alleging a breach of Forced Labour Convention No. 29, the tripartite Committee of the Governing Body of the ILO further found that work could not be considered voluntary, since a great number of persons were paid at an excessively low level and did not benefit from the protection of the legislation on labour and social security, all the more so in view of the fact that this was not an emergency solution of a provisional nature.[31] In

---

[30] I.L.O., C.E.A.C.R., *Observation on the Application of Employment Policy Convention No. 122, Chile*, I.L.C., 69th session, 1981; I.L.O., C.E.A.C.R., *Observation on the Application of Employment Policy Convention No. 122, Chile*, I.L.C., 71st session, 1983.

[31] I.L.O., *Report of the Committee Set up to Examine the Representation Presented by the National Trade Union Co-ordinating Council (CNS) of Chile under article 24 of the Constitution Alleging Non-observance by Chile of International Labour Conventions Nos. 1, 2, 29, 30 and 122*, May 1984, Vol. LXVIII, 1985, Series B, Special Supplement 2/1985); *Report of the Committee Set up to Examine the Representation Submitted by the National Trade Union Co-ordinating Council (CNS) of Chile under Article 24 of the ILO Constitution, Alleging Non-observance by Chile of International Labour Conventions Nos. 1, 2, 24, 29, 30, 35, 37, 38 and 111*, November 1986, Vol. LXXI, 1988, Series B, Supplement 1.

conformity with ILO case law, the Committee considered that indirect economic coercion invalidates formally expressed consent, if States take advantage of it.[32] Strangely, the Committee did not refer to the other defining criterion of forced labour according to Article 2, § 1 of Convention No. 29 – the menace of a penalty.

Regarding the second law, the CEACR found that the Chilean government did not manage to establish the voluntary nature of the works. It then checked if the second defining criterion of forced labour was met. It considered that the works were imposed under the menace of a penalty, more precisely the loss of a right, since they mostly targeted unemployed persons who, as former workers, had contributed to be eligible for unemployment insurance benefits.[33]

In its general report of 1997,[34] the CEACR, addressing a concern raised by Canada, developed a first and principled standpoint on the question of whether a requirement that unemployed people perform some kind of work as a condition for receiving benefits might constitute forced labour, within the sense of Convention No. 29.

It first referred to the generic definition of forced or mandatory labour specified in Article 2, § 1 of Convention No. 29: it is a work or service that is exacted from a person "under the menace of any penalty" and "for which the said person has not offered himself voluntarily".[35] It then recalled that the penalty could take the form of a loss of any right or privilege. On the basis of the criterion of the menace of any penalty, it drew a first distinction between two situations:

> If, as in most countries, unemployment and other benefits are contingent upon the recipient having worked or contributed to an unemployment insurance scheme during some minimum period, and the length of time during which benefits are paid is linked to length of time the person concerned worked,

---

[32] On this topic, see the previous chapter, I., *A.*, 1.

[33] I.L.O., C.E.A.C.R., *Observation on the Application of Employment Policy Convention No. 122, Chile*, I.L.C., 69th session, 1981; I.L.O., C.E.A.C.R., *Observation on the Application of Employment Policy Convention No. 122, Chile*, I.L.C., 71st session, 1983. See also I.L.O., C.E.A.C.R., Direct Request to Chile Concerning the Application of Forced Labour Convention No. 29, 1990, I.L.C., 77th session, 1990; I.L.O., C.E.A.C.R., *Direct Request to Chile Concerning the Application of Convention No. 29 on Forced Labour*, 1992, I.L.C., 79th session, 1992; I.L.O., C.E.A.C.R., *Direct Request to Chile Concerning the Application of Convention No. 29 on Forced Labour*, 1995, I.L.C., 82nd session, 1995; I.L.O., C.E.A.C.R., *Direct Request to Chile Concerning the Application of Convention No. 29 on Forced Labour*, 1996, I.L.C., 85th session, 1997.

[34] I.L.O., C.E.A.C.R., *General report, report III (IA)*, 1998, I.L.C., 86th session, § 106.

[35] For a detailed analysis of the defining criteria of the prohibition of forced labour, see the previous chapter.

then to impose (...) an additional requirement of having to perform work to receive these benefits would constitute compulsory labour on pain of losing benefits to which the person was entitled. However, if the benefits concerned are not an entitlement based on previous work or contributions, but a social measure granted to unemployed persons on purely social grounds, then the requirement to perform some work in exchange for the allowance would not in itself constitute forced or compulsory labour in the sense of the Convention.[36]

Thus, according to the CEACR, conditioning the granting of social benefits to the performance of any kind of work amounts to forced labour in unemployment insurance-based schemes. By contrast, when the entitlement to benefits does not rest upon a proportionate previous period of work, the legislator would be free to require some work from the unemployed, as a counterpart. This would be the case in social assistance systems where benefits are open to any person, whether he has worked or not, under a unique condition of resources. This would also be the case in unemployment benefits schemes in two specific cases, i.e. when benefits are not based on a previous period of work and when they are granted for a disproportionate duration compared with the length of time the person worked.[37] The reasoning of the CEACR seems to be that work would not be imposed under the menace of the loss of a right in those last cases. In the CEACR's perception, social benefits recipients could only claim a right to social benefits if they have previously contributed to the scheme. According to us, the definition of the notion of right as contributory appears very restrictive, particularly considering that many international instruments proclaim the right to social assistance. In that sense, the ECSR expressed very clearly that, under the right to social assistance (Article 13 of the ESC), "it is compulsory (...) to accord assistance to necessitous persons as of right; the Contracting Parties are no longer merely empowered to grant assistance as they think fit; they are under an obligation, which they may be called on in court to honour".[38]

However, the CEACR's reasoning did not stop there. Concerning non-contributory schemes, it added that "if the allowance paid were

---

[36] I.L.O., C.E.A.C.R., *General report, report III (IA)*, 1998, I.L.C., 86th session, § 106.

[37] This last hypothesis evidently includes unemployment assistance systems, but could also concern certain hybrid unemployment insurance systems. We particularly think of the Belgian unemployment insurance system. It seems to us that Belgian unemployment insurance benefits are to be included in that hypothesis when they are granted to young people without any condition of previous work but also, more generally, when their granting duration is no longer proportionate with previous period of work (since, in Belgium, unemployment insurance benefits are on principle granted for an unlimited duration).

[38] E.C.S.R., *Conclusions I, Statement of Interpretation of Article 13§ 1 of the ESC*, 31st of May 1969.

to constitute an excessively low level of remuneration for the work involved, the scheme could be tantamount to exploiting constraints by offering people who had no other options, employment on terms that would not normally be acceptable".[39] This is the second distinction that the Committee drew. This position is in conformity with the general ILO case law on the prohibition of forced labour according to which indirect coercion may invalidate formally expressed consent.[40] In the present case, the CEACR referred on the matter to the report adopted in November 1997 by the tripartite Committee of the Governing Body of the ILO, which had been asked to examine a representation introduced against Senegal.[41] Referring to the reports it had adopted following the representations introduced against Chile in 1983 and 1985,[42] the tripartite Committee had made clear in its report that the State could not be responsible for forced labour if it had not "created or exacerbated the economic constraints, nor exploited them by offering people who had no other options, employment on terms that would not normally be acceptable".[43] Thus, even in non-contributory schemes, States have obligations in respect to the prohibition of forced labour when they impose an obligation to work, in return for the granting of social benefits.

Some of the employer members of the Committee on the Application of Standards have raised concerns about the CEACR positioning. By considering that the requirement to perform work in exchange for an allowance might, under certain circumstances, constitute forced labour, the CEACR would have exceeded the terms of its mission of supervision

---

[39] *Ibid.*, § 106.

[40] On the ILO general case law on the prohibition of forced labour and the particular defining criterion of the absence of consent, see the previous chapter, I, *A.*, 1.

[41] I.L.O., *Report of the Committee Set up to Examine the Representation Made by the Senegal Teachers' Single and Democratic Trade Union (SUDES) under Article 24 of the ILO Constitution Alleging Non-observance by Senegal of the Abolition of Forced Labour Convention*, 1957 (No. 105), November 1997, GB.270/15/3.

[42] I.L.O., *Report of the Committee Set up to Examine the Representation Presented by the National Trade Union Co-ordinating Council (CNS) of Chile under Article 24 of the Constitution Alleging Non-observance by Chile of International Labour Conventions Nos. 1, 2, 29, 30 and 122*, May 1984, Vol. LXVIII, 1985, Series B, Special Supplement 2/1985; I.L.O., *Report of the Committee Set up to Examine the Representation Submitted by the National Trade Union Co-ordinating Council (CNS) of Chile under Article 24 of the ILO Constitution, Alleging Non-observance by Chile of International Labour Conventions Nos. 1, 2, 24, 29, 30, 35, 37, 38 and 111*, November 1986, Vol. LXXI, 1988, Series B, Supplement 1.

[43] I.L.O., *Report of the Committee Set up to Examine the Representation Made by the Senegal Teachers' Single and Democratic Trade Union (SUDES) under Article 24 of the ILO Constitution Alleging Non-observance by Senegal of the Abolition of Forced Labour Convention*, 1957 (No. 105), November 1997, GB.270/15/3, § 31.

and acted as a legislator.⁴⁴ Nevertheless, it needs to be underlined that the Conference, i.e. the ILO legislative organ, had already emphasised the link between mandatory work programmes for the unemployed and forced labour in Recommendation No. 176 on special youth schemes, which was adopted in 1970. This recommendation aimed at setting the goals, the methods and the guarantees of those schemes, in order to ensure their full conformity with the ILO conventions on forced labour.⁴⁵

In its last general survey on forced labour, in 2007, the CEACR has noted that conditioning the granting of unemployment insurance benefits on compulsory work requirements has become more usual in the States' legislation and practise, and raises serious concerns regarding the effective application of the conventions on forced labour.⁴⁶ It referred to the theoretical and relatively unknown position it had developed in 1997 and recalled that the requirement to perform some work *per se* constitutes a violation of the prohibition of forced labour in unemployment insurance regimes.⁴⁷ In an observation concerning the application of Convention No. 29 on forced labour adopted in 2012,⁴⁸ the CEACR recalled this case law to Albania, which imposes compulsory public work on unemployment insurance recipients. Even if this public work has an economic objective and is, at least officially, aimed at reintegrating the weaker elements of society, it constitutes, in the CEACR's view, forced labour, since it is compulsory and performed under the threat of the loss of unemployment benefits. The CEACR therefore requested Albania to bring its legislation in line with the Convention.

Finally, it must be noted that, in its 2012 observation concerning the application of Employment Policy Convention No. 122, the CEACR examined the British *Mandatory Work Activity* programme, set up in 2011. Under this scheme, the Jobseeker's Allowance recipients may be obliged to perform work for a period not exceeding four weeks of 30 hours maximum, on pain of having their benefits temporarily suspended. The CEACR requested that the United Kingdom provide information on the implementation of the programme and on its effects regarding access to productive and lasting employment opportunities. It moreover recalled that the measures taken by States under Article 2 of the Convention needed to fit in with the target of full, productive, and freely

---

⁴⁴ I.L.O., C.E.A.C.R., *General Report*, I.L.C., 86ᵗʰ session, Geneva, 1998, § 98.
⁴⁵ See the preamble to the recommendation.
⁴⁶ I.L.O., C.E.A.C.R., *Eradication of Forced Labour*, General Survey, p. xii and pp. 70 et seq.
⁴⁷ *Ibid.*, § 129.
⁴⁸ I.L.O., C.E.A.C.R., *Direct Request to Albania Concerning the Forced Labour Convention No. 29*, adopted in 2011, I.L.C., 102ⁿᵈ session, 2012.

chosen work.[49] As has been pointed out, Convention No. 122 explicitly links the positive and negative sides of the right to work. The CEACR seems to indicate that a momentary restriction of an unemployed person's right to freely chosen work could comply with Article 2 of Convention No. 122 only if it is likely to *in fine* increase his real freedom of access to a productive and freely chosen work.

2. The General Availability for Work Condition

During the 1990s, some countries started to widen the scope of the general availability for work condition in their systems of unemployment benefits, sometimes even suppressing the possibility for unemployment insurance recipients to refuse a non-suitable employment.[50] Some of these States mentioned these reforms in their reports concerning the application of the Social Security (Minimum Standards) Convention No. 102 (1952). The CEACR has thus generally examined these reforms under the angle of these conventions.[51] We will however see that the CEACR also had the opportunity to analyse the Danish reform under the Forced Labour Convention and subsequently developed a general position about reforms widening the general availability for work condition.

In its Unemployment Insurance Act 2002 reform, Denmark suppressed the distinction between suitable employment (taking into account the abilities, qualifications, experience and period in service of the jobseeker) and reasonable employment (outside the sector in which the jobseeker used to work). Under the new regulation, the unemployed were required to accept reasonable employment offers from the first day of unemployment, without any regard to their former occupational field, while under the former regulation, the unemployed had the right to refuse employment offers that did not fit with their previous occupational field during the first three months of unemployment.

In 2004, the Committee examined the compliance of the Danish 2002 reform with Social Security Convention No. 102.[52] It began by sharing the concerns expressed by the European Committee on Social Rights (ECSR), which had also examined this Danish reform in its conclusions

---

[49] I.L.O., C.E.A.C.R., *Observation Concerning the Application of Employment Policy Convention No. 122*, adopted in 2012, I.L.C., 102nd session, 2013.

[50] This is the case of, among others, the United Kingdom, Denmark and Norway. On this topic, see the references quoted in the next footnote.

[51] For an analysis of the CEACR case law on the notion of suitable employment from the angle of the ILO Convention No. 102, see E. Dermine, "Suitable Employment and Job of Quality", *op. cit.*, pp. 167-170.

[52] I.L.O., C.E.A.C.R., *Direct Request to Denmark concerning Social Security (Minimum Standards) Convention No. 102*, adopted in 2004, I.L.C., 93rd session, 2005.

XVII-1 in the light of Article 12, § 3 of the ESC.[53] As a reminder, this article commits States "to endeavour to raise progressively the system of social security to a higher level". Then, it recalled that the notion of suitable employment is central to Part IV of the Convention No. 102 dedicated to unemployment benefits. Through this notion, the unemployed are particularly guaranteed that they may refuse offers of employment that do not correspond to the skills, qualifications, acquired experience and length of service of their former occupation, at least during a minimum period of protection of 13 weeks, without running the risk of seeing their benefit suspended or definitively cut. The CEACR therefore asked the Danish government to clarify how effect was given to the Convention provisions dedicated to the notion of suitable employment. Moreover, it requested complementary details on the internal guidelines of the employment service in making offers of "reasonable employment" to the jobseekers and to determine if the interested person had reasonable ground for refusing such an offer. It particularly insisted on the extent to which account is being taken of the person's professional skills, social status and familial and personal situation in case the job offer implies a change in residence. It also asked to be given statistical information on the number of cases in which unemployment benefit had been suspended, due to refusal to accept a job offer.

Then, following a communication received from the Danish Masters' Association in 2004, the CEACR was called upon in 2005 to consider this reform from the angle of Forced Labour Convention No. 29.[54] As it has done while supervising the application of Convention No. 102, the CEACR specifically referred to the reasoning expressed by the ECSR in its conclusions XVII-1 regarding Denmark's application of Article 12, § 3 of the ESC. According to the ECSR, the rules on availability, as arising from the 2002 reform, were particularly stringent, since they were almost compelling the unemployed, on pain of loss of benefits, to accept a job regardless of the occupational field from the first day of unemployment. The CEACR expressly reproduced the very words of the Strasbourg Committee, which had considered that "one of the aims of an unemployment benefit system is to offer unemployed persons adequate protection during at least an initial period of unemployment from the obligation to take up any job irrespective of occupational field, precisely with a view to giving them the opportunity of finding a job which is suitable taking into account their individual preferences, skills

---

[53] E.C.S.R., *Conclusions XVII-I, on the Application of Article 12, § 3 of the 1961 ESC*, Denmark, Vol. 1, 28th of February 2005, § 3.
[54] I.L.O., C.E.A.C.R., *Direct Request to Denmark concerning Forced Labour Convention No. 29*, adopted in 2005, I.L.C., 95th session, 2006.

and qualifications".[55] The CEACR, in the continuation of the Strasbourg Committee, was thus willing to emphasise that unemployment benefits systems do contribute to the protection of the freedom of work. It then asked the Danish government to provide more information on the functioning of the unemployment insurance regime. In this regard, it referred to the questions asked in 2004 in the frame of the supervision of application of Convention No. 102. As a reminder, these questions aimed to assess if the new legislation and its application complied with the notion of suitable employment enshrined in Convention No. 102.

In response to the CEACR's direct request, the Danish government indicated that, in all the sanction cases except one, the employment offer the jobseeker had refused lay within his occupational field. In the case where an unemployed person was referred to a job outside his occupational field, he was referred to a job in a related field, in which he had previously received training.

In a subsequent direct request, the CEACR first referred to the comments it had adopted in the meantime in its 2007 global survey entitled *Eradication of Forced Labour*. In this document, it had observed that, in the context of growing unemployment, including long-term unemployment, industrialised countries were tending to widen the spectrum of jobs that have to be accepted by unemployed persons, on pain of having their benefits suspended, reduced or cut.[56] According to the CEACR, availability for work was of course a classic condition for receiving unemployment benefits. However, it could be in conflict with the conventions on forced labour if it were to be used as a sanction, or if the unemployed were requested to accept jobs that were not suitable, within the meaning of the Social Security Convention No. 102.[57]

After having referred to the comments of its 2007 general survey, the CEACR noted that the fact that the work did fit within the sphere of activity of the jobseeker was not sufficient to ensure its suitability as regards to Convention No. 102, "since factors such as skills, qualifications, acquired experience and length of service must also be considered". In the CEACR's view, those factors would normally be reflected in the wage level corresponding to the job. The CEACR therefore asked the government to extend its monitoring on sanctions, "beyond whether placements of unemployed persons are 'within their occupational field' to an inquiry as to whether the placements refused are 'suitable' by reference to the wage levels attached to the jobs being offered, in comparison with the person's

---

[55] E.C.S.R., *Conclusions XVII-I, on the Application of Article 12, § 3 of the 1961 ESC*, Denmark, Vol. 1, 28th of February 2005, § 3.
[56] I.L.O., C.E.A.C.R., *Eradication of Forced Labour, op. cit.*, p. 116, § 205.
[57] *Ibid.*, p. 73, § 131.

earlier earned income and the relevant collective agreement, where one exists". Referring to the government's indication that all unemployed persons were offered jobs either within their occupational field or within a related field in which they received recent training, the CEACR asked the government "to consider giving statutory effect to this practice, and to supply information on any measures taken to this end".[58] In 2008 and 2010, the CEACR noted that the Danish National Directorate of Labour would continue to monitor cases where the unemployed are sanctioned for refusing to take up a job proposed by the public employment service. It then asked Denmark to monitor in such sanction cases if placements, as it is asserted, "still take place in practice 'with due consideration' to the unemployed person, his skills and orientation towards the labour market, etc."[59]

In order to assess the compliance of the availability for work condition with the prohibition of forced labour, the CEACR thus does not refer to the general defining criteria of forced labour. Linking social security with freedom of work, it directly applies the evaluation criterion it uses to rule on the conformity of this condition with ILO Social Security Convention No. 102, that is, with the notion of suitable employment.

* * *

At the end of this ILO case law review, we can identify two guidelines that set limits to the development of activation measures for the unemployed, under the prohibition of forced labour.

On the one hand, the CEACR considers that conditioning the granting of benefits to the performance of work necessarily amounts to forced labour in real contributory unemployment benefits, while in non-contributory schemes it amounts to forced labour if the State exploits the constraints faced by recipients by imposing them to perform work on terms that would not normally be acceptable. On the other hand, the availability for work condition in unemployment benefits schemes cannot be extended to jobs that are not suitable in accordance with the meaning of Social Security Convention No. 102.

Surprisingly, the CEACR does not much refer to the general defining criteria of forced labour – i.e. the menace of a penalty and the absence of will – in the elaboration of these guidelines. They are largely based

---

[58] I.L.O., C.E.A.C.R., *Direct Request to Denmark concerning Forced Labour Convention No. 29*, adopted in 2007, I.L.C., 97th session, 2008.

[59] See also I.L.O., C.E.A.C.R., *Direct Request to Denmark concerning Forced Labour Convention No. 29*, adopted in 2008, I.L.C., 98th session, 2009; I.L.O., C.E.A.C.R., *Direct Request to Denmark concerning Forced Labour Convention No. 29*, adopted in 2010, I.L.C., 100th session, 2010.

on classical notions and the categories of our social protection systems. Concerning the first limit, the CEACR indirectly referred in a first move to the defining elements of the prohibition of forced labour. Nevertheless, in order to make them concrete, it relied on the traditional distinction in our social protection models between contributory and non-contributory social benefits. In contributory benefits schemes, the unemployed are entitled to benefits for which they have previously worked and contributed to the scheme. One cannot impose them to work, as an additional condition for the granting of benefits. The CEACR thus based on unemployment benefits conditions of eligibility to set the first limit to the development of activation measures. The second guideline construed by the CEACR under the right to feely chosen work, which is, as we recall, the right to refuse a non-suitable employment without risking a suspension or reduction of unemployment benefits, is, as for it, directly issued from international minimum standards concerning unemployment benefits.

In our view, these two minimal guidelines are not sufficient to develop a systematic and global approach to activation measures of the unemployed from the angle of the freedom of work. They offer little protection to the freedom of work of large categories of the activated unemployed, such as in particular the long-term unemployed and social assistance recipients. Besides, these guidelines focus on the restriction to the free choice of employment caused by the activation measure (formal freedom of work), without taking into account the potential effect of the activation measure on the unemployed's real opportunities to access a freely chosen work (effective freedom of work). We have seen in the first section that, in the spirit of the texts, the right to freely chosen work and the positive right to work should though be connected. In that sense, we must underline that, under Employment Policy Convention No. 122, the CEACR recently demonstrated its will to balance the restriction to the formal freedom of work with the eventual increase in effective freedom, by asking States for information on the effect of the activation measure on opportunities to access freely chosen work.

B. Activation Policies for the Unemployed and Article 1, § 2 of the European Social Charter

To this day, no collective complaint has been brought in front of the ECSR concerning the compliance of an activation measure with Article 1, § 2 of the ESC. Since the early 1990s, the ECSR has however showed an increasing interest in this issue within the framework of the reports procedure.

In their periodic national reports, States have to explain how they implement the different paragraphs of Article 1 of the ESC concerning the right to work. Under the first paragraph, States are required to show how they are conducting an employment policy aiming at reaching as high a level of employment as possible. In order to monitor the effective application of the first paragraph, the ECSR refers to various indicators, among which is the activation rate of unemployed persons, i.e. the percentage of unemployed persons taking part in active labour market policies.[60] Within this framework, States have put forward the national reforms aiming at activating social benefits recipients. Interestingly, after taking notice of these reforms through supervision of the first paragraph of Article 1, the ECSR considered that they were also likely to impact on the right to freely chosen work and therefore decided to examine their compliance with Article 1, § 2.

In its conclusions on the application of Article 1, § 2, the ECSR started to examine the reforms under the section dedicated to the prohibition of forced labour. In 2002, it created a new section in its conclusions, specifically dedicated to the supervision of States' legislation and practise concerning the loss of unemployment benefits for refusal to take up employment or training. Given this evolution, we propose to follow the historical development of the ECSR case law. In a first part, we will overview the case law elaborated under the section devoted to the prohibition of forced labour (1.). In a second part, we will concentrate on the subsequent case law concerning the loss of unemployment benefits for refusal to take up employment or training (2.).

1. Analysis of Activation Measures from the Angle of the Prohibition of Forced Labour

Between 1992 and 2002, the ECSR examined different activation measures under the section of its conclusions dedicated to the prohibition of forced labour. Numerous questions were put to the States, in order to get a better understanding of the measures, their goals and their effects. Following their replies, the ECSR either communicated new questions, or adopted conclusions of compliance. It never adopted negative conclusions on the kind of measures regarding the prohibition of forced labour. But the mere fact that it has examined those measures from the angle of the prohibition of forced labour implies notwithstanding that, in its view, some of them may, according to their design, goal or effects, contravene the prohibition of forced labour.

---

[60] On the nature and the extent of the supervision of Article 1, § 1 by the ECSR, see H. Kristensen, "Right to Employment (Article 1, § 1 of the European Social Charter): Full Employment as a State Obligation?", in N. Johanson and M. Mikkola (eds.), *Reform of the European Social Charter*, Seminar Presentations at the House of the Estates and the University of Helsinki, 8-9 February 2011, Porvoo, Bookwell, 2011, pp. 69-82.

The ECSR started by questioning the conformity of *work programmes* for social benefits recipients, with the prohibition of forced labour. In 1992, the Committee heard that a "socially useful work" obligation could be imposed on any social assistance recipient in Germany. It then requested the government to precisely explain the nature of "socially useful work"[61] and the practical application of the regulation,[62] and asked if it was a general measure targeting all social assistance recipients. In its reports, the government explained that the work programmes aimed at increasing unemployed persons' chance to develop their professional life,[63] that the unemployed could justify their refusal to perform socially useful work on the grounds of various reasons such as physical or psychological inability, or family situation, and that only between 2 or 3% of social assistance beneficiaries had concretely worked in those schemes.[64] Following these explanations, the CEACR concluded in 1996, without asking further questions, that the socially useful work that social assistance beneficiaries may be required to perform complied with the prohibition of forced labour.[65]

Subsequently, the ESCR realised that those persons refusing a suitable offer of socially useful employment ran the risk of having their social benefits reduced, by up to 25% compared to the normal rate. Moreover, within the meaning of German social assistance law, the notion of suitable employment appeared to be wider than the one used in the framework of unemployment insurance systems. Therefore, the ECSR requested more information in 1998 on the defining criteria of "suitable employment" applicable in the social assistance system and on the possibility of an appeal.[66] The government explained that, by contrast with unemployment insurance law, beneficiaries may be required to accept a job outside their previous occupational field under the Federal Social Assistance Act. However, a job is not considered suitable if the person is physically or mentally unable to perform the work or if it would unduly restrict the future prospects of a person in pursuing his previous occupation or if other important grounds may be invoked. Moreover, there was a

---

[61] E.C.S.R., *Conclusions XII-2, on the Application of Article 1, § 2 of the 1961 ESC*, Germany, 30th of November 1992.

[62] E.C.S.R., *Conclusions XIII-2, on the Application of Article 1, § 2 of the 1961 ESC*, Germany, 30th of December 1994.

[63] *Ibid.*

[64] E.C.S.R., *Conclusions XIII-4, on the Application of Article 1, § 2 of the 1961 ESC*, Germany, 30th of September 1996.

[65] *Ibid.*

[66] E.C.S.R., *Conclusions XIV-1, on the Application of Article 1, § 2 of the 1961 ESC*, Germany, 30th of March 1998.

possibility of appeal before an independent body. On the basis of these clarifications, the ECSR concluded in 2001 that the situation in Germany was in conformity with Article 1, § 2 of the Charter with respect to the prohibition of forced labour. The ECSR did not refer to the criterion of the "constraints' exploitation by the State" used by the ILO CEACR to assess the compliance of work programmes with the prohibition of forced labour.

In 1996, Belgium was invited by the ECSR to provide more details on the legal scheme according to which the long-term unemployed could have their benefits suspended if they refused to work in a local employment agency.[67] Further to the government's report, the ECSR requested Belgium to clarify the length of the suspension of benefits imposed in practice, whether there was a possibility of an appeal to an independent body against decisions on the suitability of the employment and on the length of suspensions, and the number of unemployed persons affected by the suspension.[68] Having noticed that only one person had been sanctioned in practice during the reference period and that there was the possibility of an appeal before the labour court, the ECSR stopped asking questions about this programme.[69] The ECSR did not ask any questions concerning work remuneration. This would have allowed it to realise that, in Belgium, the unemployed who work in a local employment agency sign an employment contract and receive remuneration to supplement their unemployment benefits. These questions would have typically been raised by the CEACR in order to assess if the State was exploiting the unemployed's constraints by imposing employment that would normally not be acceptable.

The ECSR also questioned Italy on a legal scheme allowing public administrations to call on the unemployed to realise projects of social utility, without the establishment of a formal work relationship.[70] The unemployed refusing to take part in the project ran the risk of having their unemployment benefits cut. In its 1998 conclusions, the ECSR did not focus on the absence of a formal work relationship but requested Italy to indicate: the period during which the benefits would be suspended; the

---

[67] E.C.S.R., *Conclusions XIII-4, on the Application of Article 1, § 2 of the 1961 ESC*, Belgium, 30th of September 1996.
[68] E.C.S.R., *Conclusions XIV-1, on the Application of Article 1, § 2 of the 1961 ESC*, Belgium, 30th of March 1998.
[69] E.C.S.R., *Conclusions XV-1, on the Application of Article 1, § 2 of the 1961 ESC*, Belgium, 30th of March 2000.
[70] E.C.S.R., *Conclusions XIV-1, on the Application of Article 1, § 2 of the 1961 ESC*, Italy, 30th of March 1998; E.C.S.R., *Conclusions XV-1, on the Application of Article 1, § 2 of the 1961 ESC*, Italy, 30th of March 2000.

criteria for assigning persons to social utility work (personal preference, qualifications, physical and intellectual abilities, transportation...); the appeals procedure, in order to determine whether the appeal body was independent; the number of refusals and imposed sanctions in practice. In its 2000 conclusions, the ECSR asked Italy to specify if the sanctioned unemployed may receive social assistance for the duration of the sanction.[71]

Under the "Project Work" scheme launched in the United Kingdom, the long-term unemployed may be obliged to attend work experience programmes, on pain of losing their unemployment benefits. Having learnt that, the ECSR asked in 1998 for more information on the suitability criteria applied in relation to the work concerned, on the sanctions imposed in practise and on the appeal possibilities.[72] The United Kingdom answered that the independent adjudication officers took into account particular circumstances such as reasons of health or safety, religion, conscientious objection or travelling, before taking a decision on the sanction. Following this answer, the ECSR asked for details on the criteria used in evaluating the jobseeker's good faith, and the suitability of his reasons, in case of refusal to take up employment.[73] At this point, the ECSR did not yet check if the unemployed were entitled to refuse an employment that did not correspond to their professional qualifications during the first period of their unemployment, which is however a central requirement of the notion of suitable employment. We will see in our next point that it later checked in 2003.

Overall, the ECSR case law concerning mandatory work programmes may seem timorous or even underdeveloped compared with the ILO case law described in the previous section. While the CEACR frequently refers to the ILO defining criteria of forced labour in its case law, the ECSR never applied them when confronting work programmes imposed on social benefits recipients. Neither did it refer to the particular jurisprudential guidelines developed by the CEACR in relation to these work programmes. The ECSR being essentially confronted with mandatory work programmes implemented in non-contributory schemes, we have particularly noticed that it did not assess if the States were exploiting the unemployed's constraints by imposing them to perform work that would not be acceptable in other circumstances. We must however underline

---

[71] E.C.S.R., *Conclusions XV-1, on the Application of Article 1, § 2 of the 1961 ESC*, Italy, 30th of March 2000.

[72] E.C.S.R., *Conclusions XIV-1, on the Application of Article 1, § 2 of the 1961 ESC*, United Kingdom, 30th of March 1998.

[73] E.C.S.R., *Conclusions XV-1, on the Application of Article 1, § 2 of the 1961 ESC*, United Kingdom, 30th of March 2000.

that the ILO position on mandatory work programmes was at this time largely unknown and has only later received a larger diffusion, through its general survey of 2007.

Besides, if the ECSR did not refer to the ILO criterion of "exploitation of constraints" and did not ask questions concerning the eventual remuneration allocated for work, it formulated a set of other questions that could be helpful to assess the said criterion. Through these questions, one can anticipate the different points the ECSR might consider problematic with regards to Article 1, § 2 of the ESC: the purpose of the work programme, the possibility for the unemployed to justify a refusal to take up employment or training, the number and the duration of the sanctions, the possibility of appeal to an independent body, the possibility of receiving social assistance for the duration of the sanction...

In its "prohibition of forced labour" monitoring, the ECSR did not only examine work programmes imposed on the unemployed. It also considered the fact that certain States condition the granting of unemployment benefits to *participation in vocational training*. Before describing this case law, we must notice that it is somewhat surprising that the ECSR has examined this type of activation measures from the angle of the prohibition of forced labour, since the CEACR, for its part, has always considered in its general surveys on forced labour that training does not constitute work, so that it cannot be constitutive of forced labour.[74]

In its XIII-3 Conclusions in 1996, the ECSR asked Luxembourg, which had indicated in its report that jobseekers might be required to participate in training courses in order to be entitled to or to retain their entitlement to full unemployment benefit, to provide more detailed information on this legislation.[75] The United Kingdom, which suspended the granting of the benefits of persons who had refused to take part in a training programme, was asked by the ECSR to specify the criteria used to assess the jobseeker's good faith and the suitability of their reasons, in cases they refuse to take up training.[76] To Norway, which had indicated that recipients of social security benefits could temporarily lose their entitlement to benefits if they refused, without valid reasons, to participate in vocational training or re-training programmes organised by the employment service, the ECSR asked in 1996 and 1998 which benefits

---

[74] I.L.O., C.E.A.C.R., *Forced Labour*, General Survey, 1968, § 26; I.L.O., C.E.A.C.R., *Abolition of Forced Labour*, General Survey, 1979, § 20; I.L.O., C.E.A.C.R., *Eradication of Forced labour, op. cit.*, p. 19, § 36.

[75] E.C.S.R., *Conclusions XIII-3 addendum, on the Application of Article 1, § 2 of the 1961 ESC*, Luxemburg, 30th of April 1996.

[76] E.C.S.R., *Conclusions XV-1, on the Application of Article 1, § 2 of the 1961 ESC*, United Kingdom, 30th of March 2000.

were concerned, what was meant by "valid reasons", who decided as to the validity of those reasons, whether there was a possibility of appeal, as well as an indication of the percentage of persons affected.[77]

While the ECSR had raised questions about mandatory training, Norway did essentially expose the rules related to the availability for work condition. It explained that given the favourable labour market situation in Norway, unemployment benefits recipients were required to accept any work for which they were physically and mentally fit. It added that participation in training courses was also compulsory. If the candidate refused without reasonable cause to take up the proposed employment or to undertake a particular training programme, their benefits may be suspended for a limited period. There was a possibility of appeal before an independent body. Considering these elements, the ECSR concluded in 2000 that the situation in Norway was in conformity with Article 1, § 2 of the Charter in relation to the prohibition of forced labour.[78] This is the only time the ECSR has examined reforms widening the scope of the general availability for work condition from the angle of the prohibition of forced labour. Contrary to the CEACR, the ECSR did not consider that requiring unemployment benefits recipients to accept any job without regard to their professional qualifications from their first day of unemployment was contrary to the prohibition of forced labour. We will see in our next point that the ECSR will however later guarantee the protection of the notion of suitable employment under Article 1, § 2 of the Charter – not in the light of the prohibition of forced labour but more broadly, with respect to the right to freely chosen work.

2. *Systematic Analysis of the Loss of Unemployment Benefits for Refusal to Take up Employment or Training from the Angle of the Right to Freely Chosen Work*

The ECSR traditionally examined two issues in its control of application of Article 1, § 2 of the Charter: the prohibition of forced labour and the prohibition of any kind of employment discrimination. In its 2002 conclusions, the Committee introduced a new item entitled: "other aspects of freely chosen work", under which it examined three issues: the loss of unemployment benefits for refusal to take up employment, the length of civilian service and the consequences of part-time work. In the framework

---

[77] E.C.S.R., *Conclusions XIII-3, on the Application of Article 1, § 2 of the 1961 ESC*, Norway, 30th of November 1995; E.C.S.R., *Conclusions XIV-1, on the Application of Article 1, § 2 of the 1961 ESC*, Norway, 30th of March 1998; E.C.S.R., *Conclusions XV-1, on the Application of Article 1, § 2 of the 1961 ESC*, Norway, 30th of March 2000.

[78] E.C.S.R., *Conclusions XV-1, on the Application of Article 1, § 2 of the 1961 ESC*, Norway, 30th of March 2000.

of its 2003 XVI-1 control cycle,[79] the ECSR has, in its words, "developed its case law" by confirming that it would now systematically examine the loss of unemployment benefits for refusal to take up employment, as well as the length of civilian service and the consequences of part-time work under a new section called "Other aspects of the right to earn one's living in an occupation freely entered upon".[80]

The ESCR motivated the systematic analysis of the loss of unemployment benefits for refusal to take up employment as follows:

"During the XV-1 supervision cycle, the Committee carried out in some cases examinations of measures taken by certain governments to support employment and reduce spending on unemployment benefits. It found that the use of such measures, which could have a significant effect on the right to earn one's living in an occupation freely entered upon, was becoming increasingly frequent".[81]

Under this new heading, the ECSR mostly examined the unemployment benefits reforms by which had been widened the spectrum of jobs that the unemployed are obliged to accept, in the name of the availability for work condition. We have seen hereinabove that the Committee had never completed an examination of this condition under the heading "prohibition of forced labour". By contrast, it established under the new heading a clear case law on the availability for work condition. In its view, it is legitimate to make the granting of unemployment benefits conditional on a real availability for work. The right to an occupation freely entered upon implies however that, "for an initial reasonable period, jobseekers may refuse offers that do not match their qualifications and experience, without running the risk of losing their entitlement to unemployment benefit".[82] This criterion thus protects the professional status of the unemployed. It does correspond to the main defining criterion of the notion of "suitable employment", as defined in the European Code of Social Security (adopted in 1964, revised in 1990 and interpreted by the Committee of Experts on

---

[79] E.C.S.R., *Conclusions XVI-1, Statement of Interpretation of Article 1, § 2 of the 1961 ESC*, 31st of October 2006.

[80] E.C.S.R., *Conclusions XVIII-1, on the Application of Article 1, § 2 of the 1961 ESC*, Sweden, 31st of April 2004.

[81] E.C.S.R., *Conclusions 2004, on the Application of Article 1, § 2 of the 1961 ESC*, Sweden, 31st of April 2004; E.C.S.R., *Conclusions XVI-2, on the Application of Article 1, § 2 of the 1961 ESC*, Latvia, 30th of June 2004.

[82] E.C.S.R., *Conclusions 2004, on the Application of Article 1, § 2 of the 1961 ESC*, Cyprus, 31st of May 2004; E.C.S.R., *Conclusions XVI-1, on the Application of Article 1, § 2 of the 1961 ESC*, Denmark, 30th of May 2003; E.C.S.R., *Conclusions XVI-1, on the Application of Article 1, § 2 of the 1961 ESC*, Germany, 30th of May 2003; E.C.S.R., *Conclusions XVII-1, on the Application of Article 1, § 2 of the 1961 ESC*, Germany, 28th of February 2005.

Social Security (CS-SS)).[83] To recap, the European Code of Social Security is an instrument adopted at the European Council level that lays down minimum standards for social security and encourages contracting parties to exceed these standards. The application of the Code is monitored through regular reports from States submitted to the CS-SS.[84]

The ECSR quickly decided to extend its analysis to the loss of unemployment benefits for refusal to undertake a training programme. Since 2004, the heading has been titled "Acceptance of a job offer or of a training offer as a condition for the maintaining of employment benefits" or "Loss of unemployment benefits for refusal to take up employment or training".[85] Nevertheless, the ECSR has practically never examined compulsory training measures under this heading.

In a 2008 statement of interpretation, the ECSR specified the respective scopes of application of Article 12, §§ 1 and 3 and Article 1, § 2.[86] As a reminder, Article 12 proclaims the right to social security, States committing themselves to establishing or maintaining a social security regime under the first paragraph, and to progressively bringing the regime to a higher level under the third paragraph. The ESCR reminded that in principle, the conditions for receiving unemployment benefits, including the obligation to take up employment, needed to be evaluated within the framework of Article 12 of the Charter. It however indicated that, under certain circumstances, the loss of benefits, following the refusal of an employment offer, "could amount, indirectly, to a restriction on the freedom to work and as such the situation would be assessed under Article 1, § 2".[87]

---

[83] On the defining criteria of the notion of suitable employment under the European Code of Social Security, see E. Dermine, "Suitable Employment and Job of Quality", *op. cit.*, pp. 170-177.

[84] On supervision mechanisms of the European Code of Social Security application, see J. Nickless, *European Code of Social Security: A Short Guide*, Strasbourg, Council of Europe Publishing, 2002; A. Gomez Heredero, *Social Security Protection at the International Level and Developments in Europe*, Strasbourg, Council of Europe Publishing, 2008.

[85] E.C.S.R., *Conclusions 2004, on the Application of Article 1, § 2 of the 1961 ESC*, Bulgaria, Cyprus, Estonia, Lithuania, Romania, 31st of May 2004; E.C.S.R., *Conclusions XVII-1, on the Application of Article 1, § 2 of the 1961 ESC*, Belgium, Czech Republic, Denmark, Finland, Germany, Greece, Netherlands, Poland, Portugal, Spain, United Kingdom, 28th of February 2005; E.C.S.R., *Conclusions XVII-2, on the Application of Article 1, § 2 of the 1961 ESC*, 30th of June 2005.

[86] E.C.S.R., *Conclusions XIX-1, Statement of Interpretation of Article 1, § 2 of the 1961 ESC*, 24th of October 2008; E.C.S.R., *Conclusions 2008, Statement of Interpretation of Article 1, § 2 of the ESC*, 24th of October 2008.

[87] *Ibid.*

During its 2012 control cycle, the ESCR realised that it had not received from the States the information required to monitor their compliance with Article 1, § 2 of the statutory obligation to take up employment present in their unemployment benefits systems.[88] It therefore specified, in a statement of interpretation,[89] the circumstances under which the loss of benefits due to a refusal to take up employment can constitute a restriction to the freedom of work. In order to determine those circumstances, it expressly referred to the Guide to the concept of suitable employment in the context of unemployment benefit, drafted in 2009 by the Committee of Experts on Social Security, in charge of the promotion of the European Social Security Code.[90] The ECSR listed a number of cases, directly inspired by the defining criteria of the notion of suitable employment set out in the Guide, in which an unemployed person cannot be compelled to accept a job on pain of seeing his freedom to work violated. According to the terms of the ECSR, cases are targeted where the job:

- only requires qualifications or skills far below those of the individual concerned;
- pays well below the individual's previous salary;
- requires a particular level of physical or mental health or ability, which the person does not possess at the relevant time;
- is not compatible with occupational health and safety legislation or, where they exist, with local agreements or collective employment agreements covering the sector or occupation concerned, and therefore may affect the physical and mental integrity of the worker;
- for which the pay offered is lower than the national or regional minimum wage or, where it exists, the norm or wage scale agreed on for the sector or occupation concerned, or where it is lower, to an unreasonable extent, than all of the unemployment benefits paid to the person concerned at the relevant time and therefore fails to ensure a decent standard of living for the worker and his/her family;

---

[88] Interview of Petros Stangos, vice-president of the ECSR, rapporteur for Article 1, § 2 during the 2012 control cycle, 5th of December 2012.

[89] E.C.S.R., *Conclusions 2012, Statement of Interpretation of Article 1, § 2 of the ESC*, December 2012.

[90] The guidelines on the concept of suitable employment have been elaborated by a working group on the basis of the practises of the States that are parties to the Code. For a comparison between those guidelines and the previous case law of Committee of experts on the Code, see E. Dermine, "Suitable Employment and Job of Quality", *op. cit.*, pp. 175-176.

- is proposed as the result of a current labour dispute;
- is located at a distance from the home of the person concerned which can be deemed unreasonable in view of the necessary travelling time, the transport facilities available, the total time spent away from home, the customary working arrangements in the person's chosen occupation or the person's family obligations (and in the latter case, provided that these obligations did not pose any problem in the person's previous employment);
- requires persons with family responsibilities to change their place of residence, unless it can be proved that these responsibilities can be properly assumed in the new place of residence, that suitable housing is available and that, if the situation of the person so requires, a contribution to the costs of removal is available, either from the employment services or from the new employer, so respecting the worker's right to family life and housing.

The ECSR will thus now pay attention to other criteria than the protection of professional status.

Moreover, the ECSR has specified that "in all cases in which the relevant authorities decide on the permanent withdrawal or temporary suspension of unemployment benefit because the recipient has rejected a job offer, this decision must be open to review by the courts in accordance with the rules and procedures established under the legislation of the State which took the decision".[91]

Since the establishment in 2003 of a systematic analysis of the loss of unemployment benefit for refusal to take up employment or training under a new section dedicated to "the other aspects of the right to an occupation freely entered upon", the ECSR has stopped monitoring activation measures under the item dedicated to "the prohibition of forced labour". One may thus wonder if the ECSR has not overturned its previous case law and started considering that work-related obligations imposed on unemployment benefits or social assistance recipients cannot, in any case, constitute forced labour.

We will first underline that the item examined under the heading "other aspects of the right to an occupation freely entered upon" is strictly defined: loss of unemployment benefit for refusal to take up employment or training. According to the different statements of interpretation, the obligation to take up employment refers to the availability for work condition in unemployment benefits systems. It does not encompass measures conditioning the granting of unemployment or social assistance

---

[91] E.C.S.R., *Conclusions 2012, Statement of Interpretation of Article 1, § 2 of the ESC*, December 2012.

benefits to the participation to work programmes[92] nor obligations to accept employment in social assistance systems. Likewise, the new heading does not encompass the obligations to undertake training in social assistance systems. Therefore, activation measures that do not fall within the scope of the new heading could still, in our view, be examined by the ECSR under the prohibition of forced labour, even if it has not done so since 2002.

The question of the potential change in jurisprudence thus only concerns the specific activation measures targeted under the new item, i.e. the availability for work condition and the obligation to undertake training in unemployment benefit systems. Does it have to be considered that these two measures can no longer be examined from the angle of prohibition of forced labour? The ECSR has not expressed any clear position on the topic so far. In favour of this interpretation, one might consider that the 2003 statement of interpretation of the ECSR is directly in line with the decision on the merits related to the collective complaint *QCEA v. Greece*, in which the ECSR had ruled that the obligation to perform an alternative civilian service could not constitute, as such, forced labour but could, in case of excessive duration, be qualified as a disproportionate restriction on the right to an occupation freely entered upon.[93] Within the framework of the reporting procedure, the ECSR would have created a new heading entitled "Other aspects of the right to an occupation freely entered upon" to analyse the questions that did not fit within the field of prohibition of forced labour. The obligation to accept employment and training in unemployment benefit systems could never equate to a forced labour relationship but could constitute, in certain circumstances, a disproportionate restriction on the freedom of access to the labour market.

---

[92] Just when it established this new heading, the ECSR however twice analysed obligations to take part in mandatory work programmes under the said heading. These examinations followed the replies given by the Italian and British governments to questions they had been asked under the "prohibition of forced labour" subtitle, during the previous control cycle. In its 2002 conclusions, the ECSR proposed new questions to Italy on the effects of refusal to take part in community work. It requested Italy to specify the length of the benefits' suspension and the number of sanctions. It no longer examined the issue during the next cycles. Concerning the participation of the unemployed to the "Project work" scheme in the United Kingdom, the ECSR judged the scheme non-compliant in 2003, since the legislation did not allow jobseekers to refuse, during a short period of time, an employment that did not correspond to their professional qualifications. Since then, the ECSR has no longer asked questions on the mandatory work programmes under the heading "Loss of unemployment benefits for refusal to take up employment or training".

[93] E.C.S.R., Decision No. 8/2000, *Quaker Council for European Affairs (QCEA) v. Greece* (decision on the merits), 25th of April 2001, complaint No. 8/1999.

But this reversal in ECSR case law would be contrary to ILO case law, according to which the loss of unemployment benefits for refusal to take up a non-suitable employment contravenes the prohibition of forced labour.[94] One should thus rather consider that the evolution of the ECSR case law simply resides in the fact that it started systematically analysing the measure from the angle of the right to freely chosen work, which does absolutely not exclude that such a measure could amount, under certain circumstances, to forced labour. This understanding of the new heading is the only one that complies with the ILO case law. Moreover, a teleological argument pleads in favour of this interpretation: the ECSR decided to systematically analyse the loss of unemployment benefits for refusal to take up employment because it had noted, during the previous cycle, that States tended to adopt this type of measures, and because it was worried by their impact on the right to an occupation freely entered upon.[95] The ECSR seems thus to have proceeded that way in order to force States to report on this specific point and to ensure a better monitoring of the phenomenon.

* * *

In the ECSR case law on the right to freely chosen work, we have identified one minimal norm that limits the development of activation measures. It concerns States' reforms aiming at widening the availability for work condition in unemployment benefits systems. Just as the ILO CEACR, the ECSR considers that these reforms may not deprive unemployment benefits recipients of the possibility to refuse an employment that is manifestly not suitable. The ECSR has borrowed this minimal norm from its case law on the right to social security (Article 12 of the ESC) and the minimal standards on unemployment benefits set in the European Code of Social Security.

Through the reporting procedure, the ECSR had formerly progressively established a standard list of questions related to activation measures. These questions concerned all kind of activation measures, whether they were implemented in unemployment benefits schemes or social assistance systems and whether they consist in work or not. Even if the States' answers had never resulted in a negative conclusion, this questioning process demonstrated the will of the ECSR to ensure a systematic monitoring of activation measures. Besides, the content of the questions revealed the Committee's desire to balance the restriction on the free choice of employment imposed on the unemployed person with

---

[94] See *supra*, II, *A.*, 1.
[95] E.C.S.R., *Conclusions 2004, on the Application of Article 1, § 2 of the 1961 ESC*, Sweden, 31st of April 2004.

general interest considerations, such as having a labour market including the highest number of working age people.

Since 2002, the ECSR seems to have focused all its questions around the notion of suitable employment. This is, in our view, somewhat disappointing. As we have seen in the previous part about ILO case law, the minimal norm of suitable employment is no doubt essential but is certainly not sufficient to apprehend the activation phenomenon in its entirety.

Conclusion

Our study started with the intuition that the right to freely chosen work could be an interesting benchmark by which to assess activation policies for the unemployed, since it protects the freedom of work, which is a key issue at stake in activation policies. The first part of the chapter aimed at tracing the outlines of the rather unknown right to freely chosen work, through the analysis of the international general case law relating to this right. We then turned, in a second part, to the specific cases in which international bodies have had to assess the conformity of an activation measure with the right to freely chosen work.

In the first part, we have shown that the right to freely chosen work offers a wider protection of the freedom of work than the prohibition of forced labour proclaimed in international covenants on civil and political rights. As has been shown in particular by the ILO Director-General, it encompasses the prohibition of forced labour, but also protects workers against less serious forms of coercion in their work relationship. Moreover, the CESCR and the ECSR case law have highlighted that it does not only protect the freedom of the individual in the work relationship. It also covers free access to the labour market, on which depends the possibility of a downstream exercise of the free choice of employment. Consequently, the right to freely chosen work constitutes a footing from which to assess the impact of all types of activation measures on the freedom of work, while some of these measures obviously cannot be evaluated under the prohibition of forced labour. Here we are referring to, for example, training schemes, but also support plans or job search assistance. These activation measures do not consist in the imposition of work, but may, in certain cases, result in restricting the free access and choice of employment.

We have also highlighted that the linkage between freedom of work and social security is patent in international instruments on economic, social and cultural rights. In these texts, the right to social security, and more particularly protection against unemployment, has been conceived as an auxiliary right to the right to work for those who have involuntarily lost their job. Besides, unemployment benefits are to guarantee a certain freedom of work to their recipients, by allowing them to refuse any employment that would not be suitable without risking losing their benefits.

The second part of the chapter evidenced that, in this general context, the CEACR and the ECSR rapidly noticed that the development of activation measures in social protection systems could have important impacts on unemployment benefits recipients' right to freely chosen work (including the prohibition of forced labour). By contrast, it has been far less evident for supervisory organs of the application of civil and political rights to admit that activation policies may hypothetically contravene the prohibition of forced labour, since they still conceive the prohibition of forced labour as disconnected from the idea that social security supports the freedom of work.

In order to determine the concrete requirements arising from the right to freely chosen work and the prohibition of forced labour regarding activation measures, ILO bodies and the ECSR have largely built on the minimum standards on unemployment benefits. ILO bodies have widely referred to part IV of Social Security Convention No. 102, which is dedicated to unemployment benefits, while the ECSR naturally turned to its case law on the right to social security (Article 12 of the ESC), whose concrete requirements are in turn determined by reference to the minimum standards on unemployment benefits developed at the level of the Council of Europe (Part IV of the European Social Security Code). By doing so, they have set two clear limits to the development of activation policies for the unemployed.

Firstly, ILO bodies consider that a requirement to perform some kind of work as a condition for receiving those benefits does constitute forced labour, when the unemployed have contributed while working to be eligible for the benefits and when the benefit duration is proportional to that of the work previously performed.

Secondly, ILO organs and the ECSR, following a common jurisprudential line, consider that the right to freely chosen work requires that unemployment benefits recipients have the possibility to refuse an employment that is not suitable in the meaning of international minimum standards on unemployment benefits. As to the notion of suitable employment, ILO bodies and the ECSR largely focus on the fact that unemployment benefits recipients must have the right to refuse jobs that do not correspond to their professional qualifications during an initial period of unemployment.

This permeability between the case law on the right to social security and the right to freely chosen work (including the prohibition of forced labour) has the significant effect of strengthening the case law related to the right to social security, since the right to freely chosen work, by contrast with the right to social security, is considered highly justiciable.

Still, these two minimal norms borrowed from the right to social security and minimal standards on harmonisation of unemployment benefits systems do not, in our view, suffice to ensure a systematic and global approach to activation measures implemented in social protection systems from the angle of freedom of work.

On the one hand, they essentially protect the freedom of work of the short-term unemployed who are entitled to unemployment benefits, all the more so if they have contributed to be entitled to benefits. It is logical since international minimal standards on unemployment benefits have been adopted to protect against unemployment, which was, at that time, a short-term risk. In the actual context of massive and long-term unemployment, increasingly wider categories of unemployed either experience unemployment for a long period or cannot even qualify for contributory unemployment benefits and rely on unemployment assistance benefits or social assistance schemes. The freedom of these categories of beneficiaries is not, or is very weakly, protected through the minimal norms, though they are also, and even increasingly, subject to activation measures. For example, the right to refuse an employment that is not suitable, which is actually the central protection afforded to the unemployed under the right to freely chosen work, does usually not offer any protection to social assistance recipients. Besides, it only protects the professional status of unemployment recipients during an initial period of unemployment, which is often not long enough for the unemployed to find a new job within the context of high and long-term unemployment.

On the other hand, the two minimal norms do only protect the unemployed's formal freedom of work, by imposing States to allow social benefits recipients to refuse offers of employment on the labour market or participation in work-related programmes, without risking losing their benefits. They fully disconnect the right to freely chosen work from the positive aspect of the right to work, despite the fact that certain activation measures intend to increase the real opportunities of the unemployed to access the labour market (effective freedom of work). At the time that unemployment was a short-term risk, only paying attention to the formal freedom of work was maybe sufficient, with the unemployed ending up anyway in most cases finding a suitable employment on their own after a few months. It is now obviously unsatisfying, all the more so in the context of the ever-faster evolution of jobs and skills required in the present day.

One has to acknowledge, though, that apart from the affirmation of the aforementioned two minimal norms, we could also identify certain elements in the CEACR and the ECSR case law that demonstrate their will to ensure a systematic and global monitoring of activation policies for the unemployed.

Firstly, the CEACR established a minimal protection of the freedom of work of all categories of social benefits recipients in relation to mandatory work programmes. According to the CEACR, whether the social scheme is contributory or not, conditioning the granting of benefits to participation in work programmes amounts to forced labour if the States appears to exploit the constraints faced by the recipients by imposing them to perform work that would normally not be acceptable.

Secondly, in the framework of its reports procedure, the ECSR developed a process of questioning the new practises of States. It has asked various questions to States, in particular on the goal of the activation measures, the possibility to justify a refusal to take up employment or training and the reasons that can be invoked, on the consideration of personal preferences in work or training assignment, on the number and the duration of sanctions, on the possibility of appeal in front of an independent body, on the possibility to rely on social assistance during the period of sanction. As for the CEACR, it recently asked for information from States on the impact of their measures on the real opportunities to return to employment, in the framework of the reporting procedure concerning the Employment Policy Convention No. 122.

In our view, those case law practises do reveal the will of international bodies to ensure an overall control of the proportionality between, on the one hand, the restriction to the right to freely chosen work imposed on the unemployed and, on the other hand, the objective of general interest pursued by the activation measures as well as the individual advantage the unemployed might obtain in terms of effective freedom of work.

In this connection, it should be recalled that the proportionality criterion has also emerged, as a defining element of the prohibition of forced labour, in situations where work is imposed by States on general interest considerations. In the previous chapter, we have showed that supervision bodies on civil and political rights have in some way mobilised the idea of proportionality to assess the conformity of activation measures with the prohibition of forced labour. The proportionality criterion is also the one that the ECSR adopted to assess the existence of a violation of the right to an occupation freely entered upon, in the *QCEA v. Greece* case. We will finally note that the two minimal norms resulting from international standards on unemployment benefits also contain this idea of proportionality. The notion of suitable employment as well as the conditions of eligibility for benefits indeed materialise the balancing test operated by States between the right of the unemployed to freely choose their work and the duty to work weighing on them in the general interest. The proportionality criterion is thus, in more or less explicit forms, present throughout all the international case law, related to the compliance of activation measures with the right to freely chosen work (including the prohibition of forced labour).

In the framework of the reporting procedure, international bodies have tended to focus their attention in the past few years on reforms that either widen or suppress the notion of suitable employment and have been less concerned by other activation measures, even though they also affect the freedom of work. By formalising a wider proportionality test, the case law could, in our view, progressively develop a systematic and effective monitoring of activation measures. It could progressively identify new criteria for assessing all activation measures, including those that target unemployment assistance and social assistance recipients. The ECSR could for example include in the proportionality test the evaluation criteria of activation measures it has developed under the right to social assistance (Article 13 of the ESC),[96] to which it does not refer in its case law on the right to freely chosen work. By this test, the case law could also connect the right to freely chosen work and the positive right to work, by balancing the restriction on the formal freedom (the right to freely chosen work) and the eventual increase in effective freedom of work (the positive right to work).

The minimal norms resulting from the right to social security and the harmonisation norms on unemployment benefits would then play as elements amongst others to be taken into consideration for the balancing test. More than the right to social security, the right to freely chosen work would then reveal all its richness and dynamism. The elements taken into account through the proportionality test would not be inflexible but could evolve in an uncertain environment, in order to best protect the social benefits recipients' freedom of work.

In the light of these considerations, we can conclude that the right to freely chosen work deserves to be invoked in front of national and international jurisdictions, in support of claims against coercive activation policies. All the more so because, contrary to the right to social security, it is considered a right with high enforceability.

---

[96] See footnote 2.

Right to Work and Individual Responsibility in Contemporary Welfare States
A Capability Approach to Activation Policies for the Unemployed

Jean-Michel BONVIN and Eric MOACHON

Introduction

For nearly three decades, socio-professional integration policies in OECD countries have undergone significant developments, calling into question the very meaning of social law. Until now, the latter has been seen as the archetype of entitlement-rights and was based on a conception of the state as a debtor, under which any member of the community could request repayment of the public authorities' debt in the form of social benefits and social services. In other words, individuals owned an entitlement that the state was required to honour by providing a certain amount of social protection in case of need, and especially in case of job loss.[1] This conception enshrined the primacy of collective responsibility over individual responsibility. But it also limited the regulatory intervention of the state in the labour market to the negative dimension of the right to work, i.e. on the prohibition of certain professional activities deemed incompatible with human dignity (forced labour, night work, child labour, etc.). As a consequence, the positive side of the right to work – which we might call the positive freedom to work[2] – was not supported by social law initiatives. Its realisation came either from trust in the labour market, which was expected to create sufficient jobs, or from the instruments of Keynesian macroeconomic policy. Social security law and labour law have indeed been developed

---

[1] On the distinction between "freedom-rights" and "entitlement-rights" and the debates it has provoked, see L. Ferry and A. Renaut, *Philosophie politique*, Vol. 3, *Des droits de l'homme à l'idée républicaine*, Paris, Presses universitaires de France, 1985, pp. 26 et sqs.

[2] We refer here to the distinction made by Isaiah Berlin between negative freedom – the freedom of not being forced to do something against one's own will – and positive freedom – the freedom to be one's own master, to have control of one's own destiny. See I. Berlin, *Four Essays on Liberty*, Oxford, Oxford University Press, 1969.

primarily in the double perspective of compensating non-employment and of protecting workers against unsuitable jobs, while supporting the positive freedom to work was not considered necessary under the law.

Since the early 1980s, Keynesian policies have been largely abandoned,[3] leaving issues of job creation and access to employment (hence the positive freedom to work) to market mechanisms alone. In this regard, the role of the state has been reduced to ensure the framework conditions allowing private economic actors to create enough jobs. Along with this withdrawal of the state from macroeconomic policies, the rise of the active welfare state has been observed, which calls into question the previous approach to social law.[4] The emphasis is now on making individuals aware of their responsibility, thereby implying that they were irresponsible under the old forms of social solidarity. According to the new conception that has emerged, it is necessary to adapt social law to eradicate the phenomena of welfare dependency and unemployment traps. The dependency trap issue, according to which individuals tend to "settle" in a state of dependency on the welfare state, provider of social benefits, was initially developed mainly in Anglo-Saxon countries. It then found a powerful relay at the international level, with the employment strategies respectively implemented by the OECD (1994) and the European Union (1997), which both recommended the revision of social benefits systems in order to eliminate any perverse incentive that would push beneficiaries to "take advantage" of public generosity rather than actively seeking a job and the financial independence that it was supposed to provide. Thus, a new common sense emerged, which presented reforming the welfare state in the direction of the activation of the unemployed as an indisputable postulate. In this perspective, it only remains to determine the actual conditions of application of this active welfare state and of its performance in making individuals responsible. The debate should therefore no longer focus on the merits of this activation turn, but on the more technical question of the means of its implementation: eligibility conditions, benefit levels, content of active labour market policies, system of incentives and sanctions, etc.

However, the transition from entitlement-rights to the responsibilisation of individuals is not self-evident and must be examined under numerous

---

[3] See for example E. Matzner and W. Streeck (eds.), *Beyond Keynesianism*, London, Edward Elgar, 1991 and B. Jessop, "The Transition to Post-Fordism and the Schumpeterian Workfare State", in R. Burrows and B. Loader (eds.), *Towards a Post-Fordist Welfare State*, London, Routledge, 1994, pp. 13-37.

[4] J.-M. Bonvin and E. Moachon, "L'activation et son potentiel de subversion de l'Etat social", in P. Vielle, P. Pochet and I. Cassiers (eds.), *L'Etat social actif*, Brussels, P.I.E.-Peter Lang (Work & Society), 2005, pp. 62-92.

aspects.⁵ Has it really been demonstrated that entitlement-rights produce irresponsibility? What is the real meaning of this "responsibilisation" of individuals? What is the relationship between the welfare state and the individual concerned? Is it about a moralistic and paternalistic state intending to discipline individuals, or about more reflexive or participative versions of the relationship between institutions and beneficiaries? Is the responsibilisation of individuals backward-looking (towards the past), in the sense of a comeback of the language of fault and imputability, or forward-looking (towards the future), in order to restore the conditions under which people act responsibly?

More specifically, the focus on the negative side of the right to work should be questioned. Wouldn't it be appropriate to also develop the positive component of this right and to provide individuals not only with the opportunity to refuse those jobs deemed unsuitable, but also with the effective (and not merely formal) right to a freely chosen work?⁶ Activation programmes could make an interesting contribution, provided they are no longer considered first in terms of compelling jobseekers to return to work (the duty to work), but also in terms of increasing their capacity to find a good quality job (the positive freedom to work). Current developments towards an active welfare state require to pay careful attention to all of these fundamental questions. This article's objective is to identify the features of the responsibilisation of individuals underlying activation policies for the unemployed. It suggests a normative grid in order to assess them.

In the first part of our paper, we propose a theoretical and analytical framework that allows a fresh perspective on these issues. This first stage of our reflection is largely inspired by the "capability approach" of the philosopher and economist Amartya Sen, of whom we will present both the thinking and vocabulary (I.). Then, we will compare the main welfare state models, as distinguished by most specialists in comparative social policy, against this analytical framework (II.). The conclusion summarises the main lessons learned in this article, highlighting the conditions for an activation and responsibilisation of the unemployed that are compatible with the requirements of the capability approach, and shows how current practices stand out from this model.

---

⁵ See D. Dumont, *La responsabilisation des personnes sans emploi en question*, Brussels, La Charte, 2012.

⁶ In this sense, see also the conclusion of the second contribution to this book by Elise Dermine ("Activation Policies for the Unemployed and the International Human Rights Case Law on the Right to a Freely Chosen Work").

I. Capability Approach, Responsibility and the Right to work

Central to Amartya Sen's work is a constant concern with developing what he calls the "capabilities" of individuals, i.e. their real freedom to lead a life that they have reason to value, following the recurrent formula in his writings.[7] The development of these capabilities requires action unfolding on two complementary sides: an enlargement of the "abilities or powers to act" of individuals (which echoes the positive freedom to work), and an increase in their "freedom of choice" (which requires, among other things, the negative freedom not to work under conditions that the person does not value).[8] This theoretical perspective thus integrates the positive and negative sides of the right to work. Let us explain more precisely what is meant by "abilities or powers to act" (A.) and "freedom of choice" (B.) in this conceptual framework, as well as the type of relationship between individuals and institutions that such a "freedom of choice" approach implies (C.).

A. Ability or Power to Act

On the first side, the positive one, developing the capabilities of individuals requires, according to Sen, the simultaneous consideration of three dimensions: resources, skills and opportunities.

Resources include all goods and services that a person can have, whether produced or offered on the market, in the non-profit sector or in the public sector. Included in this notion of "resources" are incomes perceived on the labour market, private donations or gifts, goods, and all cash benefits (compensations, replacement incomes, etc.) or in nature (social services, public transport, etc.) that individuals have access to via the welfare state. In this article, we propose to extend this concept to cover all the formal rights individuals have that may be considered as available resources in the course of action. Thus, enshrining in a constitutional or legislative text a worker's right to strike or to be consulted on a particular topic represents a resource for action, which can be used during a labour dispute or a collective bargaining. Similarly, the constitutional principle

---

[7] See for example A.K. Sen, *Inequality Reexamined*, Oxford, Oxford University Press, 1992; A.K. Sen, *Development as Freedom*, Oxford, Oxford University Press, 1999; A. K. Sen, *The Idea of Justice*, Cambridge (MA), Harvard University Press, 2009.

[8] The proximity between freedom as ability and the positive freedom to work on the one hand, and freedom of choice and the negative side of the right to work on the other hand, is not taken directly from the work of Amartya Sen. It seems, however, faithful to the spirit of the distinction he draws between "opportunity freedom" and "process freedom". See A.K. Sen, *Rationality and Freedom*, Cambridge (MA), Harvard University Press, 2002.

of gender equality is a lever on which concrete actions can be supported. We may also mention here the rights that protect the negative side of an individual's freedom to work, such as the prohibition of forced labour, the right to refuse an unsuitable job or the prohibition of discrimination in access to employment.[9]

However, the possession of resources, within this broader sense, is not sufficient to ensure conversion into the capacity for real action or the real freedom to lead a life that has value for a person. Two different people with the same amount of income or formal rights do not necessarily have the same capacity to use them wisely. Even the existence of constitutional rights does not guarantee to all citizens the equal capacity to mobilise them. It is therefore appropriate to complete these resources by other parameters, called "conversion factors" by Sen, which will enable their effective use in action. Otherwise, these resources will not be translated into capabilities or into the actual freedom to lead a quality life – or, in the case we are interested in, into meaningful employment. This is why the capability approach emphasises the need to develop, in conjunction with efforts to grant or redistribute resources in a broad sense, people's individual skills and the opportunities they are offered. Sen considers these two types of intervention in terms of conversion factors.

Firstly, the individual conversion factors designate the innate characteristics (age, sex, etc.) and acquired skills (diplomas, qualifications, work experience, know-how, self-management skills, etc.) of individuals. Here, one must make sure that these factors are considered in a way that allows the development of capabilities. From the angle of the right to work, this means ensuring that individuals have adequate skills and that they are not discriminated against on the labour market (for example because of their gender or nationality), with the goal of enabling them to find a quality job or occupation. Thus, action must be taken on both the positive and negative sides of the right to work in order to promote the capabilities of those involved. Multiple forms of rights convene here. On the one hand are what we suggest to call "constraint-rights", which are intended to prohibit discrimination on the labour market (as in conventions No. 100 and 111 of the ILO, both relating to discrimination in the workplace) or unsuitable forms of work (as in conventions No. 29 and 105 of the ILO on the prohibition of forced labour). On the other hand are "capacity-rights", which one might say are aimed at developing the skills, the know-how and the self-management skills of individuals. In Sen's view, these two forms of rights – constraint-rights and capacity-rights – do not replace conventional entitlement-rights, but rather they complement them. Joint action concerning resources and skills is a sine

---

[9] On this subject, see the two contributions of Elise Dermine in this book.

qua non for the development of capabilities, which is designed as a "goal-rights system" according to Sen.[10] The development of capabilities is indeed the ultimate goal that is pursued by the use of constraint-rights, capacity-rights and entitlement-rights. Hence, this system is the normative standard against which the impact of these three forms of rights must be evaluated.[11]

Secondly, the social conversion factors refer to the social and economic context in which the person evolves. Included here are social norms (regarding, for example, behavioural expectations towards other individuals, how one should view the place of women in society, etc.), social structures (i.e. economic, social, education and gender inequalities) and the possibilities for economic and social integration that are available to individuals (the number of jobs available, their quality, their distribution according to the economic sectors, etc.). The combination of these elements helps to define the set of real opportunities available to an individual. In fact, depending on the social norms in force, all members of a community do not have the same opportunities for professional integration, as illustrated by the example of women and foreigners. Similarly, belonging to an economically or educationally disadvantaged category of the population most often coincides with a significant restriction in possibilities on the labour market. Finally, in situations of economic difficulty, or even crisis, the scarcity of jobs reduces the capacity for professional integration of many individuals. The development of an individual's capabilities requires taking into account each of these parameters. The first factors mentioned above – social norms and social structures – are largely an issue of discrimination. The setting of constraint-rights (politics of quotas) or of incentive instruments (such as bonuses for hiring disadvantaged persons) are considered to curb the impact of these factors as much as possible. For its part, the last factor – the number and quality of jobs – depends on the economic policy concerned, whether the latter consists of the non-intervention of the state or whether it enjoys a more Keynesian inspiration. In international social law, increasing the number and the quality of jobs is not considered through constraint-rights, but takes the form of programmatic rights. One thinks,

---

[10] A.K. Sen, *On Ethics and Economics*, Oxford, Blackwell, 1987. See also J. De Munck, "Vers un nouveau paradigme du droit", in F. Eymard-Duvernay (ed.), *L'économie des conventions*, Vol. 1, *Méthodes et résultats*, Paris, La Découverte, 2006, pp. 249-262.

[11] Among the fundamental social rights, constraint-rights play an important role. Entitlement-rights are addressed in several ILO conventions (for example Convention No. 102 concerning the minimum norm of social security, and also in other instruments treating specific branches of social security), while capacity-rights are barely sketched out. See also J.-M. Bonvin, "Droits sociaux fondamentaux", in A. Jobert, M. Lallement and A. Mias (eds.), *Dictionnaire du travail*, Paris, Seuil, 2012, pp. 212-217.

for example, of Article 1 of the European Social Charter and Article 6 of the International Covenant on Economic, Social and Cultural Rights. Under these provisions, states make very broad and vague commitments, such as implementing an employment policy in order to ensure the highest and most stable level of employment possible, setting up free services for employment or even encouraging the orientation and the training of workers and unemployed individuals. Similarly, Convention No. 122 of the ILO on employment policy is limited to enacting very general objectives without stating precisely which means to mobilise in order to achieve them. The implementation of these objectives is left at the discretion of the concerned political bodies.[12] In a similar vein, Sen does not suggest a unique formula of economic policy that would have to be imposed on all states concerned. Thus, the development of opportunities can be made through various means, which must take into account the context in which they are to be deployed. The relative vagueness of these programmatic rights and the multiplicity of concrete forms they can take, fits nicely with the spirit of the capability approach. Everything seems possible, provided that the economic policy adopted fits into the overall goal-rights system, that is to say, provided that it has as its primary aim the development of the capabilities of individuals. So we cannot speak here of a perfect obligation to comply with a specific rule, but only of an imperfect obligation, that is to say, an ethical requirement.[13]

Thus, on the "ability or power to act" side – that of the positive freedom to work – the capability approach requires the consideration of resources, skills and opportunities in the same movement. Entitlement-rights or the redistribution of material, financial and legal resources are indeed not enough to ensure an improvement in the capacities of all beneficiaries. Similarly, acting on the competency of individuals is not enough either, since the social, economic and political factors are then ignored. Therefore, a public policy focused on promoting capabilities must act jointly on resources (goods, services, income and formal rights and freedoms), skills and opportunities. In terms of the right to work, such an action involves a diversity of forms of rights, combining entitlement-rights, constraint-rights, capacity-rights and programmatic rights, with all these forms being subsumed under a single objective,

---

[12] As regards the objective, economic growth and development are stimulated, work is guaranteed for all persons available and seeking a job, ensuring that such a job is as productive as possible, etc. (art. 1). The convention specifies that the chosen methods to achieve these very general objectives must be adapted to the conditions of each country (art. 2).

[13] Sen explicitly incorporates the distinction made by Kant between perfect and imperfect obligations in his article "Elements of a Human Rights Theory", *Philosophy and Public Affairs*, Vol. 32, No. 4, 2004, pp. 315-356.

namely the development of the capabilities of the persons concerned – what Sen describes as a "goal-rights system".

The issue of responsibility is at the heart of the "ability or power to act" side of Sen's approach. He believes that a person who is not equipped with the adequate resources, skills and opportunities cannot be held responsible for the situation in which s/he is. This conception of responsibility requires resolute action from public authorities in terms of the positive right to work, which involves the pluralisation of the instruments of law mentioned above. The distinction between two forms of responsibility introduced by J.-L. Genard can clarify this point.[14] According to Genard, one should distinguish between responsibility as willingness to answer for one's own actions, which is oriented towards the past, and responsibility as capacity to start, which is oriented towards the future and therefore requires that the conditions for responsible action are actually given. The first perspective insists on the necessity of taking responsibility for one's own actions and their consequences. Responsibility is then considered primarily in terms of imputability. The second perspective assumes that it is necessary to determine the conditions under which humans are responsible for their actions, in order to restore their ability to act responsibly. The capability approach can be clearly situated in the second of these two perspectives: a person can only be held responsible if s/he has the necessary capacities to act. A competent individual, endowed with resources and having access to numerous opportunities can be summoned to answer for his actions: in this case, the conditions for responsible action are met. In short, the capability approach argues that the issue of imputability comes second and is legitimate only insofar the conditions for the realisation of the positive right to work are met. In Bovens' terms,[15] an "active" conception of responsibility ("what should be done to promote responsible behaviour?") should be promoted, and only afterwards should "passive" responsibility – "why did you do that?" – be invoked, which aims to identify those who are culpable and deliver sanctions on them. To this end, the right to work, or, in Sen's words, the capability for work, should include all the dimensions laid out in the preceding pages (resources and individual and social conversion factors). Otherwise, it is likely to remain, at least in part, formal, and the demand for responsibilisation will appear as an injunction that is impossible to achieve, since the conditions for responsible action are not being met.

---

[14] J.-L. Genard, *La grammaire de la responsabilité*, Paris, Cerf, 1999.
[15] M. Bovens, *The Quest for Responsibility. Accountability and Citizenship in Complex Organisations*, Cambridge, Cambridge University Press, 1998.

However, the "ability or power to act" aspect is not by itself enough to ensure the capability for work: it is a necessary but not a sufficient condition. If the capability approach stopped there, it would not necessarily differentiate itself from certain other conceptions of "human capital" or of "employability" developed, for example, in Scandinavian countries.[16] Individuals could benefit from large endowments in terms of resources, skills and opportunities, but they would not be free in their use. The second dimension of the Senian capability approach – freedom of choice – introduces a decisive distinction in this regard.

B. *Freedom of Choice*

In his writings, Sen frequently insists on the importance of distinguishing functionings, or a person's achievements (i.e. who I am or what I am actually doing), from capabilities, or the real freedom of being and behaving in a certain manner (the actions and the choices that I can make). This terminological precision may seem trivial, but it is nonetheless far-reaching. Indeed, two people who find themselves in the same situation or perform the same acts do not necessarily have the same degree of real freedom. Here Sen uses the example of the state of nutritional deficit.[17] If someone lives in an area affected by food shortage or famine, the fact they are not eating is part of a constraint, while a person living in an environment of abundance can choose between eating or not eating. Between famine and voluntary fasting, there is a gap in terms of real freedom, which can be captured by the distinction between "functionings" and "capabilities". The relevance of this distinction also applies to less extreme examples. A person having abundant resources (via the welfare state or other channels) may choose to work or not. They will have therefore a significant capability for work, while a person without resources will be forced to perform a professional activity to ensure their subsistence.[18]

Generally speaking, the real freedom of individuals depends on the comparative feasibility of the alternatives placed in front of them. In a context where individual liberties are guaranteed, any choice is theoretically possible: to choose paid employment or volunteering, to

---

[16] See I. Lødemel, "Discussion: Workfare in the Welfare State", in I. Lødemel and H. Trickey (eds.), *An Offer You Can't Refuse. Workfare in International Perspective*, Bristol, Policy Press, 2001, pp. 295-344, and I. Lødemel and H. Trickey, "A New Contract for Social Assistance" in I. Lødemel and H. Trickey (eds.), *An Offer You Can't Refuse, op. cit.*, pp. 1-40.

[17] See for example A.K. Sen, *Development as Freedom, op. cit.*

[18] Here we see the importance of a guarantee of resources (such as that provided by social insurances) to increase the real freedom of individuals with regard to the labour market.

participate in training or not, to take care of one's own children or not, to work part-time or full-time. But in practice these choices most often induce very unequal costs for those involved. Thus, according to the legal framework or the social norms in effect, the choice between a part-time position or volunteering may be more or less feasible. A person's degree of freedom of choice depends basically on his/her ability to opt for choices in which the cost remains within bearable limits. This point is of crucial importance in the context of the active welfare state: if the legislation provides a strong incentive, with penalties, to return to work as quickly as possible, this binding framework does not allow the consideration of alternatives like long-term training in order to restore the conditions for sustainable professional integration (via the resumption of a better suited and open-ended job) – or only at too high a price. In fact, individuals who choose such options are likely to have to give up their social benefits for a certain period or to simply content themselves with minimum benefits such as those paid by the social assistance system. In this context, the alternatives are clearly unbalanced. This example shows that the conditions of access to entitlement-rights play an important role in the development of capabilities or real freedom to lead a good life or have a good job. If these conditions are too restrictive, they are likely to lead to a downwards adjustment of a person's individual preferences, which can mean a restriction of the negative side of the freedom to work.

The "freedom" dimension of the capability approach is specifically designed to avoid this pitfall and to ensure that the positive right to work is not transformed into a duty to work. We propose to assume that this "freedom of choice" dimension implies the existence of three possible alternatives for each person benefiting from entitlement-rights, subject to certain eligibility and granting conditions: the person should be able to choose to be loyal to the requirements that are collectively issued (loyalty), but also and especially to challenge or negotiate these requirements without incurring an unbearable punishment (voice) or, where appropriate, to opt for the path of defection (exit) at an acceptable cost to them. The effective presence of this triple alternative[19] ensures real freedom of choice. If, for example, a worker has no say in how to manage the wages, conditions and pace of his work and does not benefit from an option to defect at an affordable cost (for example in the form of unemployment benefits at an acceptable level), he finds himself, so to speak, constrained to loyalty. In the contrary case, when the presence of the other two alternatives is guaranteed (exit and voice), loyalty may be interpreted as the result of a freely made choice. From the perspective

---

[19] A.O. Hirschman, *Exit, Voice, and Loyalty. Responses to Decline in Firms, Organizations, and States*, Cambridge (MA), Harvard University Press, 1970.

of capabilities, a person who only has the choice between a low-quality job and the suspension of his/her right to social benefits does not have the necessary degree of freedom to act in a truly responsible way and thus s/he cannot be held responsible for that choice. Therefore, granting freedom of choice requires that available opportunities are provided in sufficient quantity: if a person only has the choice between two options of poor quality or between one satisfactory option and another of low value, his/her real freedom of choice will be limited.

In Sen's eyes, the capability for work depends not only on the "opportunity" dimension. It also requires that a person has a certain "process" freedom that allows him/her to be as much as possible the author of his/her choices.[20] This does not mean that individuals can always make their individual preferences prevail, but that they must have the possibility to express them and have them taken into account when a decision concerning them is being made. We refer to this possibility with the notion of capability for voice.[21] An important prerequisite of the capability for voice lies in the incompleteness of law. The more complete and comprehensive legal rules and administrative guidelines are, the less room is left for individual freedom of choice. By contrast, the more incomplete the law, the more interpretative leeway the beneficiaries have, as well as other local actors. However, too much incompleteness may lead to arbitrary behaviour, such as abuse of power, from welfare state civil servants.[22] It is therefore important that the law guarantees the fairness of the relationship between the beneficiary and the representative of the active welfare state. The capability approach is therefore not a plea for a radical incompleteness of the regulatory framework (which should then be limited to enunciate major principles), but it requires a reflection on the necessary conditions for the establishment of an adequate procedural framework. If the law should be enacted as much as possible at the local level and by those involved, it is necessary to establish procedural rights to give all participants the necessary conditions for their capacity for expression or capability for voice to blossom.[23]

---

[20] This distinction between "opportunity freedom" and "process freedom" is explained, among others, in A.K. Sen, *Rationality and Freedom, op. cit.*

[21] J.-M. Bonvin, "La démocratie dans l'approche d'Amartya Sen", *L'économie politique*, No. 27, 2005, pp. 27-36; J.-M. Bonvin, "Individual Working Lives and Collective Action. An Introduction to Capability for Work and Capability for Voice", *Transfer. European Review of Labour and Research*, Vol. 18, No. 1, 2012, pp. 9-18.

[22] V. Dubois, *La vie au guichet*, Paris, Economica, 1999.

[23] J. Browne, S. Deakin and F. Wilkinson, "Capabilities, Social Rights and European Market Integration", in R. Salais and R. Villeneuve (eds.), *Europe and the Politics of Capabilities*, Cambridge, Cambridge University Press, 2006, pp. 205-221; S. Deakin and A. Supiot (eds.), *Capacitas. Contract Law and the Institutional Preconditions of a Market Economy*, Oxford-Portland, Hart Publishing, 2009.

A new field of activity opens here for law, which encompasses all the dimensions that may influence the possibility of each and every person to speak and to ensure the effectiveness of this speech in the process of collective decision-making.[24] The ILO has also perceived the importance of these procedural rights by raising to the status of fundamental labour rights, the rights of freedom of association and collective negotiation (cf. ILO Conventions No. 87 and 98). The importance given to these procedural rights is consistent with an approach that we can call "situated", in the regulation of the labour market. Everything should not be decided by a central regulator: room should be left for action by the persons concerned, while ensuring at the same time that each of these actors (or groups of actors) is provided with the necessary capabilities to exercise their capability for voice. In this respect, the rights to associate and organise are not sufficient. Other forms of procedural rights should also be developed aiming to promote effective participation in the collective decision-making process (for example the right to be informed, consulted or to be co-decider), the possibility of producing one's own information about a given situation (which we could call "cognitive rights", that would translate for example into the possibility of consulting experts), the right to challenge a decision *ex post* (via a right of appeal), etc.

The development of such rights, which equips actors for democratic debate, arises as a key condition of the fairness of regulation processes that falls in line with what Dorf and Sabel refer to as "democratic experimentalism".[25] In order not to fall into a libertarian version of capabilities where everyone can do what they want (that is to say, where individual preferences should always prevail everywhere), and by contrast favour a vision of freedom of choice rooted in democratic deliberation and debate, everyone should be able to effectively represent their point of view. Procedural rights and the incompleteness of law appear as the sine qua non of such an interpretation of the capability approach, which differs from a libertarian conception, and endorses a perspective based on democratic deliberation and recourse to public debate. The next section shows the implications of such a conception of freedom of choice on active labour market policies.

---

[24] J. Bohman, *Public Deliberation, Pluralism, Complexity and Democracy*, Boston, MIT Press, 1996; J.-M. Bonvin, "La participation à l'aune de l'approche par les capacités d'Amartya Sen", in F. Claisse, C. Laviolette, M. Reuchamps and C. Ruyters (eds.), *La participation en action*, Brussels, P.I.E.-Peter Lang (Méthodes participatives appliquées), 2013, pp. 41-53.

[25] M. Dorf and C. Sabel, "A Constitution of Democratic Experimentalism", *Columbia Law Review*, Vol. 98, No. 2, 1998, pp. 267-473.

C. The Individual-Institution Relationship at the Heart of the Active Welfare State

In the framework of the active welfare state, the key issues are the relationship between the institution and the individual and the space left in this framework for the development of the capability for voice of the beneficiaries. As with other areas of public policy, the active welfare state is the result of a collective decision-making process that leads to impose, in a more or less authoritarian or top-down manner, collective norms on individuals. Thus, there is a threat of a tyranny of the majority. If this risk were to be achieved, the "freedom" side of the capability approach would not materialise. Focusing on the real freedom of everyone to choose a lifestyle that they value requires that this threat vanishes and that public action impinges as little as possible on individual freedom.

The incompleteness of social law and of the directives that frame its implementation is essential in this context. Only then will it be possible to deploy forms of reflexive governance,[26] which guarantee a space for the unfolding of the capability for voice. Indeed, no normative reference can be considered the best in absolute terms, since there are several possible evaluative frameworks,[27] thus many possible goals could be assigned to an activation policy for beneficiaries of the welfare state. This may be a quick return to employment, but also an improvement of their employability in the long-term, the restoration of their confidence and of their sense of autonomy, etc. All these objectives carry their own vision of the right to work and of individual responsibility. If a quick return to work is privileged, the capacity and freedom sides of the right to work lose their importance in the face of the duty to work. Increasing employability gives more importance to the ability or power to act side but may neglect the freedom side. Various conceptions of the articulation of the right to work and responsibility are thus possible. Collective choices should make a place for this plurality of legitimate points of view. In fact, for some beneficiaries a quick return to work is relevant, while for others further training could be much more necessary, and for some others a far longer process, including so-called "low threshold" programmes, would be essential. The existence of this diversity requires a certain incompleteness of the adopted rules, which allows taking into account individual characteristics and local circumstances at the time of the implementation of these rules.

---

[26] O. De Schutter and J. Lenoble (eds.), *Reflexive Governance. Redefining the Public Interest in a Pluralistic World*, Oxford-Portland, Hart Publishing, 2010.

[27] L. Boltanski and L. Thévenot, *De la justification*, Paris, Gallimard, 1991.

However, it is necessary to regulate this "process freedom" and to ensure that it does not lead to arbitrary forms of local justice. The active welfare state is thus exposed to two symmetrical pitfalls: on the one hand, too much completeness of legal prescription that leaves little or no room for action; on the other hand, too much incompleteness that could lead to abuses of power by officials at the local level. The challenge is to ensure the fairness of the actions expected at the local level within a framework of incompleteness of the law enacted by the central authorities.

In practice, the most common response to this challenge is to use tools inspired by new public management, such as provision agreements, performance indicators or management by objectives, which set specific and binding objectives while allowing, at least in theory, flexibility on how to achieve them.[28] However, such a managerialist version of reflexive governance is not without ambiguity: indeed, the more specific the managerial injunctions are and the more quantitatively determined, the less they leave room for interpretation by local actors. For example, requirements for a high success rate in the reinsertion of the unemployed will often lead to a creaming of the beneficiaries (in order to exclude from the statistics those persons with the least chance of finding a job) and to focus interventions on those persons who are already the closest to the labour market, in order to achieve the performance expected. A requirement for increased employment rates will lead to a focus on quick professional reintegration rather than on job quality. In this context, local actors will have the task of adapting or adjusting the individual preferences of the beneficiaries so that they best meet official expectations.

In contrast, local actors enjoy a greater margin of manoeuvre when top-down directives are less binding. Thus, more modest goals in terms of employment rates or the recognition of other objectives such as the restoration of self-confidence, or the provision of a wider catalogue of measures, are in line with truly reflexive governance and with the concept of "constructive democracy".[29] According to the latter, any social construction, i.e. any social rule, social norm, collective decision, etc., should be as much as possible part of a process of democratic deliberation and not be imposed from above. It is therefore important, in the spirit of the capability approach, that the managerial instruments are also stamped with a seal of incompleteness in order to leave room for the deployment of situated action.

---

[28] F. Varone and J.-M. Bonvin (eds.), "La nouvelle gestion publique", *Les politiques sociales*, 2004, No. 1-2 (special issue).

[29] A.K. Sen, "Democracy as a Universal Value", *Journal of Democracy*, Vol. 10, No. 3, 1999, pp. 3-17.

The concept of a "goal-rights system" is crucial here: it is not, indeed, in the light of (or through) quantified objectives or managerial precepts that action must be evaluated (or framed), but in the light of its impact on the development of beneficiaries' capabilities. In this perspective, incompleteness is therefore not a complete void, insofar as there remains a prominent reference that local actors have to pursue. Thus, this reference is deliberately designed in very vague terms ("the freedom to live the life that we have reason to value"), which can take into account the actors' preferences.

II. Types of Active Welfare States and Approaches to Responsibility and the Right to Work

Now, we will confront the main types of active welfare state with the analytical and normative framework that has just been presented and that emphasises the necessary complementarity between the "ability or power to act" and "freedom" dimensions. Our presentation favours a diachronic perspective that shows how recent developments have affected the conception of the right to work and the responsibility that exists in each of these models. It revolves around the following three questions: a) what abilities are provided by the concerned active welfare state to the beneficiaries in terms of resources, skills and opportunities (positive right to work)?, b) to what extent is the relationship between the individual and the institution concerned with the promotion of the individual freedom of choice (negative side of the right to work)?, c) how does the promoted conception of responsibility combine backward-looking and forward-looking orientations?[30]

The transition to an active welfare state shows an evolution towards another way of envisioning the relationship between individuals and social institutions and towards the formulation of other expectations with respect to individuals and public institutions. Thus, the emergence of the active welfare state coincides with the imposition of a new normative reference for the welfare state. It is no longer about organising compensation for people who have lost their jobs through the occurrence of a social risk (illness, disability, etc.). Now it is about restoring an individual's capacity for action, which coincides in most cases with their ability to find a place on the labour market. Such an evolution profoundly changes the traditional concept of the welfare state, as highlighted

---

[30] The distinction between backward-looking and forward-looking forms of responsibility is taken from R. Goodin, "Social Welfare as a Collective Social Responsibility", in D. Schmitz and R. Goodin (eds.), *Social Welfare and Individual Responsibility*, Cambridge, Cambridge University Press, 1998, pp. 97-195. It is very similar to the reflections of Genard and Bovens, mentioned above.

by François Ewald.[31] On the one hand, the notion of risk, which had supplanted, or even removed, the notion of fault, is questioned insofar as it is accused of comprising incentives for irresponsibility. On the other hand, the division of labour between beneficiaries and social institutions has been newly rethought out.

We will successively consider the three welfare state models that are usually distinguished in the field of comparative social policy.[32] We will discuss each of them in terms of their specific conception of the right to work and responsibility.[33] Reading between the lines of the following analysis, it will become clear what one could present as being a capability-friendly approach to responsibility and the right to work. Its main outlines will be summarised in the conclusion to this article.

A. *The Liberal Model*

The normative foundations of the first welfare state model, the liberal one, belong to the tradition of liberal thought. This model shows a marked preference for market mechanisms. The welfare state only assumes a residual function, since benefits are paid only to those persons unable to make out a private insurance. In addition, these benefits are means-tested and are very modest in order to encourage a quick return to the labour market. Despite their paucity, they are still considered a possible dependency factor and their beneficiaries are subject to important stigmatisation.

In terms of "ability or power to act", public interventions are confined to this low redistribution of financial resources, with little or nothing being done with respect to the development of skills and opportunities. In fact, Anglo-Saxon countries, which are the closest to this model, are characterised by a high and constant proportion of low-skilled persons. With respect to opportunities for professional integration, it is up to the market to create them. For this purpose, the main strategy consists in lowering labour costs. Thus, in times of economic difficulty, the fight against unemployment uses the lowering of wages rather than increasing the employability of jobseekers. The goal is to improve the value for money of those excluded from the labour market, not by increasing their attractiveness and competitiveness on the labour market, but by reducing the cost of their hiring for employers. This restrictive definition

---

[31] F. Ewald, *Histoire de l'État-providence*, Paris, Le Livre de Poche, 1996.
[32] In continuation of the seminal work of G. Esping-Andersen, *The Three Worlds of Welfare Capitalism*, Cambridge, Polity Press, 1990.
[33] The analysis presented here should not be applied as such to national situations, which in most cases are much more mixed.

of opportunities, which are usually reduced to poor quality jobs, explains why the action in terms of resources and skills also remains limited. A redistribution of resources above the threshold represented by the wages paid for such jobs would act as a powerful deterrent, which would go against the principle of "making work pay" that is at the heart of the activation strategy of this model. In this context, the reference to rights is almost absent (especially in terms of entitlement-rights and capacity-rights) to the extent that the solution to socio-professional integration problems lies primarily in market mechanisms.

The rise of the active welfare state (also called workfare in the countries close to this model) from the early 1990s led to a strengthening of the characteristics of the liberal model, by further reducing the redistributed resources and by shortening the period of their payment. In the United States, for example, welfare programmes have been accused of having massive perverse effects.[34] This prompted the legislator to introduce more restrictive provisions, in the form of work requirements, of time limits for the length of granting and of setting up an administrative apparatus of coercion based on the new paternalism advocated by the intellectual Lawrence Mead,[35] where an unemployed person must be followed and even harassed until s/he returns to work.[36] The welfare reform act signed by President Clinton in 1996 embodies these developments. It removed the main federal welfare programme, instead transferring to the states the competency to define the content of social programmes, provided that they comply with a general framework imposing the principle of conditionality of social assistance. To be financially supported at the federal level, the state programmes must especially comply with the following rules: (1) requirement must be made on adult members of a beneficiary family to perform services such as work of general interest; (2) in any case, it is not possible to receive benefits for more than five years during an adult lifetime.

The fundamental change resulting from the emergence of workfare, or welfare-to-work, programmes is the strengthening of the duty to work at the expense of the freedom of choice of the beneficiaries. Whereas previously the rapid recovery of employment was prompted by the modest level of benefits available, it is now supported, and if necessary imposed, by administration officials. Since the equation "less

---

[34] P. Bénéton, *Le fléau du bien*, Paris, Robert Laffont, 1981.
[35] L. Mead, *Beyond Entitlement. The Social Obligations of Citizenship*, New York, Free Press, 1986; L. Mead, *The New Politics of Poverty. The Nonworking Poor in America*, New York, Basic Books, 1992.
[36] On the American case, see the chapter of Dumont in this book.

redistributed resources = more incentive to quickly return to work" does not materialise, the legislator decides to further reduce resources and sets up a system of administrative control to eliminate the adverse effects of dependency produced by the previous system. Responsible action is required here on the dual basis of reduced capacity (via the redistribution of reduced resources) and negation of the freedom of individuals who are ordered to comply with the injunctions of the officials. In this context, the relationship between individual and institution is highly unbalanced. There is no possibility for the individual to negotiate the services delivered or to request an additional service (which would correspond to the "voice" option of Hirschman). Instead they must either comply with the requirements of the administrative authority (loyalty) or simply waive their rights to benefits (exit).

The underlying conception of responsibility remains constant over time: the responsible individual is always the one who takes a job quickly, whatever the wage and working conditions. But the means used for fostering this responsible action have changed. Whereas previously the state did not exercise direct pressure on the individual, but instead subjected him to benefit levels that prevented him to make choices and imposed to take the first job he found, it now directly constrains the individual and exerts pressure on him/her in order to shorten the perception of public support as much as possible. Thus, the responsible individual is the one who complies with further injunctions from the state (in the framework of the new paternalism) and from the market (s/he agrees to adapt his/her preferences to opportunities offered on the labour market). Such a definition does not result from a deliberative process between beneficiaries and representatives of the administration, but is an imposition of the public will to promote as quick a return to the labour market as possible. These conditions illustrate the evolution of social law in the liberal model towards a strengthening of constraint-rights and the promulgation of specific objectives leaving little room for a genuine "democratic experimentalism".[37]

In this model, backward-looking responsibility comes first: the condemnation of past attitudes justifies the intensity of the exerted pressure taking the form of financial restrictions or constraints to return to work. Overall, the liberal model gives few abilities, tends to deny the freedom of individuals by subjecting them to injunctions from public authorities and from the market, and emphasises responsibility as imputability and a source of punishment.

---

[37] J. Handler, *Social Citizenship and Workfare in the United States and Western Europe. The Paradox of Inclusion*, Cambridge, Cambridge University Press, 2004.

B. The Social-Democratic Model

Equality and the redistribution of resources are the fundamental principles of the social-democratic model, the Scandinavian countries being those that are the closest to it. A key objective is to reduce inequalities through the redistribution of large amounts of compulsory levies. Therefore, fiscal imposition is presented as a mechanism of social solidarity benefiting from strong legitimacy. Welfare benefits cover a wide range of social risks; they attain a high level with generous replacement rates and they are open to all citizens, regardless of their individual responsibility over the situation and lack of resources that affects them. The right to benefits is not based on need (as in the liberal model), but on citizenship or residence in the national territory.

This determined action in terms of redistributing resources is accompanied by a resolute intervention with respect to both skills and opportunities. In this perspective, the fight against unemployment does not take the form of a reduction in benefits in order to produce incentives to return to work, but instead involves the combination of three complementary forms of action: a) ensuring the flexibility of the labour market (conceived as a condition for economic competitiveness), b) serving generous benefits to those temporarily excluded from the labour market due to economic difficulties or obsolete skills, c) promoting the rapid reintegration of these individuals through active labour market policies focused on improving skills and therefore attractiveness in the eyes of potential employers. What is meant here is the establishment of a virtuous triangle that revolves around a generous redistribution of resources, a proactive policy to improve skills and the development of opportunities made possible through the flexibility of the labour market.[38]

On the side of the "abilities or powers to act" provided by the welfare state, two other components play a central role in the social-democratic model. On the one hand, a wide range of services are offered almost for free by the public sector, resulting in a major development of employment opportunities for all family members, especially for women, who can also transfer the care of their children and other dependents to these services. The social-democratic model is thus distinguished by its egalitarian voluntarism, not only in terms of the redistribution of resources, but also in terms of the opportunities actually provided. The existence of these services, their high quality, and the fact that they are almost free, aim at making work a real opportunity for all members of the community. On the other hand, the public sector is presented in this model as a last

---

[38] This virtuous triangle remains partly theoretical. In fact, this model developed by the Swedish trade unionists Rehn and Meidner was only partially implemented (until the early 1990s), particularly with regard to active labour market measures.

resort employer: since the flexibility of the labour market does not allow the absorption of all the available workforce, the public sector takes over. In general, the public employment rate is nearly 30% in the Nordic countries, more than double the average of OECD countries.[39] Thus, all forms of rights mentioned in the first part of this article are mobilised on a large scale in the social-democratic model, especially generous entitlement-rights and a meaningful action in creating opportunities, which concretely implements the programmatic rights contained in Article 1 of the European Social Charter, Article 6 of the International Covenant on Economic, Social and Cultural Rights and the Convention No. 122 of the ILO. It should be noted that, until the early 1990s, action on the side of capacity-rights (activation measures) was less extensive.

In terms of freedom of choice, the constraints put on benefit recipients before the rise of the active welfare state in the early 1990s were very limited. Denmark and its unemployment insurance system were an emblematic case. In the late 1970s and throughout the 1980s, the opinion that there was not enough work for all Danish people was widespread. The solution to this unemployment problem was to share jobs and improve the protection of the unemployed by guaranteeing them a high replacement income (between 80 and 100% of their previous salary, albeit capped) for an extended period of time (up to 9 years). Participation in facultative training programmes and in community work was treated as employment, in order to allow the long-term unemployed to access new rights to benefits. In addition, law enforcement was relatively flexible: there was little control over job searching as well as over whether people respected the obligation to accept suitable employment. So there was no political will to impose a normative reference or a specific conception of responsible action, but rather to provide opportunities that individuals could freely choose to use or not.

We are here in a very similar configuration to that proposed by the capability approach: allocating abundant resources and opportunities and recognising an extended area of freedom (in an environment where the predominance of "work ethos"[40] has a significant influence) are at the heart of the conception of responsibility that characterises this model. However, there was limited development of activation policies before the 1990s, which allows us to conclude a low consideration for capacity-rights. The sustainability of this model depends on its financial viability, which is embodied in the permanence of a very high employment rate,

---

[39] See G. Esping-Andersen, *The Three Worlds of Welfare Capitalism*, op. cit.
[40] This sociological concept inspired by the work of Max Weber refers to the internalisation by individuals of the work norm as the foundation of their identity. See for example C. Lalive d'Épinay, *Les Suisses et le travail*, Lausanne, Réalités sociales, 1990.

allowing citizens to pay important taxes and social charges to finance the system. The goal of full employment (male and female), which finds strong support in the predominance of the "work ethos" in the Scandinavian countries, presents itself as the sine qua non for the success of this conception of the right to work and of responsibility.

This requirement for full employment was jeopardised in the early 1990s when there was a significant increase in unemployment rates in the Scandinavian countries. The decision was then taken to strengthen measures within the active welfare state in the triple sense of multiplication of activation programmes, reduction of redistributed resources (including the maximum duration of benefit receipt) and, especially, introduction of strong conditionalities rooted in the principle of duties and mandatory counterparts from beneficiaries.[41] On the "abilities and powers to act" side, this evolution entails the tendency of the social-democratic welfare state (based on entitlement-rights and opportunities) to move towards an activation strategy aiming to influence the individuals' capacity to take action (capacity-rights). But the most profound transformation concerns the "freedom of choice" side, where a different kind of relationship between the individual and the institution is established. Collective decisions define a more binding framework for beneficiaries and the welfare state acts henceforth as a powerful relay of "work ethos" supporting the goal of full employment. A new feature of responsible action is established, where the redistribution of resources is largely conditioned by the adoption of appropriate behaviours. We can observe both a rebalancing of the components of the positive right to work (with a focus on capacity-rights) and important restrictions on the right to freely chosen employment, or the negative side of the right to work.[42]

This evolution coincides with a change in the temporal orientation of responsibility. Resolutely focused on the future before the adoption of more stringent activation policies during the 1990s, responsibility is henceforth characterised by the combination of both backward-looking and forward-looking dimensions: on the one hand, the mechanisms of imputability recently introduced (where it is about punishing past behaviours); on the other hand, the strengthening of programmes aiming to restore the capacity of action of beneficiaries.

---

[41] See for example N. Kildal, *Workfare Tendencies in Scandinavian Welfare Policies*, Geneva, International Labour Office, 2000.

[42] It should be noted that the so-called "social investment" perspective shares a similar orientation. See G. Esping-Andersen (with B. Palier), *Trois leçons sur l'Etat-Providence*, Paris, Seuil, 2008; G. Bonoli and D. Natali (eds.), *The Politics of the New Welfare State*, Oxford, Oxford University Press, 2012.

C. The Conservative Model

The main goal of the conservative welfare state model, to which the countries of continental Europe seem to resemble the most,[43] is the maintenance of incomes and statuses through the use of social insurances. Thus, a person who loses his/her job for recognised reasons (disability, occupational accident, illness, old age, maternity, unemployment) receives a benefit equal to a percentage of his/her previous salary. The issue of individual responsibility in the occurrence of social risk is not taken into account in the calculation of the benefit. As long as s/he meets the envisaged eligibility criteria (usually relating to the duration of previous work), the individual is an unconditional beneficiary.[44] For example in the case of sickness insurance, not only are the hygienic behaviour or lifestyle of the individuals not held responsible for their poor health, but moreover the receipt of benefits will not include injunctions for adopting healthier or more hygienic behaviours. In this model, individual responsibility is somewhat absent from the manner in which social insurance works. The individual receives benefits as a member of a category affected by social risk (the disabled, the unemployed, etc.) and not by virtue of his/her personal characteristics.

Replacement benefits are more or less abundant depending on the level of previous earnings. Persons who are not in employment do not have direct access to social insurance benefits. Within families, only employees (usually fathers) have their own rights to be compensated for loss of income, while other household members only have derived rights. In case of proven need, non-workers who do not enjoy derived rights or who have exhausted their rights, may resort to social assistance, the benefits being smaller and subject to more restrictive conditions. The conservative model is rooted in a particular conception of the division of family roles that sees the man dealing with the financial needs while the woman is responsible for childcare and household chores. The social policies developed in this framework confirm and reinforce the gender division of labour within the traditional family.[45] Thus, on the side of resources and entitlement-rights, the amount and the degree of conditionality of benefits greatly vary. The amounts are higher or lower

---

[43] The relevance of this model is very controversial in the literature, as the countries of continental Europe present contrasting situations. It is however not the purpose of this article to get into this controversy and therefore we refer to this classification without discussing it here.

[44] Note, however, that the attribution of unemployment benefits has been, from the outset, subject to compliance with various obligations meant to ensure that the beneficiary has not voluntarily left the labour market and, eventually, to reinstate him. The effective implementation of these requirements appears variable depending on the context.

[45] See M. Daly, *The Gender Division of Welfare*, Oxford, Oxford University Press, 2000.

depending on previous earnings under the social insurance schemes and very modest for social assistance benefits. Their degree of conditionality varies from quasi-inconditionality in the case of social insurance to a stricter conditionality for women – derived rights rather than proper rights – and for beneficiaries of social assistance.

Financial compensation is at the heart of the conservative welfare state model, which shows little investment in terms of skills development and other activation programmes. In general, until the mid-1980s, the issue of unemployment was tackled in the conservative welfare states by encouraging a withdrawal from the labour market rather than actively promoting the return to work.[46] The absence of active measures (or capacity-rights) does not mean that the question of opportunities was neglected in this model, insofar as macroeconomic policies in support of the goal of full employment were implemented. It is also worth noting the weak development of services for persons in this model, where the family remains the traditional provider of these services, with all the limitations entailed in terms of increasing employment opportunities for women.

In sum, on the "abilities or powers to act" side, we can observe a differentiated action in terms of entitlement-rights (generous to those who fall within the standard of full-time and male employment, and more modest for the others), a limited intervention on the side of capacity-rights and of the development of skills (as evidenced by the virtual absence of active measures in most continental European countries until the early 1980s) and often an important action on opportunities, which belongs primarily to the domain of macroeconomic policies.

On the "freedom of choice" side, the social insurance schemes of the conservative model do not seek to impose a particular behaviour onto their beneficiaries. The welfare state does not appear here as a normalisation factor, but as the provider of a guaranteed compensation irrespective of the question of the responsibility of the beneficiaries, i.e. their past behaviours.[47] In contrast, social assistance offers only conditional benefits often accompanied by actions aimed at making assisted persons comply with applicable social norms, particularly for the beneficiaries who are able to work. The beneficiary of social assistance is considered responsible

---

[46] J.-C. Barbier and J. Gautié (eds.), *Les politiques publiques d'emploi en Europe et aux Etats-Unis*, Paris, Presses universitaires de France, 1998.

[47] The social social insurance state does not impose onto individuals a predetermined specific behaviour, but it ensures that certain conditions to act responsibly are met (through the compensation of persons and the setting of employment macroeconomic conditions, for example through Keynesian policies acting on demand). However, we can observe that the development of capacity-rights is not really taken into account in this model, at least until the mid-1980s. All the conditions of responsible action and of positive freedom to work were therefore not met.

for his/her fate. As such, s/he has to accept second-rate compensations and is subject to strict behavioural injunctions. Thus, we are faced with two very different situations, which can be summarised as follows: firstly, the individual of social insurances, well endowed in terms of resources (but deprived of capacity-rights) and whose freedom of action is barely constrained; secondly, the individual of social assistance, less generously compensated and for whom the focus is on compliance with social norms.

The emergence of the active welfare state entails an in-depth upheaval of the model, which modifies the conception of the right to work and of the responsibility that prevails in the mechanisms of social insurance. This transformation is essentially reflected in three aspects. Firstly, income received under social insurance is subject to more stringent conditions, especially for the young unemployed, long-term unemployed and disabled.[48] Secondly, many active measures are introduced with the aim of enabling the unemployed towards employment. At first, these measures were less stringent than in countries belonging to the social-democratic and liberal models, but since the early 2000s, the trend has moved towards a strengthening of the behavioural conditions and expectations imposed on social insurance beneficiaries.[49] Thirdly, action regarding the creation of opportunities has been much more restrained since the emergence of the active welfare state, to the extent that balanced budget and zero inflation requirements have overtaken macroeconomic management instruments and investment policies. For the same reasons, the development of those services (structures for taking care of infants, care for the elderly, etc.) that would relieve women of some of the domestic work traditionally ascribed to them, and which would help create the conditions for the positive right to work for all family members, often remains at an embryonic stage. Overall, there is a significant development of capacity-rights, but with a strong emphasis on the duty to work, and a more timid action with regard to opportunities.

The beneficiaries' freedom of choice is clearly reduced by these developments, which are coupled with a greater coercion exerted against them and with a greater completeness of law, insofar as the use of resources, skills and opportunities granted by the welfare state is no longer left to the discretion of the beneficiary, but is subject to more stringent injunctions.

---

[48] See J.-M. Bonvin, "The Rhetoric of Activation and its Effects on the Definition of the Target Groups of Social Integration Policies", in A. Serrano Pascual (ed.), *Are Activation Policies Converging in Europe? The European Employment Strategy for Young People*, Brussels, ETUI, 2004, pp. 101-127.

[49] The German law Hartz-IV is emblematic of this evolution towards a reinforcement of the duty to work of unemployed individuals.

Regarding the temporal orientation of responsibility, the conservative model is characterised by its duality. Social insurance, with its system of taking care of socialised risks, is based on setting aside the issue of fault.[50] Thus, there is an explicit commitment not to charge individuals with responsibility for their past behaviours, but rather to ensure that they are appropriately compensated, regardless of the cause of their current situation. This intervention is oriented towards the future insofar as the compensation paid to individuals allows them to more easily overcome their difficulties and to reintegrate the labour market in better conditions. In contrast, social assistance favours imputability, emphasising individual responsibility and the need for sanctions and discipline to make individuals more faithful to social norms. With the emergence of the active welfare state, there is a clear trend towards erasing boundaries between assistance and insurance, as illustrated by the development of the rhetoric of fault in certain social insurance schemes (in particular the unemployment insurance system).

Conclusion

The capability approach emphasises the multiplicity of forms of rights (entitlement-rights, constraint-rights, capacity-rights, procedural rights, programmatic rights, all discussed in the context of a certain incompleteness promoting the deployment of specific modalities of the right to work) that should be put at the service of an ultimate objective, namely the development of the capability for work of the persons concerned. Proposed here is a complex architecture of law, with "goal-rights" at the top of the pyramid, which indicate the purpose of the action and set forth imperfect obligations. It is then up to each public authority to establish the appropriate mix of "means-rights" in order to best fulfil this imperfect obligation. The yardstick by which public action in the field of the right to work must be assessed is its contribution to the realisation of the goal-rights system, i.e. to the development of capabilities. Proposed here is a radical change of perspective. The normative standard is no longer an increase of employment rates, which lies, for example, at the heart of the OECD and EU strategies, but the capability for work seen as a human right. Therefore, the point is not simply to determine the most effective ways to increase employment rates, which could legitimise forms of "instrumentalisation" of the right to work and justify violations of the right to freely undertaken work (namely the negative component of the right to work, or the "freedom of choice" dimension in Sen's words).

---

[50] See F. Ewald, *Histoire de l'Etat-providence*, op. cit. However, this conception of social insurance is debatable (see for example D. Dumont, "Activation rime-t-elle nécessairement avec stigmatisation?", *Droit et Société*, No. 78, 2011, pp. 447-471).

From the perspective of capabilities, it is rather about determining which combination of "abilities or powers to act" and "freedom of choice", in other words which combination of the positive and negative sides of the right to work, should be favoured for promoting the human right of the individual to perform the work that is most of value for him. The capability approach does not imply a reconceptualization of the right to work as understood in the international human rights law, on the contrary it allows better visibility of the complementarity of the two sides – positive and negative – found in the various international instruments that proclaim the right to work.

In this respect, the active welfare state models analysed in this article are in contrasting situations. In terms of "means-rights", either on the "abilities or powers to act" or "freedom" sides, or on the temporal orientation of responsibility, the approaches are very different. The liberal model tends to give more salience to the equation "less redistributed resources = more power to act" and the interventions in terms of skills and opportunities come to a very large degree under individual responsibility or market mechanisms. The welfare state appears here as an increasingly powerful factor of normalisation of behaviours, primarily following a logic of imputability and punishment of deviant behaviours (i.e. those who fail to integrate into the labour market by themselves). The duty to work takes precedence over the right to work, in both its positive and its negative sides. In contrast, the social-democratic model is distinguished by its resolute action in favour of the redistribution of resources and the development of skills and opportunities. The cost of these diverse interventions in a tense economic and budgetary context has prompted authorities to introduce stronger constraints that have changed the balance of the relationship between the institutions and the beneficiary individuals, in the sense of a greater supervision of individual freedoms. In the same movement, the orientation towards the future that characterises this model is complemented by imputability mechanisms that can lead to severe sanctions (even if they are applied with moderation). Here, an initial situation of significant development with regard to the positive and negative sides of the right to work must come to terms with a desire to strengthen the duty to work. Finally, the conservative model is characterised by a desire to establish more ambitious activation measures, which are able to increase an individual's employability and attractiveness to employers. However, this evolution coincides with much more modest action in terms of development of opportunities and there are fears that this new emphasis on skills and employability is not sufficient, in the absence of real opportunities on the labour market, to effectively promote the right to have a job. The positive right to work has been strengthened, but in an ambiguous way that opens the door to many drifts in the direction of duty to work.

Beyond these differences, there is, in terms of finality, a broad convergence around the goal of increasing employment rates and accelerating reintegration, which coincides with a relative neglect of the issue of the quality of employment. This convergence results in a tendency, common to all three models, towards a decrease in the redistributed resources and their increased conditionality, by the introduction of mandatory counterparts that are more strictly framing individual freedom and by strengthening the retrospective orientation of responsibility. These evolutions have a huge impact on conceptions of the right to work and the underlying responsibility of the welfare state, whether in substantive or procedural terms. On the substantive side, the balance between entitlement-rights, capacity-rights and opportunities is weighted in the direction of strengthening capacity-rights and a more or less pronounced tendency, depending on the case, towards questioning the other components. It seems that the development of employability policies (labour supply) is not accompanied by such a determined action in terms of employment policies (labour demand). On the procedural side, the strengthening of the duty to work coincides with the rise of managerial precepts that too often leave little room for local experiences and reflexive governance. Thus, on these two sides, individual responsibility does not enjoy all the necessary conditions for its deployment.

We believe that a strong reference to the capability for work understood as a human right, and thus a "goal-rights system" alternative to the increase in employment rates, could better allow the active welfare state to fulfil its promises, to curb its possible drifts towards exacerbating the duty to work, and to promote a more reflexive and democratic vision of public action in the field of the right to work.

IV. Debating Ideas: The Basic Income Guarantee and the Employment Guarantee

The Tensions of Welfare State Reform and the Potential of a Universal Basic Income

Yannick VANDERBORGHT

Introduction

The idea of granting every individual a universal basic income (UBI) has a long history. Since the end of the 18th century, various thinkers in Europe and North America have advocated the implementation of an income by right as a fair compensation for the private appropriation of natural resources. In 1848, for instance, the Belgian Fourierist Joseph Charlier published his *Solution du problème social* (*Solution to the Social Problem*), in which he claimed that everyone should be entitled to a modest cash transfer, or "territorial dividend".[1] Similar proposals can be found in the writings of several other so-called "utopian" socialists throughout the 19th century.[2] Interestingly, much later the same idea of a compensation for unequal access to resources was also at the core the *Alaska Permanent Fund Dividend* (PFD), launched in the early 1980s. The PFD, today's only existing UBI scheme, is paid out of the oil revenues under the justification that oil is a common property of all residents of the State of Alaska.[3]

During the 20th century, and especially after the 1960s, UBI gradually entered the mainstream discussion on welfare reform. Since then, it has left the marginal circles to which it was mainly confined, and has been advocated by several prominent economists, including John Kenneth Galbraith, James Tobin, Milton Friedman, Herbert Simon, or Anthony Atkinson. It has been widely discussed in the academic literature,[4] and has been included in the platform of several important political parties

---

[1] J. Cunliffe and G. Erreygers, "The Enigmatic Legacy of Charles Fourier: Joseph Charlier and Basic Income", *History of Political Economy*, Vol. 33, 2001, pp. 459-484.

[2] J. Cunliffe and G. Erreygers, *The Origins of Universal Grant. An Anthology of Historical Writings on Basic Capital and Basic Income*, New York, Palgrave Macmillan, 2005.

[3] K. Widerquist and M. Howard (eds.), *Alaska's Permanent Fund Dividend: Examining its Suitability as a Model*, New York, Palgrave Macmillan, 2012.

[4] See K. Widerquist, J.A. Noguera, Y. Vanderborght and J. De Wispelaere (eds.), *Basic Income: An Anthology of Contemporary Research*, New York, Wiley-Blackwell, 2013.

across the world. Furthermore, experiments have been launched in a few countries.[5]

It is not part of the purpose of this chapter to give a detailed account of these historical developments, full of stimulating stories and fascinating figures. My intention is rather to show that there were, and still are, many good reasons to think about a UBI while exploring the issues of welfare state reform in developed countries. It is especially true in the context of an increasing emphasis on activation – or even workfare – in almost all welfare states. In particular, I intend to show how the discussion about UBI forces us to think about three key tensions of welfare state reform: the tension between universalism and selectivity (I.), between in-cash and in-kind benefits (II.), and between conditionality and unconditionality (III.).

In the remaining of this chapter, I will use the following background definition of UBI: an income paid by a political community to all its members, on an individual basis, without means-test or work requirement. As it is made clear by this definition, a UBI differs from a minimum income scheme, or social assistance, in three crucial ways. Conventional minimum income schemes are restricted to the poorest (i.e. they are means-tested), take into account the recipient's family situation, and are conditional upon availability to work. By contrast, a basic income is granted to all, rich and poor (universal), on an individual basis (individual), without any work requirement (unconditional). In principle, a UBI would be paid to all adult residents, but a basic universal pension, or a universal child benefit, can be considered to be part of the same league of proposals.

I. The Tension Between Universalism and Selectivity

Discussing the idea of a UBI first offers a welcome opportunity to examine into some detail a central tension in social policy, the tension between universalism and selectivity. Should the welfare state provide the same benefits to all legal residents on a universal basis, or should it target benefits in order to cover the needs of some specific categories only?

Since the early 1990s, strong pleas in favour of increased selectivity have been heard, especially on the left side of the political spectrum. The case of child benefits is quite illustrative in this respect. While Canada had already ended the universal character of its Federal Family

---

[5] See for instance E. Forget, "The Town with no Poverty: The Health Effects of a Canadian Guaranteed Annual Income Field Experiment", *Canadian Public Policy*, Vol. 37, No. 3, 2011, pp. 283-305.

Allowance in 1989, other countries started to discuss similar reforms in the 1990s. In France, for instance, the Socialist Prime Minister Lionel Jospin made an attempt at turning the universal child allowance into a selective system in the late 1990s (see below). After the election of Socialist President François Hollande in 2012, the French government was again considering the end of universalism in child support policies. The French case is illustrative of many similar moves in other countries.

The main arguments in favour of increased selectivity always refer to budgetary constraints (universal schemes are said to be too costly), but also to fairness: universal benefits are allegedly unfair, since rich households or individuals do not need them. In November 2012, in the context of an intense discussion about the child benefit reform, a Belgian columnist phrased it as follows: "Why would someone who is earning as much as Kris Peeters [the then Prime-Minister of the Flemish regional government] receive the same amount of child benefit as a lone mother"?[6]

To some extent, it sounds self-evident: why should a welfare state opt for universalism, whereas some of the recipients, be it in the middle-class or the wealthy upper class, do not need the benefits? In other words, a universal benefit such as UBI seems to waste valuable tax and payroll revenues by distributing equally among all what some do not need in the least. This is an often-heard objection to UBI: why pay Bill Gates?[7]

Obviously, I would not argue that selectivity, or targeting, is always wrong. It is sometimes required, especially when one has to meet certain specific needs, such as those of the disabled. But contrary to what one might think at first sight, universalism matters a great deal when we think about progressive welfare reform. Not only does universalism "express our common membership of society";[8] it is also, crucially, more efficient against poverty (A.), more efficient in guaranteeing access to the labour market (B.), and more resilient against welfare retrenchment (C.).

A. *Poverty*

Universalism is, somewhat paradoxically, important if we want welfare programmes that are efficient in tackling poverty. Of course, the concrete distributive impact of a universal scheme will always depend on how it is financed. Let us assume that, as is the case for most existing universal programme in Europe, a UBI would be funded through progressive general taxation (i.e. not via flat-rate social contributions). If

---

[6] B. Eeckout, "Hervorm de kinderbijslag", *De Morgen*, 13 November 2012.

[7] F. Block, "Why Pay Bill Gates?," in P. Van Parijs *et al.* (eds.), *What's Wrong with a Free Lunch?*, Boston, Beacon Press, 2001, pp. 85-89.

[8] T. Horton and J. Gregory, *The Solidarity Society*, London, Fabian Society/Webb Memorial Trust, 2009, p. 135.

it were the case, the fact that both rich and poor receive a UBI would not mean that its implementation makes the rich richer. The richest will have to finance both their own basic income, and a considerable portion of the basic income of the poorest. More interestingly, universalism is a key to anti-poverty policies for the three following reasons.

First, selectivity tends to be hampered by severe administrative problems. Selective programmes typically have to rely on means-tests in order to get a more or less accurate picture of who is to be counted as poor: caseworkers control the actual income of potential recipients, as well as their other assets such as the income of other members of the household, properties, and savings. In some cases, claimants even have to prove that they cannot count on the resources of their extended family. These complex controls take time. As a result, eligible recipients might ultimately get the benefit with some delay, or be denied access to the benefit altogether because they failed to pass the tests. In other words, selective schemes operate *ex post*, on the basis of a complex prior assessment of the beneficiaries' means, whereas universal programmes operate *ex ante*, providing a more stable basis for income security.

The second reason is closely related to the first. Given the above-mentioned complexity, potential recipients are often unable to pass the means-tests because they even ignore what their exact rights consist in. In other words, "targeting rules often tend to exclude the neediest potential recipients because they are the ones who have the most difficulty complying with program rules".[9]

Third, selective programmes also tend to stigmatise recipients, a fact that is well-documented by sociologists. For this reason, a significant proportion of the eligible recipients do simply not claim the benefits, especially in countries where cultural norms tend to make individuals ashamed to apply for assistance. This does not only raise a problem in terms of efficiency against poverty but is also, and perhaps more importantly, a problem of justice, assuming that self-respect is an important social primary good in the sense of John Rawls.[10]

Along with the administrative complexity, the stigma attached to targeting explains the relatively low take-up rate of all social assistance programmes: in a nutshell, targeted programmes often miss their target. Studies conducted in France after the 2009 thorough reform of the minimum income scheme (see the chapter by Diane Roman in this volume) have shown that almost 50% of the potential recipients of the scheme do simply not claim it. Ironically, estimations also show that this

---

[9] J. Currie and F. Gahvari, "Transfers in Cash and In-Kind: Theory Meets the Data", *Journal of Economic Literature*, Vol. 46, No. 2, 2008, p. 348.

[10] J. Rawls, *A Theory of Justice*, Oxford, Oxford University Press, 1971.

low take-up rate amounts to massive savings for the budget of French public authorities.[11]

B. *Labour Supply and the Right to Work*

A universal benefit is not only more efficient against poverty, it is also more efficient in guaranteeing access to the labour market, a key objective for supporters of activation policies. Somewhat paradoxically, a UBI can thus perfectly be discussed within the framework of a reflection on the "active welfare state" and the "right to work".

Selective programmes always tend to generate traps. Means-tested minimum income schemes, for instance, generate deep poverty traps. They penalise those who succeed in finding a low-paid job, since the gains from taking up work are offset by the reduction, or complete withdrawal, of the benefit. In some cases, when different means-tested transfers are combined, including subsidies for public housing or free public transportation for instance, access to employment becomes financially unattractive, as marginal tax rates get close to (or even exceed) 100%.

Policymakers across Europe are of course aware of this issue. Some of them argue that one solution might consist in lowering the benefits, in order to increase the incentives to take a low-paid job. However, since in all European countries minimum incomes are already below the at-risk-of-poverty threshold, this option does not seem very promising. The idea of increasing the minimum wage looks more attractive, and is supported by a vast majority of workers' representatives. In most countries, however, there is not much room for such a reform since the labour market is already under pressure at the bottom end of the income distribution.

In such context, UBI supporters argue that one should start with turning selective schemes into universal ones. A universal benefit, such as the existing child benefits in most EU countries, can be fully kept when one takes a low paid job.[12] In means that a UBI, contrary to targeted schemes, gives incentives to seek work, because it improves the net income of the individual worker as compared with what she receives when she is inactive. Disregarding mechanisms for its subsequent recovery through taxation, the basic income is retained in full by the recipient whatever the

---

[11] The studies were conducted by Philippe Warin. In English, see for instance P. Warin, "Non-Demand for Social Rights: A New Challenge for Social Action in France", *Journal of Poverty and Social Justice*, Vol. 20, No. 1, 2012, pp. 41-55. See also the following interview (in French) with P. Warin: "La moitié des personnes qui ont droit au RSA ne le demandent pas", *Le Monde*, 17 January 2013.

[12] On the impact of universal child benefits, see the illustrative Belgian case in B. Cantillon and T. Goedemé, "Les allocations familiales dans le régime des travailleurs salariés: rétrospective axée sur l'avenir", *Revue belge de sécurité sociale*, Vol. 48, No. 1, 2006, p. 9.

circumstances. It can be compared to a stable, permanent employment subsidy, available to everyone, regardless of prior employment record. Contrary to the complex schemes of job subsidies that are implemented on a yearly regular basis by all governments across Europe, it accordingly avoids creating income inequalities at the bottom of the wage structure, while being far more transparent as regards conditions of entitlement.

A UBI is sometimes presented as the ideal alternative to full employment. Some criticise it for this very reason, as they fear that paying a basic income will amount to pay the lazy, whereas our goal should be to guarantee a right to work – perhaps through a guaranteed job (see the chapter by Philip Harvey in this volume). However, the discussion about the differences between universal and selective schemes shows that in order to have an effective right to work, it is essential to guarantee the right to an income. By focusing on the inactive only, conventional means-tested schemes definitely help to reduce poverty, but also create a genuine trap as they tend to penalise people who manage to find a job. The introduction of a UBI guarantees that even a poorly paid job can provide individual workers with a higher net income than they would have if unemployed.

C. Resilience

The final way to explain why universal schemes perform better that selective ones has to do with the politics of income support. To put it briefly, data show that "the greater the degree of low-income targeting, the smaller the redistributive budget".[13] The distribution of power resources is key to understanding this mechanism, and can be summarised as follows: the probability that universal programmes will be defended against a potential backlash is much higher than in the case of selective programmes, simply because the former are more inclusive than the latter.[14] Selective programmes establish a clear divide between net recipients and net contributors, and the middle class is less prone to support them.

The French universal child benefit offers a perfect illustration of this: in the past two decades, several governments attempted to turn it into a selective programme. As already mentioned, the socialist Prime Minister Lionel Jospin, for instance, tried to reform the universal child benefit in the late 1990s. In 1998, he managed to introduce a short-lived income-test. However, as he had to face the fierce opposition of major

---

[13] W. Korpi and J. Palme, "The Paradox of Redistribution and Strategies of Equality: Welfare State Institutions, Inequality, and Poverty in the Western Countries", *American Sociological Review*, Vol. 63, No. 5, 1998, p. 672.

[14] See the discussion in Korpi and Palme for further details and additional references.

political and social forces, in 1999 he had to make the transfer universal again.[15] By contrast, the U.S. case is paradigmatic of the perverse effects of selectivity: targeting tend to assign some specific social identity to recipients, especially since a significant proportion of the worst-off are Black or Hispanic (see the chapter by Daniel Dumont in this volume). No surprise, therefore, to see little support for welfare within the white middle class.

"Not only the poor":[16] this is a crucial element of welfare reform, at least if we believe, as I do, that sustainable and resilient programmes are of key importance.

II. The Tension Between In-Cash and In-Kind Benefits

Suppose we agree on the fact that, for the above-mentioned reasons, universal benefits are superior to selective transfers. The next question then becomes: should we opt for universal benefits in-cash or in-kind?[17] This question, which was already raised during the early stages of welfare state development, is also at the core of the discussion between UBI supporters and advocates of a job guarantee.

According to supporters of in-kind benefits, some form of mild paternalism is required in order to protect individuals against themselves, or in order to protect their dependent relatives (especially their children). By directing their consumption choices, in-kind benefits help to avoid suboptimal spending on some specific goods and services. For instance, by providing free universal education, public authorities avoid parent's (potential) suboptimal spending on children's education. Similarly, as illustrated by the comparison between Europe and the United States, a free public health care system is more efficient than a largely privatised one, because it helps to avoid individual's suboptimal spending on preventive health care services. In almost all OECD countries, health care and free basic education are two universal programmes that provide in-kind benefits, and still represent a very large share of public spending. It should also be noted that several means-tested (i.e. non-universal) schemes, such as public housing programmes, or the U.S. *Supplemental Nutrition Assistance Program*, also rely on this mildly paternalistic view through the provision of in-kind benefits.

---

[15] However, on October 24, 2014, the French House of Representatives adopted an important reform of the child benefit, which mainly consists in paying lower benefits to higher income groups.

[16] Following the title of a famous book: R.E. Goodin and J. Le Grand, *Not Only the Poor: the Middle Classes and the Welfare State*, London, Allen & Unwin, 1987.

[17] An excellent overview of this discussion can be found in J. Currie and F. Gahvari, "Transfers in Cash and In-Kind: Theory Meets the Data", *op. cit.*, pp. 333-383.

Another related argument in favour of in-kind benefits focuses on the broader issue of the legitimacy of public transfers. Even when income inequalities are seen as justified, for instance because they are considered to be the result of individual merit, many people will nevertheless stick to some sort of "specific egalitarianism": they will tend to think that everyone, regardless of his or her past choices, should have a guaranteed access to some basic necessities. The expression "specific egalitarianism" was coined by American economist and UBI-advocate James Tobin, and refers to the widespread view that "scarce commodities should be distributed less unequally than the ability to pay for them". According to Tobin, "candidates for such sentiments include basic necessities of life, health, and citizenship".[18] In other words, most of us would agree with the fact that access to these basic necessities should be guaranteed to all, on a universal basis.

To some extent, both arguments apply to the proposal of a "job guarantee" supported by Philip Harvey (see his contribution in this volume). The job guarantee includes some form of mild paternalism, since its advocates want to make sure that people are going to work; and it includes some form of specific egalitarianism, since it assumes that everyone should get access to the labour market, be it only because it guarantees access to other "social primary goods" such as income and self-esteem.

By contrast, a UBI is paid in cash, as in the case of existing conditional schemes of means-tested income support, without restrictions as to the nature or timing of its consumption. The key argument here is based on considerations of individual freedom, since such a benefit leaves everyone fully free to decide how to spend it. In this vein, philosophers of the liberal-egalitarian school insist on the importance of combining egalitarian transfers with a great degree of freedom. In-cash is then justified on grounds of justice; this is what Philippe Van Parijs, one of the most prominent UBI advocates, calls "real freedom for all".[19] In order to be really free, and pursue one's own conception of the good life, some form of minimal income security is required.

But in-cash benefits can also be defended for efficiency reasons, referring to what economists usually call "consumer sovereignty": "At the heart of the economist's love affair with cash transfers is the doctrine of

---

[18] J. Tobin, "On Limiting the Domain of Inequality", *Journal of Law and Economics*, Vol. 13, No. 2, 1970, p. 264. Tobin's argument is also discussed in J. Currie and F. Gahvari, "Transfers in Cash and In-Kind: Theory Meets the Data", *op. cit.*, p. 340.

[19] P. Van Parijs, *Real Freedom for All. What (if anything) Can Justify Capitalism?*, Oxford, Oxford University Press, 1995.

absolute consumer sovereignty."[20] This argument is best phrased in terms of imperfect information of public authorities: in-cash is superior to in-kind, because the government has limited information about individual preferences and consumption choices. In other words, following this argument, individuals are supposed to be "the most qualified judges of how to best maximize their own utility."[21]

These arguments about justice and efficiency of in-cash transfers should be carefully discussed, as they are not decisive; in fact, in-kind transfers also have obvious positive features. It certainly means that, in the end, welfare states have good reasons to combine both in-kind and in-cash benefits. Let me focus on two last arguments in this respect.

First, in the framework of any discussion about activation policies and the right to work, one should pay attention to any possible impact on the labour supply. Leaving aside the normative question of the work ethic (work as being intrinsically important), if transfers are aimed at reducing the poverty rate, providing poor individuals with cash benefits might not be enough, even when it has a positive impact on the inactivity trap (see above). The difference between childcare facilities (in-kind) and a universal child benefit (a basic income for children, in-cash) is quite illustrative in this respect. According to the above-mentioned arguments, on grounds of justice and efficiency one should obviously opt for the highest level of in-cash child benefit. But if we want to promote employment in the framework of activation policies, universal services such as childcare facilities might also be considered, as they could positively affect the labour supply of mothers.

This is a tricky issue, as there is no clear-cut evidence about the fact that in-kind benefits really have better effects on labour supply, at least in the short-term. Most American studies actually found minor effects: on the whole, "there is little evidence that in-kind programs have positive short-run effects on labor supply" of mothers.[22] In a detailed study on the European Union (EU27), Wim Van Lancker gives a more balanced picture of this relationship, as he examines inequalities in childcare use.[23] But evidence also shows that an expansion of childcare services will not necessarily translate into an increase of women's employment rate among

---

[20] L. Thurow, "Cash Versus In-Kind Transfers", *American Economic Review*, Vol. 64, No. 2, 1977, p. 193.

[21] L. Thurow, "Government Expenditures: Cash or In-Kind Aid?", in G. Dworkin (ed.), *Markets and Morals*, New York, Wiley, 1977, p. 96.

[22] J. Currie and F. Gahvari, "Transfers in Cash and In-Kind: Theory Meets the Data", *op. cit.*, p. 365.

[23] W. Van Lancker, "Putting the Child-Centred Investment Strategy to the Test: Evidence for the EU27", *European Journal of Social Security*, Vol. 15, No. 1, 2013, pp. 5-27.

all social groups. In fact, childcare services are widely used by high-income groups, but to a much lesser extent by least well-off families. Hence, the impact of such services on the employment of mothers of disadvantaged children is also much lower in the short-term.

If one considers a long-term perspective, however, and especially when employment patterns tend to converge as least well-off mothers gradually enter the labour market, there might be good reasons to support in-kind services such as childcare facilities. To some extent, "the relationship between childcare use and maternal employment is presumably reciprocal: availability of childcare services gives mothers of young children a better option to engage in paid employment, which will in turn induce a higher demand for childcare places".[24] Childcare services also tend to have a positive effect on the human capital of young children, hence providing them with better opportunities to access the labour market when they become young adults.[25] Furthermore, such services might also have a positive effect on the socialisation of mothers, which in turn – due to the positive impact of networks and social capital – might improve their chances to find a job.

Second, we have seen that according to one classic view in economics, individuals are said to be best qualified to make decisions that will satisfy their preferences and maximise their own utility. This is a strong argument in favour of in-cash benefits without any restriction as to nature or timing of consumption. However, as was rightly stressed by Thurow, "real public policies must face up to a modification of this simplistic view – there are individuals who are incompetent to make their own decisions".[26] If this is true, and especially at young age, some mild paternalism might be required after all. It might also mean that some decision-aiding services are justified for the management of in-cash benefits.[27]

This point implies at least one important consequence: it means that payments of in-cash transfers should be made in small instalments, rather than once a year, for instance. In fact, while they often argue against any form of paternalism, almost all UBI advocates opt for a monthly payment of the basic income. In other words, even if UBI supporters are attached to individual freedom, they seem to be aware of the fact that individuals have to be protected against themselves. For this reason, contrary to what one might think at first sight, mild paternalism is not totally absent from the design of their proposal.

---

[24] *Ibid.*, p. 15.
[25] J. Currie and F. Gahvari, "Transfers in Cash and In-Kind: Theory Meets the Data", *op. cit.*, p. 367.
[26] L. Thurow, "Cash Versus In-Kind Transfers", *op. cit.*, p. 193.
[27] See L. Thurow, "Government Expenditures: Cash or In-Kind Aid?", *op. cit.*, p. 98.

In principle, one could of course pay a UBI as a lump-sum, as was proposed by Ackerman & Alstott in the U.S. context. Their idea was to give every American a "stakeholder grant" of 80,000 US$ at the age of 18.[28] But the whole of such an endowment could be spent on luxuries or unnecessary items, rather than invested in studies, training, or housing. Hence, a vast majority of UBI advocates have been very critical of this proposal, arguing that its design was bound to make such a capital grant "far less opportunity-egalitarian" than a UBI. Philippe Van Parijs, for instance, argued that young people already favoured along various dimensions, such as talent, parental attention, or school quality, would be "the most likely to make the best possible use of their stakes", while others will likely take wrong decisions.[29]

In the end, it seems that the tension between in-kind and in-cash remains intact, partly because of the conflicting objectives we have in mind when we think about welfare state reform. Clearly, as was already stressed by Thurow, transfer systems probably need a continuum "ranging from cash, cash with advice, vouchers, in-kind provision, and, finally, compulsion."[30] In any case, what is often overlooked by UBI opponents is the fact that the introduction of an universal benefit in cash is, of course, fully compatible with the maintenance and even reinforcement of universal benefits in kind, such as free basic education, free healthcare, or free access to public services in general.[31] Some universal social policies already in place rely on such combination, like is the case in countries where universal child benefits are combined with universal access to subsidised childcare facilities.

III. The Tension Between Conditionality and Unconditionality

Finally, let me briefly deal with the third tension, the tension between conditionality and unconditionality. If the idea of paying everyone a UBI

---

[28] B. Ackerman and A. Alstott, *The Stakeholder Society*, New Haven, Yale University Press, 1999.

[29] P. Van Parijs, "Basic Income Versus Stakeholder Grants: Some Afterthoughts on how Best to Redesign Distribution," in B. Ackerman, A. Alstott and P. Van Parijs (eds.), *Redesigning Distribution. Basic Income and Stakeholder Grants as Cornerstones for an Egalitarian Capitalism*, London, Verso, 2006, pp. 199-208.

[30] L. Thurow, "Government Expenditures: Cash or In-Kind Aid?", *op. cit.*, p. 98.

[31] Given the fact that governmental resources are limited, some left-wing critics of basic income conclude that "state provision of a long list of expensive services, plus targeted cash payments to those in special circumstances, has a higher priority" (B. Bergmann, "A Swedish Welfare State or Basic Income: Which Should Have Priority?," in B. Ackerman, A. Alstott and P. Van Parijs (eds.), *Redesigning Distribution, op. cit.*, London, Verso, 2006, p. 130.

sounds radical, it is probably not due to its universal or to its in-cash nature. The most controversial feature of this proposal rather lies in the fact that, by contrast with activation schemes, the benefit is not linked to any work requirement. In other words, even if most of us would agree that the very idea of a "right to work" deserves closer attention, there might be a broad consensus about the idea that there should still be some form of "duty to work", at least for the able-bodied. Note, however, that in developed welfare states unconditionality – under the form of an absence of work requirement – is already at the core of several existing universal in-cash benefits (such as child benefits and basic means-tested pensions), and of several universal in-kind benefits (such as health care and education).

How can we justify this feature of the proposal, especially in the light of the discussion of active welfare policies? One obvious way to answer this question consists in referring, once again, to the liberal-egalitarian framework already mentioned. In this perspective, providing everyone with an unconditional cash grant of equal value is a good way – indeed, the best way – to achieve social justice in terms of "real freedom". But some would object that social justice also has to do with the idea of reciprocity, or with the idea of merit: somehow, access to benefits should be deserved, since there are no rights without related duties. In other words, why would we pay the lazy? Shouldn't we force them to reciprocate through some form of participation in the labour market? Facing this widespread "reciprocity objection", UBI supporters have at least three different replies.[32]

First, forcing individuals into the labour market, be it through workfare policies or through a job guarantee programme, might prove counter-productive. Many entrepreneurs are reluctant to support activation programmes, as they do not want unproductive workers who are not motivated to do the job. In general terms, for obvious reasons, the average productivity of forced labour is quite low. By contrast, the cost of workfare and job guarantees programmes is quite high, perhaps higher than the net cost of a UBI. Proponents of activation might counter-argue by saying that within the OECD most activation programmes are of a much softer nature, as they rather focus on vocational training, guidance, or positive incentives intended at "making work pay". An increasing proportion of UBI supporters, as we will see below, do not necessarily oppose this softer approach. They advocate a progressive activation strategy, of which a guaranteed income is the main component.

---

[32] Leaving aside the numerous replies that are inspired by political theory. For an overview, see Part III ("Reciprocity and Exploitation") of K. Widerquist, J.A. Noguera, Y. Vanderborght and J. De Wispelaere (eds.), *Basic Income: An Anthology of Contemporary Research, op. cit.*, pp. 79-140.

Second, UBI proponents argue that one should not be afraid of an alleged "nightmare scenario", in which everyone stops working and live off their basic income. Paradoxically, they can even rely on one of the most-often heard arguments against UBI. Sceptics like to say that a UBI makes no sense because individuals are not looking for an income as such, but for social recognition and self-esteem through a valuable occupation. If this is really the case, i.e. if the non-monetary benefits of work are so important, why should we fear the nightmare scenario with the implementation of a modest income guarantee?

Third, and perhaps most importantly, one should stress the fact that a UBI is an essential component of a progressive activation strategy. As was made clear in the above discussion about the tension between universalism and selectivity, selective schemes definitely help reduce poverty but also create a genuine trap, because they penalise people who manage to find a job. Since the introduction of a UBI guarantees that even a poorly paid job can provide people with a higher net income, it can be considered as a job subsidy. Some UBI opponents, especially within the trade-union movement, counter-argue by saying that taxpayers would then actually subsidise "bad jobs", i.e. degrading jobs. But precisely because of its unconditional nature, with a UBI workers get the right and the power to refuse jobs that they consider as degrading. The fact that there is no work requirement provides the most vulnerable with a negotiating power, enabling them to reject job offers that (in their own view) have no future. In other words, because it is universal, basic income functions as a subsidy for less productive work, but because it is unconditional it does not serve as a subsidy for degrading jobs. Basic income favours employment, but not under any conditions. It makes it possible to offer and accept poorly paid jobs, but these will only find takers if they are sufficiently pleasant, stimulating, and formative, or offer real career prospects, not if they are repulsive, degrading and lead nowhere. It makes it also much easier to accept such transitions as training and apprenticeship, provided they correspond to one's individual aspirations, not to the will of a civil servant.

Conclusion

Fundamentally, the driving idea behind the proposal of an unconditional basic income is to improve the situation of the worst-off in at least three key dimensions: income security, freedom, and self-esteem. Even if conventional social policies often share similar objectives, the careful examination of the tensions at the core of welfare reform shows that a UBI performs much better, even when one takes progressive activation strategies into account. UBI supporters do not, in fact, deny the idea that there should be some sort of "right to work" or, at least, the right to get access to a meaningful activity. What they dispute is that the best way to realise such a right consists in implementing a "duty to work". Instead, they force us to think about the idea that there might be a (somewhat unexpected) connection between the right to work and the right to an income.

In this chapter, I did not explore the financial and political feasibility of basic income, although I am aware of the fact that these are key elements in the assessment of its potential from the perspective of welfare reform.[33] However, whatever the results of such exploration, I firmly believe that in the long-term a UBI indicates the direction into which developed welfare systems should evolve. But in the short-term, this proposal can – and should – inspire more modest reforms, that might prove more realistic in times of economic downturn; some potential advantages of a UBI can be incorporated into less radical policies, which might even include existing mainstream activation schemes. It could, for instance, inspire reforms aimed at facilitating transitions between the school system and the labour market, if it is implemented as a direct subsidy for students and apprentices.

In particular, one should pay attention to the possible drawbacks of a move towards increased selectivity, which is on the agenda in most European countries. Such move might be detrimental to the interests of the worst-off. On the contrary, as this brief discussion of the potential of a UBI shows, universalism is required in order to achieve a welfare reform that bridges concerns of justice with concerns of efficiency and sustainability.

---

[33] On the potential of basic income in a changing welfare state, see for instance Y. Vanderborght and T. Yamamori (eds.), *Basic Income in Japan. Prospects for a Radical Idea in a Transforming Welfare State*, New York, Palgrave Macmillan, 2014.

Securing the Right to Work and Income Security

Philip HARVEY

Introduction

For approximately three decades following the end of the Second World War progressive reformers believed they knew how to achieve full employment in developed market economies – a condition they originally equated with 2 per cent unemployment.[1] Recessions no longer scared them because of their confidence in Keynesian anti-cyclical policies. They were equally confident that these same policies could insure the availability of enough jobs to provide work for everyone who wanted it in a manner that supported rather than undermined efforts to improve job quality via labour market regulation and collective bargaining. The elevated unemployment rates suffered by disadvantaged population groups cast a cloud over this scenario, but progressives believed they could solve this problem with a combination of anti-discrimination legislation, offers of special labour market assistance, and the promotion of investment in the communities where disadvantaged workers lived. The achievement of full employment, or close to it, also supported the growth of the welfare state by reducing the number of people who needed government income assistance while simultaneously increasing the resources available to expand both targeted and universal social welfare benefits.

The overall success of this reform strategy depended on the success of its full employment leg – not because insuring adequate job availability was viewed as inherently more important than other elements of the reform agenda, but because of the functional role it played in facilitating the achievement of other progressive goals. As United States President Franklin D. Roosevelt commented in his last State of the Union Address,

---

[1] See J.M. Clark *et al.*, *National and International Measures for Full Employment*, report by a group of experts appointed by the Secretary General of the United Nations, New York, Lake Success, 1949, p. 14. William Beveridge's often-cited 3 per cent estimate was not out of line with the consensus reported by Clark *et al.*, since he included not only frictional unemployment (which he estimated at 1%), but also seasonal unemployment and unemployment attributable to fluctuations in international trade in his estimate. See W. Beveridge, *Full Employment In A Free Society*, London, Allen and Unwin, 1944, pp. 127-129.

the right to work is the "most fundamental" of all economic and social rights, because it is the "one on which the fulfilment of the others in large part depends".[2]

That is why the entire progressive reform project suffered a crippling blow when the "stagflation" crisis of the 1970s shattered the confidence of progressives in the full employment leg of their overall strategy. Keynesian theory, which provided clear guidance for responding to recessions or weak economic growth at the bottom of the business cycle and to inflationary tendencies at the top of the business cycle, proved helpless in explaining how to respond to a recession or sluggish economic growth that was accompanied by persistently high rates of inflation.

Conservative economists were quick to seize the initiative with promises of a cure for inflation and a reinvigoration of the engines of economic growth. But the policies they favoured for achieving these goals required the abandonment of both the progressive full employment goal and further welfare state expansion. Progressives resisted but were not able to stem the conservative tide. They had no credible strategy for achieving full employment with price stability, and they were susceptible to claims that welfare state expansion, labour market regulation and trade union power actually aggravated the inflation problem in developed market economies by encouraging excessive deficit spending by governments and by encouraging resistance by workers to productivity-enhancing changes in business practices. Neo-liberalism became the new orthodoxy in market economies.

Over the next several decades, progressive thinking itself was influenced by this neo-liberal trend. The progressive reform agenda turned defensive, and progressive reformers came to accept certain tenets of the neo-liberal policy regime as unavoidable. Most importantly for the purposes of our inquiry, the pursuit of full employment was effectively abandoned.[3] Rather than go back to the drawing boards and ask whether full employment could be achieved by means other than the now discredited Keynesian strategy, growing numbers of progressive economists reconciled themselves to the idea that full employment, as it was understood in the immediate post-Second World War era, simply could not be achieved. They were loath to admit, however, that they had no strategy for achieving full employment, so they instead began using

---

[2] Franklin D. Roosevelt, State of the Union Address, 6 January 1935, retrieved 19 September 2014 from <http://www.presidency.ucsb.edu/ws/?pid=16595>.

[3] The evidence of this trend in the platforms of Democratic candidates for president in the United States is quite striking. See P. Harvey, "Is There a Progressive Alternative to Conservative Welfare Reform?", *Georgetown Journal on Poverty Law and Policy*, Vol. 15, No. 2, 2008, p. 173, note 49.

the term in a different way. Rather than conceiving of full employment in terms of job availability – as a labour market condition in which the aggregate demand for labour equalled or exceeded the aggregate supply of labour – they began using the term to refer to the lowest rate of unemployment they considered achievable consistent with the maintenance of reasonable price stability.[4] Unfortunately, they have done this without explaining to the people who rely on their advice that the "full employment" goal they aim to achieve is not the full employment goal that progressives promoted in the immediate post-Second World War era and which progressive activists still associate with the term.[5]

To bring clarity to a policy discourse whose goals have been obscured by this tendency, I have long argued that progressives should recognise the goal of securing the right to work as the basis of their definition of full employment or as a substitute for the full employment goal.[6] For benchmarking purposes, I have described this right as having four dimensions. The *quantitative* dimension requires that enough suitable jobs be readily available to provide freely chosen, paid employment for everyone who wants it. The *qualitative* dimension requires that all of these jobs must satisfy certain conditions of decency. The *distributive* dimension requires that these employment opportunities be made available on an equal basis to all workers without regard to irrelevant personal characteristics. The *scope* of the right requires that persons engaged in non-waged work be accorded the same or equivalent rights as wage workers, even though the form in which those rights are secured may differ.[7]

---

[4] For recent examples, see, e.g., P. Krugman, "Stimulus Arithmatic (Wonkish but Important)", *Conscience of a Liberal*, New York Times Web Log Post, 9 January 2009, retrieved 31 July 2013 from <http://krugman.blogs.nytimes.com/2009/01/06/stimulus-arithmetic-wonkish-but-important/?_r=0>; J. Bernstein, "Where Have All the Jobs Gone?", *New York Times*, 3 May 2013, op-ed article, retrieved 31 July 2013 from <http://www.nytimes.com/2013/05/04/opinion/where-have-all-the-jobs-gone.html>; R. Pollin "A Debate on Back To Full Employment, Round Two," *Back to Full Employment*, Web Log Post, 26 March 2013, retrieved 31 July 2013 from <http://backtofullemployment.org/2013/03/26/a-debate-on-back-to-full-employment-round-tworobert-pollin-and-phillip-harvey/?subscribe=success#blog_subscription-3>.

[5] See G.S. Goldberg, P. Harvey and H.L. Ginsburg, "A Survey of Full Employment Advocates", *Journal of Economic Issues*, Vol. 41, No. 4, 2007, pp. 1161-1168.

[6] See P. Harvey, *Securing the Right to Employment. Social Welfare Policy and the Unemployed in the United States*, Princeton (N.J.), Princeton University Press, 1989, pp. 11-16; P. Harvey, "Why Is the Right to Work so Hard to Secure?", in A. Minkler (ed.), *The State of Economic and Social Human Rights. A Global Overview*, New York, Cambridge University Press, 2013, pp. 168-170.

[7] See P. Harvey, "Benchmarking the Right to Work", in A. Minkler and S. Hartel (eds.), *Economic Rights. Conceptual, Measurement and Policy Issues*, New York, Cambridge University Press, 2007, pp. 123-124.

Defining full employment as the realisation of all four of these dimensions of the right to work highlights the unevenness of our efforts to achieve that goal. Labour law has been assigned the task of securing the qualitative and distributive aspects of the right to work, and considerable progress has been made in that effort despite the countervailing influence of our failure to secure the quantitative dimension of the right. Extending the rights associated with wage employment to non-wage workers is still in its rudimentary stages, but that too is a task largely assigned to labour law – mainly via the use of social welfare benefits to subsidise parenting and other care activities. In contrast, the only role played by the law in enforcing the quantitative dimension of the right to work operates at the collective level via mandates to policy makers that they strive to minimise unemployment rates and promote job creation in various contexts. And, as noted above, these mandates have little effect in a policy environment in which neither conservative or progressive economists believe it is possible to achieve genuine full employment, i.e., full employment conceived in the way it was when the goal was expressly embraced as a goal that all members of the United Nations had a duty to pursue under international law.[8]

When considering the legal nature of the right to work, though, and particularly the quantitative dimension of that right, I think it is important to recognise the aspirational character of human rights law.[9] The historical road is a long one from the first articulation of a new human rights claim, through its formal recognition, and finally its routine enforcement; but that does not mean such claims acquire the status of law only when they are enforced or when a means of enforcing them is acknowledged to exist. As I have argued elsewhere,

> Human rights are a form of aspirational law by means of which humans establish goals for themselves concerning the kinds of species they are committed to becoming (a species that respects these rights) and the kind of societies they are committed to creating (the kind of societies that secure and protect these rights).
>
> To argue, as legal positivists might, that what the [South African] antiapartheid movement did was force a change in the law, creating legal rights where only moral claims had existed before, is nothing but a linguistic shuffle. The reality is that non-white South Africans living under apartheid claimed that they possessed legal rights of a higher order than those granted by South African law; and when the South African government refused to recognize

---

[8] This duty is articulated in Articles 55 and 56 of the United Nations Charter.
[9] P. Harvey, "Aspirational Law", *Buffalo Law Review*, Vol. 52, No. 3, 2004, pp. 701-726.

those rights, they called upon supporters of their claims inside and outside South Africa to enforce their human rights by extra-judicial means. It took decades, but this "enforcement" action ultimately proved successful.

Language is a product of usage, and definitions (even in legal theory) should not ignore usage. People consistently use the term "human rights" in a way that connotes a special category of entitlements that is distinct from other moral claims and that may, under certain circumstances, be more authoritative than mere legal rights. Who are the positivists to say that this usage is mistaken? Was it simply a linguistic mistake to assert that apartheid violated the human rights of non-white South Africans or for Thomas Jefferson to assert that "all men are created equal"? I don't think so. The usage is too widespread and, more importantly, too consequential to be dismissed as confused. Something special and unique is going on when people assert or accept the existence of unenforced human rights that is not adequately captured in the positivist distinction between legal rights and moral claims.[10]

My purpose in this chapter is not to parse the enforceability of the four dimensions of the right to work identified above. It is to assert that all four dimensions share the same status as constituent elements of the right, and that public policy relating to the right should be judged based on its ability to secure all four dimensions.

Accordingly, unless the context indicates otherwise, when I use the term "full employment", or "genuine full employment" in this chapter, I will be referring to a labour market condition that fully secures the quantitative dimension of the right to work with jobs that also satisfy the other three dimension of the right. This is the traditional meaning of the term, the one ascribed to it in popular parlance, professional economic discourse and international law during the 1940s.[11]

But if the achievement of full employment was viewed as more or less synonymous with securing the right to work, why didn't progressives emphasise that linkage in their advocacy of the full employment goal? Why in the post-Second World War era did they pursue a concerted campaign to achieve full employment while hardly ever mentioning the right to work – at least in their domestic policy discourse? I have puzzled over this question and still do. Nevertheless, I believe the failure of progressives to promote the achievement of full employment as a human rights struggle in the decades following the Second World War can be at least partly explained by practical political considerations.

---

[10] *Ibid.*, pp. 723, 714 and 701-702.
[11] P. Harvey, "Why is the Right to Work so Hard to Secure?", *op. cit.*, pp. 156-160.

The rapidity and ease with which war-time spending lifted the U.S. economy out of the Great Depression was widely viewed as confirming both the truth of Keynesian economic theory and the practical ability of Keynesian macroeconomic policy to achieve full employment.[12] The post-Second World War experience of Western European countries in rebuilding their economies reinforced this view of the efficacy of Keynes's teaching. Since the full employment goal and the Keynesian strategy for achieving it were thus strongly associated with one another, it was natural for progressives in both the United States and Western Europe to view them as a package. In contrast, the goal of securing the right to work was not associated with any particular strategy for achieving the goal. Indeed, since the drafters of the Universal Declaration undertook to produce a document that could be deemed acceptable to all the world's cultures, they took pains not to presume or suggest the means by which the rights proclaimed in the document should be secured. Nor was the ability of rights-based claims to mobilise progressive social movements widely appreciated as of yet.

Of course progressives could have cited the right to work in promoting the Keynesian full employment strategy; but there were good reasons to regard the achievement of the latter goal to be an easier political "lift" if it was not associated with the former goal. Conservatives knew that full employment was a progressive Trojan horse, but it was a harder goal to oppose than the promotion of a "new" human right would have been. After all, the full employment goal aimed to achieve no more than what conservatives claimed the economy would achieve on its own if governments left it alone. This tended to shift the debate to a dispute over means rather than ends, and the perceived effectiveness of the Keynesian strategy gave progressives confidence that they could win that debate.

Progressives who were drawn to the claim that access to decent work was a human right could take solace in the fact that achieving full employment in conjunction with the rest of the progressive reform agenda, would secure the right in fact whether or not the goal was acknowledged. Why throw down the gauntlet with a highly-charged human rights claim

---

[12] John Kenneth Galbraith described the effect this experience had on Keynesian economists during World War II in the following terms. "One could not have had a better demonstration of the Keynesian ideas, and I think it's fair to say that as a young Keynesian in Washington, in touch with the other Keynesians there, we all saw that very clearly at the time." J.K. Galbraith, interview conducted 28 September 2000, originally broadcast on *Commanding Heights: The Battle for the World Economy* [television series, 2002], PDF transcript of interview retrieved 31 July 2013 from <http://www-tc.pbs.org/wgbh/commandingheights/shared/pdf/int_johnkennethgalbraith.pdf>, p. 6.

when there was good reason to believe the right to work could be secured more easily by not mentioning it?

Advocacy of the right to work accordingly played little role in the advocacy of full employment following the Second World War, and by the 1970s, the original association between the two goals was a receding memory. For the generation of progressives whose views were shaped by the social struggles of the 1960s, it was not even a memory.

The linkage between securing the right to work and achieving full employment was not even promoted by human rights advocates. What little attention they paid to economic and social human rights in the decades following the Second World War was devoted, at least in the United States, to philosophical debates over whether social welfare entitlements could properly be termed human rights at all. By the time mainstream human rights organisations began paying attention to the failure of governments to secure economic and social human rights – a trend I date to the 1990s in the United States – progressives had largely reconciled themselves to their inability to achieve full employment. Advocacy of the right to work by human rights organisations accordingly has tended to focus on the goal of securing rights *at* work (the qualitative and distributive dimensions of the right to work and to some degree its scope) rather than the right *to* work (the quantitative dimension of the right). Law reform efforts have also largely ignored the goal of securing the quantitative dimension of the right to work, leaving that task to economic policy makers.

What has this got to do with activation policies for the unemployed and basic income proposals? The answer is that both of these policy innovations owe their popularity, at least in part, to the failure of the Keynesian full employment strategy. Much of their attractiveness, at least to progressives, rests on the hope that they may provide a solution to the problem of unemployment that does not depend on the achievement of full employment.

In the balance of this chapter, I will consider whether these hopes are well founded. However, in keeping with my efforts to reaffirm the linkage between full employment and the right to work, I will frame my discussion as an inquiry into their ability to provide an acceptable substitute for securing the right to work rather than the achievement of full employment (I., II. and III.). Also, because it would serve little purpose to criticise these strategies for their inability to attain an unachievable goal, I will also describe an alternative response to the problem of unemployment that would not only secure the right to work, but also would provide stronger support for the rest of the progressive reform agenda than the achievement of full employment by Keynesian means ever did (IV.).

I. Activation Policies for the Unemployed in a Job Short Economy

It is clear that activation measures can help individual workers find work they otherwise would not have obtained. The more difficult question is whether such measures help secure the right to work of the labour force as a whole. They may not because of what I call the "musical chairs effect" – the fact that unemployed individuals who find work in a job short economy may simply displace other individuals who otherwise would have occupied the jobs in question.

For activation measures to reduce the level and rate of unemployment in an economy (as opposed to merely changing who is and who is not unemployed at a particular moment in time), the measures in question have to result in jobs being filled that otherwise would remain vacant.

This could happen, for example, if there were more vacant jobs requiring a particular set of qualifications than there were unemployed workers possessing the qualifications required to fill them. Economists describe unemployment caused by this phenomenon as *structural*. Activation measures can help eliminate structural unemployment by providing unemployed workers with the skills needed to fill these otherwise unfillable jobs.

Alternatively, job openings could remain vacant because it takes time and effort for qualified job seekers and employers with job openings to find one another and complete a hiring. Economists describe unemployment caused by this phenomenon as *frictional*. A certain amount of frictional unemployment is unavoidable, but to the extent it is caused by inadequate job search effort on the part of unemployed workers, activation measures may reduce it by helping or pressuring unemployed workers to look harder for suitable job openings.[13]

To assess the effectiveness of activation measures in reducing the level of unemployment in an economy, we accordingly must ask whether there is reason to believe that structural or frictional factors of the sort described above would cause a noticeable increase in the level of unemployment in the economy if the activation policies were terminated.

The first point that needs to be made in addressing this question is that neither structural nor frictional factors are likely to have much effect on the level of unemployment in an economy that is suffering from a

---

[13] For a more extended discussion of the nature of "structural" and "frictional" unemployment, see P. Harvey, "Combating Joblessness: An Analysis of the Principal Strategies that Have Influenced the Development of American Employment and Social Welfare Law During the 20th Century", *Berkeley Journal of Employment and Labor Law*, Vol. 21, No. 2, 2000, pp. 699-707.

significant job shortage or "job gap" – i.e., a deficit in the number of jobs relative to the number of job wanters in the economy. The reason is simple. When there are multiple job seekers competing for every available job, the chances diminish that there will be a lack of qualified candidates applying for available jobs.

Figure 1 portrays three different measures of the job gap in the U.S. economy. The bottom line in the figure (job openings) shows how many vacant jobs employers were seeking to fill on a monthly basis between December 2000 (when this data series was first reported) and May 2013. The line immediately above it (official unemployment) shows how many people were totally unemployed and actively looking for work over the same time period. The third line from the bottom adds to official unemployment the number of people who were working part-time but wanted full-time jobs (involuntary part-time workers). Finally, the top line adds to these two groups the number of people who said they wanted a job and were available to accept one even though they were not actively looking for work. I call these individuals "discouraged workers", even though the U.S. Bureau of Labor Statistics uses that term more narrowly.

Figure 1: Job Wanters and Job Openings in the U.S. Dec. 2000-June 2013 (in millions, except unemployment rate in parentheses)

Source: Author's Calculations from BLS Data

As one would expect, Figure 1 shows that the U.S. economy's job gap mushroomed as a result of the so-called Great Recession. But it also shows that a persistent, if much smaller job gap existed before the recession. Indeed, a positive job gap was a permanent feature of the American labour market during this period, and the same is true of earlier periods for which job vacancy data is available.[14] Jay Zagorsky, concludes that there were only five years between 1923 and 1994 when there were more job vacancies than unemployed individuals in the United States: 1923, 1926, and the last three years of the Second World War.[15]

It also is worth noting that the unemployment burden created by this job gap is not equally shared. Some population groups bear a much larger share of the burden than other groups. Table 1 illustrates this point by showing the comparative unemployment rates of various population cohorts and metropolitan areas in June 2013 when the overall official unemployment rate in the United States was 7.8 per cent. The disparities shown in this table are typical of those that exist at all times in the U.S. economy.

Table 1: Comparative Unemployment Rates in the United States: National Averages, June 2013

Overall Unemployment Rate	7.8
Metropolitan Areas	
Bismark, North Dakota	2.8
Washington, DC	6.0
New York City	8.2
Detroit, Michigan	10.3
Yuma, Arizona	31.8
Youths aged 16-19	
Black aged 16-19	43.6
White aged 16-19	20.4
All persons aged 16 & over	
Black or African American	13.7
Hispanic or Latino	9.1
White	6.6
All Persons aged 25 and Older	
Less than high school diploma	10.7
High School Graduates, No College	7.6
Some College or Associates Degree	6.4
Bachelor's Degree and Higher	3.9

Source: BLS

---

[14] *Ibid.*, pp. 706-709.
[15] J. Zagorsky, "Job Vacancies in the United States: 1923 to 1994", *Review of Economics and Statistics*, Vol. 80, No. 2, 1998, pp. 338-345.

I have not compiled similar data for Europe, but there is no reason to believe the facts are different there.[16] Indeed, I posit that significant job shortages are the norm in market economies and that they always have been. In earlier centuries and in most of the world still, the existence of a job gap is effectively guaranteed by the latent supply of labour residing in rural areas where employment is both seasonal and intermittent. The number of workers migrating in search of steadier and higher paying work in urban areas always tends to exceed the demand for it. In modern economies where this latent labour supply has been substantially absorbed, the business cycle and the efforts of governments to control inflation by slowing economic growth continue to insure the existence of the kind of job gap shown in Figure 1.

This latter point is especially important. It means the governments of virtually all developed market economies pursue a *de facto* policy of preventing unemployment from falling anywhere near the full employment level – which probably still lies in the neighbourhood of 2 per cent as progressive economists assumed in the immediate post-Second World War period. How do we know that still constitutes the unavoidable frictional unemployment floor in market economies today? Because that is the level to which unemployment still consistently falls when, for brief periods of time, jobs truly are plentiful relative to the supply of labour in some momentarily lucky country or local labour market.

In the United States, for example, the national unemployment rate at the end of 2000 was 3.9 per cent – as Figure 1 shows. However, the unemployment rate that month in the Bridgeport-Norwalk-Stamford metropolitan area in the state of Connecticut was 1.6 per cent. When jobs are truly plentiful, that is the level to which unemployment rates tend to drop.[17] Clearly this is not a phenomenon that can be attributed to unemployed workers suddenly acquiring the skills needed to fill vacant jobs. Nor can it be attributed to a sudden increase in the intensity of their job search efforts. What happens is that when employers have job openings they cannot otherwise fill, they lower their standards and engage workers whom they previously dismissed as unqualified. They may complain in these circumstances about unqualified job applicants and drag their heels

---

[16] The European Union has inaugurated a project to establish a common methodology for the collection of job vacancy data suitable for comparison with U.S. data. Job vacancy data produced as a result of this initiative can be accessed at <http://epp.eurostat.ec.europa.eu/portal/page/portal/labour_market/introduction>. For a discussion of the statistical relationship between full employment and job vacancies, see P. Harvey, "Combating Joblessness", *op. cit.*, pp. 702-709.

[17] Norway's unemployment rate was 2.3 per cent in April 2008, and since that was an average for the entire country there were almost certainly places where it was under 2.0 per cent.

in adjusting their standards; but their behaviour in finally hiring workers they previously viewed as "unqualified" demonstrates that the workers in question are good enough to earn their keep. No one forces employers in these circumstances to hire workers whose productivity is so low that it is unprofitable to employ them.

With unemployment rates as high as they have been in developed market economies over the past several decades, there is ample reason to doubt that structural and frictional factors account for any significant part of the problem. And that being the case, the effectiveness of activation policies in reducing the aggregate level and rate of unemployment also appears doubtful. At the very least this doubt should place a burden of proving otherwise on the shoulders of those who justify the activation strategy on these grounds.

Unfortunately, empirical evidence concerning the level of frictional or structural unemployment in an economy and the possible effectiveness of activation policies in reducing it is inherently difficult to collect. Evidence concerning the placement success of various activation measures is useless, because it cannot tell us whether the jobs in question would have remained vacant in the absence of the activation measures. What we need to settle the question is evidence of a causal relationship between the introduction of activation measures and a decline in aggregate levels of unemployment or, alternatively, between a cessation of activation measures and an increase in aggregate levels of unemployment. Regrettably, since so many factors can and do affect the level of unemployment in a particular labour market, it is hard to imagine how the requisite data could be collected other than by experimentally introducing or terminating activation measures in appropriately selected samples of local labour markets.

It may be, however, that supporters of activation policies are pursuing a different goal. Instead of reducing the level or rate of unemployment suffered by workers (i.e., trying to secure the quantitative aspect of the right to work), they may be attempting to equalise the unemployment burden workers are forced to bear by giving the least advantaged among the unemployed a leg up in their quest for work (thereby trying to secure the distributive aspect of the right to work). If the unemployment burden caused by a market economy's job gap were equally distributed among all workers, it might impose a small enough burden that it would be deemed an acceptable alternative to securing the right to work.[18] A 5 per cent unemployment rate, if equally shared, would require

---

[18] For a more extended discussion of this possibility, see P. Harvey, "Human Rights and Economic Policy Discourse: Taking Economic and Social Rights Seriously", *Columbia Human Rights Law Review*, Vol. 33, No. 2, 2002, pp. 438-445.

each member of the labour force to endure only about 2 ½ weeks of unemployment a year.

The problem is that activation policies are not well designed to ration unemployment in this way. Their immediate goal is to reduce the length of individual unemployment spells, and their target population does consist of disadvantaged job seekers. However, even if the activation measures deployed to assist these workers is 100 per cent effective in placing them in jobs, the individuals who lose those employment opportunities (via the musical chairs effect) will not be drawn from a cross section of the labour force. They will tend to be workers who suffer from the same or equivalent disadvantages as the assisted population – since they are the people most likely to lose out in the competition for available jobs when someone else in their circumstances moves closer to the front of hiring queues. The net result is likely to be an increase in the number of marginally qualified workers who experience unemployment, with that population experiencing more frequent but briefer spells of unemployment.

It is possible, of course, that this outcome will produce less harm in the aggregate than having a smaller number of workers experience less frequent but longer unemployment spells. Demonstrating that this is the case, however, requires more than a recital of data on the negative effects of long-term unemployment. The additional harm caused by the increased incidence and frequency of unemployment spells must be set off against the reduction in harm caused by the shortened duration of those unemployment spells. Unfortunately, such a calculation would require interpersonal comparisons of suffering, something that it is no more possible to do in practice than interpersonal comparisons of utility. Moreover, even if it were possible to show that activation policies reduce the net harm attributable to an economy's job gap, it is highly unlikely that the limited spreading of the unemployment burden they may achieve is capable of generating enough of a reduction in the harmfulness of that burden to render the activation strategy an adequate substitute for securing the quantitative as well as the distributive aspect of the right to work.

There is one more way to rationalise the reliance market economies have placed on activation policies in recent decades. Rather than reducing the level or rate of unemployment, or spreading its burden more widely, perhaps their contribution lies in raising the employment rate – i.e., the proportion of the working age population that is employed. This could be achieved by successfully discouraging workers from withdrawing from the labour force – a common consequence of long-term unemployment. By itself, of course, discouraging labour market withdrawal would tend to increase the unemployment rate, but a higher rate of unemployment would allow for further economic expansion at the top of the business cycle before central bankers stepped in to slow the rate of economic growth (to keep inflation in check). The result would then be a higher labour force participation rate and a higher level of employment, but without any reduction in the unemployment rate.[19]

The goal of raising the employment rate in Europe was famously embraced in the so-called Lisbon Agenda of 2000, but the role assigned to activation policies in that strategy was to increase labour productivity and reduce unemployment, not to create more leeway for macroeconomic expansion by increasing the pool of active job seekers.[20] Nevertheless, this may be the only way in which labour activation policies can be expected to reduce joblessness in a job short economy – not by reducing official unemployment but by reducing the number of people who may want jobs but are no longer actively seeking work, the group identified as discouraged workers in Figure 1. On the other hand, even if activation policies do have this effect (and it is an empirical question whether they do or not) the strategy cannot be said to provide a very good substitute for securing the quantitative aspect of the right to work. It would, at best, reduce the number of labour market dropouts.

Except for this last effect, activation policies are unlikely to reduce the unemployment problem in market economies. They certainly cannot be deemed an adequate substitute for securing the quantitative aspect of the right to work – no matter how effective they may be in assisting individual workers in finding jobs. This may be hard to accept, especially for people who provide this assistance for the best of reasons – to help people in need. But that is the hard lesson of the musical chairs effect in job short economies. Doctors may eradicate illness one patient at a time, because the help they provide is not subject to the musical chairs effect. Unfortunately, the problem of unemployment in a job short economy is different.

II. The Right to Work and to Income Security

Because a basic income (BI) guarantee can be understood as addressing the right to income security – either instead of or in addition to the right to work – it will be useful to preface our discussion of BI proposals with a brief review of the characteristics of the right to income security. As recognised in the Universal Declaration of Human Rights,[21] it has two pillars or branches. One of these addresses the income security needs of workers and the other addresses the income security needs of persons who are unable to earn their own livelihood.

---

[19] Assuming the rate of unemployment remained the same, the level of unemployment would grow proportionately as much as the labour force grew.
[20] Presidency Conclusions, Lisbon European Council, 23 and 24 March 2000, § 28-30.
[21] Universal Declaration of Human Rights, G.A. Res. 217 (III), U.N. Doc. A/811, 1948.

The first of these pillars is set forth in Article 23, § 3 of the Declaration, which describes the right to income security that workers enjoy: "Everyone who works has the right to just and favourable remuneration ensuring for himself and his family an existence worthy of human dignity, and supplemented, if necessary, by other means of social protection".[22]

In passing, we should note that the gendered language of this provision does not mean the right in question is limited to men. Article 2 of the Declaration makes that clear.[23] It also is important to note that the right is described in terms that are not limited to wage employment. It speaks of "remuneration" rather than "wages," and similarly broad language is used to describe other aspects of the right to work. The drafters probably had non-waged, agricultural producers in mind when they chose this language, but it does raise the question of what other types of employment and what other types of remuneration are properly included within the right to work. This is why I describe the "scope" of the right to work as one of its four aspects or dimensions.

The substantive content of the "just and favourable remuneration" to which workers are entitled according to Article 23, § 3 is clarified by Articles 22 and 25, § 1. The first phrase of Article 25, § 1 describes the standard of living to which "everyone" is entitled, including workers and their families. I shall refer to this as the "adequacy standard": "Everyone has the right to a standard of living adequate for the health and well-being of himself and of his family, including food, clothing, housing and medical care and necessary social services".[24] For a worker's remuneration to be deemed "just and favourable", it accordingly must satisfy this adequacy standard, and it must do so for both the worker and the worker's family – with the caveat that achieving this goal may require that the worker's remuneration be "supplemented [...] by other means of social protection." This could include, for example, government-funded health care benefits, housing subsidies for larger families, or even cash wage supplements.

Article 22 further elucidates the meaning of both the "just and favourable" standard set forth in Article 23, § 3 and the adequacy standard

---

[22] Universal Declaration, Art. 23, § 3.
[23] Article 2 states that

"Everyone is entitled to all the rights and freedoms set forth in this Declaration, without distinction of any kind, such as race, colour, sex, language, religion, political or other opinion, national or social origin, property, birth or other status. Furthermore, no distinction shall be made on the basis of the political, jurisdictional or international status of the country or territory to which a person belongs, whether it be independent, trust, non-self-governing or under any other limitation of sovereignty".

[24] Universal Declaration, Art. 25, § 1.

set forth in Article 25, § 1 by making it clear that the economic and social rights recognised in the Universal Declaration are intended to do more than guarantee people a minimally adequate physical subsistence. Their purpose is to make it possible for "everyone" to live in "dignity" and to achieve the "free development of [their] personality".[25]

To satisfy this requirement, the standard of living guaranteed by Articles 23, § 3 and 25, § 1 must accordingly do more than secure the worker's physical survival. It must be sufficient to permit the worker and each member of the worker's family to live as full, equal and respected members of society possessing the practical capacity to develop, express and enjoy their own individuality within a framework of mutual respect for the universality of these rights.

The second pillar of the right to income security is the right of "everyone" to "security in the event of unemployment, sickness, disability, widowhood, old age or other lack of livelihood in circumstances beyond his control."[26] This clearly establishes the right of persons who are unable to earn their own livelihood to a level of income support consistent with the adequacy standard described in Article 22 and the first phrase of Article 25, § 1 as described above. At the same time, however, the right to "security" in this context may be interpreted as possessing an insurance connotation entitling people who lose their livelihood as a result of circumstances beyond their control to the maintenance, within reasonable bounds, of their prior standard of living, or at least to accommodate a gradual enough adjustment in their standard of living to preserve their dignity along with their physical and emotional well-being.

What about people who are capable of earning their own livelihood but would prefer not to have to? Are they entitled to societal support? It can be argued that they are based on the unqualified language of the first

---

[25] The inherent and equal dignity of all persons is referenced five times in the Universal Declaration – twice in the Preamble and three times in the Declaration's substantive provisions, including Article 22. The recognition of everyone's right to live a life consistent with this principle is a foundational principle underlying the entire Declaration.

The goal of facilitating the "free and full development of the human personality" is another foundational principal of the Declaration. It is mentioned three times in slightly different form in the economic and social provisions of the document, and as one commentator has noted, "the right to 'the full development of the human personality' was seen by most delegates to the committee that drafted the Universal Declaration as a way of summarizing all the social, economic, and cultural right in the Declaration" (J. Morskink, *The Universal Declaration of Human Rights. Origins, Drafting, and Intent*, Philadelphia, University of Pennsylvania Press, 1999, p. 212).

[26] Universal Declaration, Art. 25, § 1.

phrase of Article 25, § 1,[27] but that phrasing could also be interpreted as meaning that everyone has the right to obtain an adequate standard of living – either by exercising the right to work recognised in Article 23 or the right to income security recognised in the second half of Article 25, § 1. The most authoritative account we have of the drafters' intent concludes that the latter was what they had in mind.[28]

Accepting this interpretation of Article 25, § 1, however, does not mean it would be improper for a society to provide an income guarantee to persons who cannot claim it as a human right. The right to work recognised by the Universal Declaration is not accompanied by any duty to work. Proposals to recognise such a duty in the Declaration were considered and expressly rejected.[29] Moreover, virtually all developed market economies do provide unconditional income guarantees to certain population groups. Many elderly people and the vast majority of children in their teenage years would be capable of earning their own livelihood if society expected it of them, but most societies do not. There may be sound policy reasons for conferring such a benefit on the young and the old, but there may also be sound policy reasons for offering such a benefit more broadly. The point is that it is not improper for a society to do so, and that being the case, there is no impediment grounded on human rights doctrine that would prevent a society from granting an unconditional BI guarantee to all its members, as BI advocates propose.

III. The Basic Income Strategy as a Remedy for Unemployment

The connection between the failure of the Keynesian full employment strategy and the increased popularity of labour activation policies is fairly obvious. Its connection to the increased popularity of the BI idea may not be. Still, the link is readily recognised by proponents of the BI idea. Philippe Van Parijs, the BI movement's most influential theoretician, has noted it in the following comment on the origins of the Basic Income European Network (BIEN) in the mid-1980s.[30]

> The first point of departure, and the most concrete one, is that it was becoming clear that we in Europe were beginning to experience a kind of mass

---

[27] See, e.g., G. Standing, "About Time: Basic Income Security as a Right", in G. Standing (ed.), *Promoting Income Security as a Right: Europe and North America*, London, Anthem Press, 2005, p. 14.

[28] J. Morsink, *The Universal Declaration of Human Rights, op. cit.*, pp. 191-194.

[29] *Ibid.*, pp. 157-190.

[30] In response to the idea's growing international popularity, BIEN was renamed the Basic Income Earth Network in 2004.

unemployment which could not be interpreted as conjunctural or cyclical in nature but which rather resulted from central features of our socio-economic system. The preferred remedy for unemployment at the time (and a number of years afterwards) was growth. But, along with a number of other more or less Green-oriented people on the left, I felt that this could not be the right solution. So the pro-growth consensus or grand coalition of the left and right had to be broken by providing a solution to the unemployment problem that would not rely on a mad dash for growth.[31]

The BIEN website similarly attributes much of the popularity of the BI idea to its promised effectiveness as a solution to the unemployment problem facing market economies.

> Liberty and equality, efficiency and community, common ownership of the Earth and equal sharing in the benefits of technical progress, the flexibility of the labour market and the dignity of the poor, the fight against inhumane working conditions, against the desertification of the countryside and against interregional inequalities, the viability of cooperatives and the promotion of adult education, autonomy from bosses, husbands and bureaucrats, have all been invoked in its favour.

> But it is the inability to tackle unemployment with conventional means that has led in the last decade or so to the idea being taken seriously throughout Europe by a growing number of scholars and organizations. Social policy and economic policy can no longer be conceived separately, and basic income is increasingly viewed as the only viable way of reconciling two of their respective central objectives: poverty relief and full employment.[32]

Is the claim that a BI guarantee would solve the unemployment problem in market economies warranted? I think not, but I want to emphasise two points before setting forth my argument. The first is that my criticism is not based on any philosophical objection to providing all members of society an unconditional BI guarantee. I agree with BI advocates that such a guarantee would confer a significant benefit on the members of society, and I have already noted that there is no impediment based on international human rights law that would prevent a society from granting its members such a benefit. My criticism of BI proposals is based on more practical considerations.

The other preliminary point I want to make is that my criticism does not apply to all possible BI proposals. My criticism is directed at the universal grant and equivalent negative income tax proposals upon which BI advocates principally rely in their promotion of the BI strategy.

---

[31] P. Van Parijs, "The Need for a Basic Income: An Interview with Philippe Van Parijs," *Imprints*, Vol. 1, No. 3, 1997, p. 5.

[32] Basic Income Earth Network, "About Basic Income," Retrieved 31 July 2013 from <http://www.basicincome.org/bien/aboutbasicincome.html>.

I would have no objection to a BI guarantee configured in a manner that addressed my criticism, and I have described elsewhere how such a benefit could be included in the strategy I advocate for securing the right to work and income security.[33]

According to BI advocates, an unconditional BI grant distributed individually to all members of society would secure the right to work by making it possible for people to choose the kind of life they want to live, including the kind of "work" they want to do, without having to rely on wage employment. Indeed, it would secure the right to work better than the achievement of full employment because it would allow people to choose from a more varied and personally satisfying set of occupations. As one commentator has noted,

> To conceive of work only as those activities through which a monetary consideration is obtained is to have a very limited idea of what work means, and it is even worse to rely on the market to determine what is and what is not work. [...] It is necessary to distinguish between work and its commercial appraisal. Work can be defined as all those activities that combine creativity, conceptual and analytic thought and manual or physical use of aptitudes. It consists of every activity that human beings carry out in which they combine their intelligence with their force, their creativity with their aptitudes.[34]

Conventional income transfer programmes do not allow for this because the provision of benefits to able-bodied adults is invariably linked to their continued pursuit of wage employment, and this expectation results in the imposition of behavioural requirements that are freedom restricting and demeaning. The consequent stigmatisation of the recipient population (who are perceived at best as "losers" and at worst as "shirkers") visits further harm on them.

Basic income advocates believe this problem would be eliminated if all members of society were provided an unconditional BI grant without any accompanying work obligation.[35] First, it is claimed that receipt of

---

[33] P. Harvey, "The Right to Work and Basic Income Guarantees: Competing or Complementary Goals?", *Rutgers Journal of Law and Public Policy*, Vol. 2, No. 1, 2005, pp. 55-58; P. Harvey, "Is There a Progressive Alternative to Conservative Welfare Reform?", *op. cit.*, pp. 196-197; P. Harvey, "More for Less: The Job Guarantee Strategy", *Basic Income Studies*, Vol. 7, No. 2, 2013, p. 13.

[34] J.L. Rey Perez, "El Derecho Al Trabajo, ¿Forma De Exclusión Social? Las Rentas Mínimas De Integración Y La Propuesta Del Ingreso Básic", *Revista Icade*, No. 62, 2004, pp. 247-248. See also P. Van Parijs, *Real Freedom for All. What (if anything) Can Justify Capitalism?*, Oxford, Oxford University Press, 1995, p. 126; G. Standing, *Beyond the New Paternalism: Basic Security As Equality*, London, Verso, 2002, pp. 255-261.

[35] In this analysis, I shall refer exclusive to universal BI grant proposals, but a negative income tax could be configured to achieve exactly the same effect. See P. Harvey,

the grant would allow people to create their own jobs, compensated by their BI grant. In other words, unemployed workers would no longer need waged employment to secure their right to work.[36] Second, it is argued that it would be easier for workers to find satisfying waged work if they had a BI guarantee, because they could accept lower wages in exchange for the opportunity to work in a more desirable job.[37] Third, it is argued that receipt of a BI guarantee would empower workers to reject substandard work and thereby force low-wage employers to improve the quality of the jobs they offer.[38]

I believe all of these claims are unfounded – that even a generous BI guarantee would constitute an inadequate and unsatisfactory substitute for wage employment, that it would not make it easier for unemployed job-seekers to find satisfactory wage employment, and that it would not pressure low-wage employers to improve the quality of the jobs they offered. I shall explain each of these contentions in turn.

First, would a generous universal BI grant allow people to create their own jobs, compensated by their grant? Consider the following hypothetical. Jane and John Doe both live in a society that provides all its members an unconditional BI grant of 200 monetary units (MUs) per month, an amount sufficient to support a modest but acceptable standard of living. Then Jane is laid off and suffers involuntary unemployment while John does not. Does Jane's continued receipt of her BI grant compensate her for the job she has lost? I do not think so. Her income has been cut in half, and her BI grant does not replace a penny of her loss, because she already received the full value of the grant before she was laid off. Since Jane's BI grant gives her nothing at all that she did not already have before she was laid off, how can it compensate her for being laid off?

Now suppose that Jane, supported by her BI grant, decides to turn her back on the world of waged employment and instead devote her time to caring for her invalid mother or working as a volunteer for a local Oxfam project. Would her BI grant convert her service work into a form of self-directed employment? Once again, I do not think so. Jane's continued receipt of her BI grant makes it easier for her to follow her heart, but she

---

"The Relative Cost of a Universal Basic Income and A Negative Income Tax", *Basic Income Studies*, Vol. 2, No. 2, 2006, pp. 1-24.

[36] See, e.g., P. Van Parijs, *Real Freedom for All, op. cit.*, p. 126.
[37] See, e.g., P. Van Parijs, "The Need for a Basic Income: An Interview with Philippe Van Parijs," *Imprints*, Vol. 1, No. 3, March 1996), pp. 5-22, retrieved 19 September 2014 from <http://eis.bris.ac.uk/~plcdib/imprints/vanparijsinterview.html>.
[38] See, e.g., Guy Standing, *Beyond the New Paternalism: Basic Security as Equality*, London, Verso, 2002, p. 259.

will receive absolutely nothing to replace the wage she lost when she was laid off from her paying job. Her BI grant does not compensate her for the work she is doing because she was receiving it before she lost her job.

If, alternatively, we view her BI grant as compensation for whatever she chooses to do with her time, then it is equally compensation for John's decision to keep his job, and the difference between a paying job and time spent in activities that do not pay remains exactly the same as it would in the absence of a BI guarantee. A paying job provides you with compensation in excess of whatever resources you may independently possess. Volunteer work does not. Jane's BI grant fails utterly to provide her the equivalent of a paying job. What she needs to secure her right to work is another paying job to substitute for the one she lost – not continued receipt of her BI grant.

The same problem undermines claims that a BI guarantee would empower workers to obtain desirable jobs in exchange for lower wages or win improvements in the quality of substandard jobs by refusing such employment. Both of these claims rest on the same assumption – that having a BI guarantee would empower workers to obtain better quality wage employment by allowing them to refuse undesirable work or trade a lower wage for better working conditions.

The circumstances in which John (Jane's former co-worker) finds himself illustrate the problem with this assumption. He retained his job. Jane took the layoff bullet. But suppose the reason he was kept on rather than Jane was because he loved the job and his BI guarantee made him feel able to accept a cut in wages from 200 MUs a month to 175 MUs, whereas Jane was unwilling to make that sacrifice because she did not find the job as desirable as John did. It is certainly true, in this circumstance that John's receipt of a BI guarantee has helped him secure his individual right to work (provided we ignore the question of whether his 175 MU salary qualifies as "just and favourable" remuneration), but has it helped secure the right to work in general or does it merely illustrate the musical chairs effect discussed above in reference to activation policies? Although clothed in the claim that a BI guarantee would empower workers to obtain more desirable jobs, the only way BI advocates can argue that accepting reduced wages in exchange for such employment will help secure the right to work is to embrace the neo-classical claim that reducing average wage levels will result in job growth.

Suppose alternatively that John's job offers substandard employment, and the reason Jane left was not because she was laid off but because their employer refused her reasonable demand for an increase in pay. Is this going to put pressure on the employer to raise John's wages for fear he too will quit? That depends, of course, on whether there are other job seekers willing to take Jane's place? If there are – and in a job short economy there generally will be – Jane will be replaced and neither John nor Jane's replacement will experience any improvement in the quality of their jobs. With a surplus of labour competing for available jobs, employers who offer substandard work are unlikely to have much trouble replacing dissatisfied employees. Indeed, that's what permits them to offer substandard work in the first place. What John needs to secure the qualitative aspect of his right to work (i.e., improvements in the quality of his job) is not a BI guarantee. It is what full employment would give him – the ready availability of enough jobs to make it impossible for employers to find workers who have no choice but to accept unfavourable conditions of employment. The one caveat to this conclusion is that John's receipt of a BI guarantee would make it easier for him to go on strike if his workplace was unionised and if his employer was unable to replace striking workers.

Isn't it possible that the distribution of a universal BI grant would make workers in general more resistant to accepting sub-standard employment – that there would be enough Jane Does willing to quit substandard jobs that employers actually would be forced to improve job quality? The problem with this hypothesis in a job short economy is that it is just as possible that the BI grants would end up functioning as a wage subsidy for low wage employers. If the existence of a BI guarantee meant that low wage employers would no longer have to pay enough to satisfy even the minimum subsistence needs of their workers, the wages they paid could sink below the minimum subsistence level. It would all depend on the size of the economy's job gap and the downward flexibility of wage standards.

This does not mean the BI grant Jane and John receive is worthless. It insures that their standard of living will not fall below whatever level the grant supports, whether or not they have a job. It makes it easier for them to survive unemployment spells without the qualifying conditions that limit the availability and duration of both unemployment insurance and means-tested social welfare benefits. It makes it easier for them to pursue non-waged work if they want to spend their time that way and are willing to adjust their standard of living accordingly. And, if they are unionised, it will strengthen their union's bargaining power. What it cannot do is provide a satisfactory substitute for securing the right to work.

That is why I have suggested that a BI guarantee is more appropriately viewed as a strategy for securing the right to income security rather than the right to work.[39] That is its express purpose after all. Claims that it would secure or at least help to secure the right to work represent an understandable but nonetheless forced attempt to offer a solution to the

---

[39] P. Harvey, "The Right to Work and Basic Income Guarantees", *op. cit.*, pp. 14-15.

problem of unemployment as well as that of poverty. Moreover, viewed as a strategy for securing the right to income security rather than the right to work, the BI idea has great appeal based on the widespread assumption (which advocates of the idea have done little to dispel) that a universal BI grant could guarantee all members of society an adequate standard of living.

In fact, sophisticated BI advocates recognise that it is unrealistic to expect a one-size-fits-all BI guarantee to achieve this goal because the needs of differently situated individuals vary too greatly. They also recognise that for either economic or political reasons a BI grant could be fixed below the level required to secure a decent standard of living. Accordingly, they acknowledge the need to retain "publicly organized social insurance and disability compensation schemes that would supplement the unconditional income while remaining subject to the usual conditions."[40]

The fact that different people have different needs is one of the reasons the Universal Declaration does not presume that the wages workers receive will necessarily cover all their needs. Instead, their right to "just and favourable remuneration" is accompanied by a right to have that remuneration "supplemented, if necessary, by other means of social protection".[41] The same recognition of differential needs is implicit in the partial list of essentials comprising the adequate standard of living recognised in Article 25, § 1. Moreover, as noted above, Article 25, § 1 may also mandate income support linked to a worker's prior earnings following a loss of livelihood in circumstances beyond the worker's control.

The inability of the BI strategy to adequately secure the right to income security all by itself would not matter if it were an inexpensive benefit to provide. Then it could be supplemented by other measures that would fill the gap, just as the Universal Declaration contemplates that wage income will require supplementation. The problem is that a universal BI grant is a very expensive benefit to provide, and any significant diversion of public revenues to fund such a benefit would not only diminish the pool of resources available to provide need-based supplementation; it could also leave the poor worse off.

The EU has adopted a poverty threshold equal to 60 per cent of median disposable income for purposes of measuring member states' progress in eliminating poverty and social exclusion.[42] According to the

---

[40] P. Van Parijs, "A Basic Income for All," *Boston Review*, 1 October 2000, retrieved 19 September 2014 from <http://bostonreview.net/forum/ubi-van-parijs>.
[41] Universal Declaration, Article 23, § 3.
[42] See European Union Social Protection Committee, "Report on Indicators in the Field of Poverty and Social Exclusion", 5 November 2001.

EU Social Protection Committee, this standard is based on a definition of the "poor" as "those individuals or households whose resources are so low as to exclude them from the minimum acceptable way of life in the country where they live."[43] The concordance between this description of poverty and the Universal Declaration's conception of what an "adequate" standard of living requires suggests that the 60-per cent standard can also be used as a rough measure of a nation's success in securing the universal component of the right to income security.[44]

I have not estimated what it would cost the EU to secure this right with a universal BI grant, but the price tag in the United States would have been about $5.1 trillion in 2011[45] before counting the additional transfer benefits required to satisfy the special needs of persons for whom the BI guarantee alone would be insufficient to secure their right to an adequate income. Aggregate social welfare spending by all levels of government totalled only $1.7 trillion in 2011, with more than half of that total consisting of old age pension benefits. Even if this entire $ 1.7 trillion in social welfare spending was reallocated to fund a universal BI guarantee, the grant would provide only a third of the EU's prescriptive poverty threshold – while leaving nothing at all to supplement anyone's BI grant. The arithmetic is simple. Large numbers of elderly persons would be thrust into poverty and large numbers of the non-elderly poor would almost surely be left worse off than they are under the existing system – simply because a resource pool that previously had been devoted to their support was now being divided among all members of society. I am confident that BI advocates would never accept that outcome, but

---

[43] European Union Social Protection Committee, *The Social Dimension of the Europe 2020 Strategy. A Report of the Social Protection Committee*, Luxembourg, Publications Office of the European Union, 2011, p. 16.

[44] By the "universal component of the right to income security", I mean the right of "everyone" to an adequate standard of living that is clearly stated in the first phrase of Article 25, § 1 of the Universal Declaration. I distinguish this from what might be called the "insurance component" of the right to income security, which is arguably recognised in the second phrase of Article 25, § 1. Whereas the "universal component" of the right to income security guarantees at least a minimally adequate standard of living for everyone, the purview of the "insurance component" is narrower – a promise that individuals who have lost their livelihood through no fault of their own will not be forced to suffer a precipitous reduction in their standard of living.

[45] This estimates is based on the methodology reported in P. Harvey, "The Relative Cost of a Universal Basic Income and a Negative Income Tax", *op. cit.* In that article, I estimated what it would cost to fund a universal BI grant providing everyone in the United States an income at least equal to the U.S. government's official poverty thresholds. Since these thresholds are currently pegged at about 30 per cent of median income, a universal BI grant capable of guaranteeing people an income satisfying the 60-per cent-of-median-income standard would cost approximately twice as much.

given the obviousness of the problem, it is surprising how little attention they have devoted to explaining how they believe it should be addressed.

Brazil's *Bolsa Familia* (family allowance) provides another example of this conundrum. Although the programme is widely praised by BI advocates as a model for introducing a BI guarantee in middle and low income countries,[46] its benefits are income-tested rather than universal, and I assume most BI advocates would agree that this arrangement is preferable to the distribution of the same pot of money in the form of a much smaller grant to all families in the country.[47]

And that being the case, does the *Bolsa Familia* really demonstrate the superiority of the BI idea or is it simply an attractive model for providing targeted social welfare benefits in a resource-constrained society? This is not an issue that confronts only middle and low income countries. The cost of a universal BI grant capable of satisfying the adequacy standard of the right to income security is high enough that it cannot help but raise questions as to whether it is the best way of securing that right – in wealthy as well as poor countries. If alternative strategies do exist for securing the right – and they do – can the advantages of a universal BI grant possibly justify its relative cost measured in terms of the opportunities society would have to forgo to pay for it?

IV. The Direct Job Creation Strategy for Securing the Right to Work and Income Security

Progressives have been too willing to accept the assumption that the only way to secure the right to work is to somehow induce the private sector to close the economy's endemic job gap. Progressives do not assume that market economies are capable of satisfying peoples' needs for education, health care or income support without substantial government provision of the benefits in question. Why assume that market economies are capable of providing all the jobs people need without substantial government provision?

---

[46] See, e.g. E. Suplicy, "From the Family Scholarship Program towards the Citizen's Basic Income in Brazil", paper presented at the 12th International Congress of the Basic Income Earth Network, Dublin, Ireland, June 20-21, 2008, retrieved 20 September 2014 from <http://www.basicincome.org/bien/pdf/dublin08/4bisuplicybibrazil.doc>.

[47] At a BI conference in New York City in February 2011 I asked Eduardo Suplicy, the author of the paper cited in the immediately preceding footnote, what he would choose to do if a pot of money became available that could be used either to double the size of the Bolsa Familia grant (which is not currently adequate to lift a family out of poverty by itself) or establish a small universal BI grant for the entire Brazilian population. He immediately and unhesitatingly answered that he would double the size of the Bolsa Familia grant.

Instead of asking economists how to fix what ails market economies in the hope that their job gaps will then somehow disappear, we should instead be asking them how governments can close their economy's job gaps at least cost in terms of adverse side-effects. Accepting any other outcome should be viewed as unacceptable, just as it would be unacceptable to accept that we can provide an education for only 90 per cent of our children, or health care for only 90 per cent of our population, or income support for only 90 per cent of those people who are incapable of supporting themselves.

The means I advocate for achieving this goal is an updated version of a strategy conceived and implemented by New Deal social welfare planers before Keynes's *General Theory* was even published. This strategy consists of the following five elements.

(1) Everyone (with appropriate limitations on the employment of children) would be given a legally enforceable right actually to be employed in a private or public sector job consistent with their qualifications and experience.

(2) In order to secure this right, a publicly-funded direct job creation programme would be established to eliminate the job shortages that are a normal feature of market economies. This programme could administer job-creation projects itself, fund not-for-profit agencies to operate such projects, or place unemployed workers in temporary positions within existing public sector agencies. All three strategies would likely be included in a well-designed programme.

(3) The employment provided or funded by the job creation programme would pay wages comparable to those paid similarly qualified workers performing comparable work in the private and regular public sectors of the economy. Everyone employed in the programme would also enjoy the same legal rights and protections as other workers, except that the tenure of their employment would be subject to the continued unavailability of suitable employment in the private or regular public sectors of the economy.

(4) To the extent the hourly wages individual workers received were insufficient to support a standard of living satisfying the Universal Declaration's adequacy standard, they would be supplemented by cash and/or in-kind supplements furnished by the state; and the same supplementation would be provided to workers employed in the private and regular public sectors of the economy.

(5) Persons who were either unable or not expected to be self-supporting would receive conventional transfer benefits guaranteeing them a similarly adequate standard of living.

Having discussed this strategy in detail elsewhere,[48] the only thing I will add to this five-point description is a brief explanation of the kind of jobs that could be created using the strategy, its cost, and why it would be capable of closing a market economy's job gap without the inflationary effects that doomed the Keynesian full employment strategy.

What Kind of Jobs Would the Programme Create? It is widely assumed that unemployed workers lack employable skills. People accordingly wonder what kind of jobs a programme like the one I advocate could provide.

This perception of unemployed workers is badly distorted. The groups portrayed in Figure 1 are not a fixed population. They have, on average, suffered far more than their fair share of unemployment, but they share that fate with a much larger pool of currently employed workers who cycle in and out of employment. The fact that unemployment rates drop below 2 per cent when jobs are truly plentiful shows that the vast majority of these individuals are fully capable of earning their keep when jobs are available.

This population also possess a broader range of skills than is commonly recognised. I have estimated that the last wage earned by the programme's workforce in non-programme employment would be only a couple of dollars per hour less than the mean earnings of all production and non-supervisory employees in the U.S. economy.[49] In short, it is a workforce that can be hired to do many things, and with training the possibilities are even greater.

Rather than asking what kind of jobs this workforce could reasonably be expected to take on, the proper way to approach the job planning question is to ask what goods and services we would like them to produce. What additional tasks would we assign to government agencies if they had larger staffs? What improvements in the services they provide would we like them to undertake? What free standing projects have we wanted but have not had the resources to fund? What additional services could the not-for-profit sector provide with a major influx of workers whose wages were paid by the jobs programme?

---

[48] See, e.g., P. Harvey, *Securing the Right to Employment, op. cit.*; P. Harvey, "Back To Work: A Public Jobs Proposal for Economic Recovery," Demos, March 2011, retrieved 31 July 2013 from <http://www.demos.org/publication/back-work-public-jobs-proposal-economic-recovery>; P. Harvey, "Securing the Right to Work at the State or Local Level with a Direct Job-Creation Program," Big Ideas for Jobs Initiative, Institute for Research on Labor and Employment, University of California at Berkeley, November 2011, retrieved 31 July 2013 from <http://www.bigideasforjobs.org/wp-content/uploads/2011/09/Harvey-Full-Report-2-PDF.pdf>.

[49] *Ibid.*

I have assumed in my cost estimates that 75 per cent of the programme's budget would be devoted to direct labour costs (wages and benefits) with the remaining 25 per cent reserved for non-labour costs (materials, supplies, transportation, etc.). This assumes that a strong preference would be shown for labour intensive over capital intensive projects, but the ratio would be an average, so projects with higher capital intensities could be undertaken. Supplemental funding could also be arranged for more capital-intensive projects (e.g., mortgage financing to support the construction of low-and moderate income housing). Naturally projects would be selected with an eye to how well their labour requirements matched the skills profile of the programme's workforce. Still, a wide range of projects could be undertaken.

There also might be special job-creation ideas or opportunities that shout out for implementation. One of my favourite ideas is to turn the U.S. Government's existing "Work-Study Program" into an entitlement programme available to any and all students. Government subsidised jobs created and supervised by post-secondary educational institutions are currently made available on a means-tested basis. Millions of jobs for otherwise unemployed or underemployed students could be created both during the school year and over vacation breaks by expanding the programme. Moreover, a similar programme could be established to provide work for university graduates who are unable to find employment.

Other examples of possible projects in the United States might include a major expansion in the number of child-care slots made available to working parents; a commitment to renovate the nation's stock of low-income housing and to build new low-rise housing; a concerted campaign to rehabilitate and enhance the ambiance and safety of outdoor spaces in low-income neighbourhoods; a special initiative directed at giving the nation's parks and recreational areas the kind of attention they received from the New Deal era Civilian Conservation Corps. Cultural projects and special green projects also could be supported. Environmental research and monitoring activities could be expanded. Community gardens and local food distribution systems could be subsidised. School buildings could be renovated, expanded and redecorated. School support staff could be augmented. Educational and recreational programing could be added to the school day, and school year.

What Would It Cost: I have estimated the cost of using the strategy outlined above to reduce unemployment in the United States from its July 2011 level of 9.1 per cent to its pre-recession level of 4.5 per cent and, alternatively, to the full employment level of 2 per cent.[50] I estimated the first year cost of achieving genuine full employment at $753 billion.

---

[50] *Ibid.*

However, after taking into account a partial list of the additional revenues and savings the job programme would have generated, that estimate fell to $389 billion.[51] Also, since the U.S. economy was already experiencing a modest recovery at the time (with the unemployment rate falling 0.8 per cent over the course of the year) the true net cost of the initiative would have been even lower than this estimate.

Because securing the right to work would reduce both the number of people needing transfer benefits and the average level of their need, only about $70 billion in added funding would be required to secure the right to income security using conventional transfer benefits.[52] Hence, the total cost of securing the right to work and income security using the strategy outlined above would have added something in the neighbourhood of $459 billion to total government expenditures between July 2011 and June 2012. That is only one tenth the cost of a universal BI grant pegged at the 60-per cent-of-median-income level.

Because the fiscal stimulus provided by this additional spending would have accelerated the economy's recovery, the second year cost of the strategy would have been significantly smaller than its first year cost, but its precise level is hard to predict because it would have depended on how quickly consumer borrowing and private sector investment would have recovered from their previously depressed levels.

In the long run, I have estimated the baseline cost of securing the right to work and income security using this strategy at under $200 billion per year over and above current levels of government expenditure. Moreover, a fuller accounting of the savings generated by the job creation programme could very well show that it would actually save taxpayers money.[53] In short, the cost advantage of the direct job creation strategy over the BI strategy is overwhelming.

---

[51] The additional revenues and savings counted for this purpose included (1) the income and payroll taxes that programme workers would pay on their programme wages, (2) the unemployment insurance benefits that programme workers would forfeit because of their employment in the jobs programme, (3) the means-tested health insurance benefits that programme workers would not need because of their receipt of employer-provided health insurance benefits through the jobs programme, and (4) the revenues the jobs programme would collect from the sale of at least some of the goods and services it produced (a figure I estimated conservatively at 10 per cent the value of programme output).

[52] P. Harvey, "Is There A Progressive Alternative to Conservative Welfare Reform?", *op. cit.*, p. 191; P. Harvey, "More for Less", *op. cit.*, p. 7.

[53] P. Harvey, "Securing the Right to Work at the State or Local Level with a Direct Job Creation Program", *op. cit.*, p. 11.

Wouldn't It Be Inflationary? There are three reasons why the direct job creation strategy would not be subject to the same inflationary tendencies that prevent the Keynesian full employment strategy from achieving genuine full employment.[54] First, unlike the Keynesian strategy, it is capable of closing the economy's job gap at the top of the business cycle without increasing either aggregate demand or private sector labour demand – thereby inhibiting the emergence of demand pull inflation as full employment is approached. This is due to the strategy's low net cost and the wide range of options that exist for funding it. Indeed, a direct job creation programme could be implemented in a manner that was fiscally deflationary and still achieve full employment.

Second, there is a natural tendency for spending on the direct job-creation strategy to be concentrated in communities where unemployment rates are highest. This is in marked contrast to market driven (including multiplier driven) economic growth, which tends to cause disproportionate expansion in "hot" economic sectors and regions while leaving unemployment to fester in depressed economic sectors and communities. This unbalanced expansion of the economy is one reason inflationary tendencies tend to emerge in expanding market economies before full employment is reached. A direct job creation programme configured to achieve full employment by securing the right to work would mitigate this problem by automatically limiting programme expenditures to places where surplus labour supplies existed.

Third, a well-designed direct job creation programme could also perform a price-stabilising, "buffer-stock" function. By remaining available for private sector employment, programme workers would restrain wage and price inflation the same way a "reserve army" of unemployed workers would – but without requiring anyone to actually suffer unemployment.

Conclusion: Providing for the Full and Free Development of the Human Personality

The focus of this chapter has been on the progressive quest for a solution to the problem of unemployment, but our attention has been drawn as well to the closely related task of eliminating poverty and income insecurity. I have argued that the assessment and design of policies directed at achieving these goals should be premised on an affirmation of the duty to secure the right to work and income security

---

[54] For a more extended discussion of this point, see P. Harvey, "Funding a Job Guarantee", *International Journal of the Environment, Workplace and Employment*, Vol. 2, No. 1, 2006, pp. 114-132.

recognised in the Universal Declaration of Human Rights. I have further argued that a strategy of direct job creation combined with conventional transfer benefits could succeed in securing these rights whereas the Keynesian strategy, activation policies and BI proposals all lack the capacity to do so. There is, however, one facet of the Universal Declaration's conception of the right to work and income security that we have not expressly addressed in our analysis – how well the policies we have considered would serve the goal articulated in Article 22 of the Universal Declaration of providing support for the "free development of the human personality."

Since providing support to individuals in furtherance of this purpose is one of the goals of both BI proposals and progressive versions of activation policies, I will conclude this chapter with an account of how the direct job creation strategy described above would help achieve this goal. First, it would remove the profound impediment that unemployment and poverty themselves pose to the achievement of the goal. Second, by providing an effective means of eliminating substandard employment it would make it possible for all workers to enjoy the opportunities for personal development that "good jobs" furnish. Third, it would enhance both the effectiveness and attractiveness of vocational training and retraining programmes by promising actual jobs to successful graduates. Fourth, it would guarantee everyone easy re-entry to the labour force when they wanted or needed paid employment, thereby reducing the risk and anxiety associated with withdrawing from the labour force to pursue other interests on either an intermittent or regular basis. Fifth, it would provide an easy means of expanding the availability of personally fulfilling work opportunities in a wage range of community service endeavours. Sixth, because persons with disabilities have the same right to work as other individuals, they could waive their right to a disability pension if they would prefer to have their right to work accommodated – even if it would cost society more to provide them a job with accommodations than it would to send them their disability pension. This would be liberating for many people with disabilities. Finally, the income support component of the strategy would also guarantee a standard of living capable of supporting the individual development rights of those persons who chose to rely on their entitlement to such benefits for their livelihood.

I believe that these features of the direct job creation strategy would provide substantially greater opportunities for the "free and full development of the human personality" than either the receipt of a universal BI guarantee or the operation of a well-functioning set of activation policies in a job short economy. My last claim, therefore, is that the direct job creation strategy would not only solve the problem of unemployment and income insecurity better than these alternative strategies; it also would do more to enhance the real freedom of people to develop and live lives of their own choosing within communities that accept the mutual burden of ensuring that everyone enjoys a similar right.[55]

---

[55] See Universal Declaration, Art. 29, § 1, which declares that "Everyone has duties to the community in which alone the free and full development of his personality is possible".

CONCLUSION

Activation Policies for the Unemployed: Redefining a Human Rights Response

Olivier DE SCHUTTER

The activation of employment policies that has developed in a wide range of OECD countries since the mid-nineties consists in coupling unemployment benefits and social assistance with certain services or requirements to improve one's "employability" by going through training, requalification, or work experience. Elise Dermine and Daniel Dumont, the editors of this volume, chose to frame the debate on the thus understood spread of activation by putting forward three theses. First, they note, activation *per se* is not *necessarily* to be denounced as a "recommodification" of work or social protection. In modern societies, work is not simply a constraint imposed upon individuals to achieve a decent standard of living; as Fernand Tanghe reminds us in his contribution, it is also, and simultaneously, a means of social integration and of personal fulfilment. Therefore, insofar as activation policies seek to strengthen individuals' abilities to join the employment market and access decent work, they may be seen potentially as progress towards the full realisation of the right to work.

Second, however, whether or not activation represents a step forward or a step backward in the fulfilment of the right to work and the freedom to choose employment depends on which balance each regime strikes between the conflicting values at stake. On the one hand, activation may result in an expanded set of opportunities for individuals, whose quest for a decent job may be supported by social services (including in particular placement services), by access to vocational training throughout the lifecycle to reduce the risks of skills depletion associated with globalisation and technological change, and by individualised counselling. On the other hand, activation is not without its own dangers, when it results in reduced levels of social protection as an incentive to return to employment, in the introduction of stronger forms of control to assess whether the jobseeker is actively searching for work, or in the imposition of a duty to take up employment that is not suitable. It is because activation policies have this dual character that they cannot be unambiguously either condemned or welcomed: unilateral and ideological statements are not a substitute for the careful study of its various institutional regimes, in the comparative approach that is proposed, for instance, by the contributions of Daniel Dumont on the United States or of Diane Roman on the French version of activation in this volume.[1]

The third hypothesis that is made is at the same time more implicit and apparently the most obvious: that human rights, particularly the prohibition of forced labour and the right to work and to freely chosen employment, may provide an adequate benchmark by which to assess the introduction of activation policies. This concluding chapter unpacks the implications of this hypothesis. The human rights instruments that are most relevant to this debate, after all, were drafted under very different circumstances, when the achievement of full employment was still seen as a real long-term possibility,[2] and when economic growth was strong enough to compensate for the jobs destruction resulting from technological progress. But these circumstances have changed dramatically. Is the resulting human rights regime well suited to meet the challenges of today? Or should we rethink the human rights framework in order to take into account the changes that have taken place since the post-Second World War period? Is there a danger that, unless we thus redefine the contribution of human rights, human rights will be dismissed as an obstacle to much-needed reforms of social and employment policies – and seen as irrelevant at best, or ignored entirely, at worst?

In seeking to answer these questions, this chapter recalls the role of human rights in the establishment of the post-Second World War international order (I.). It then suggests that certain dimensions of human rights may need to be revived in order to support the search for an adequate balance between activation as a means to realise the right to work, and activation as a threat to the freedom to choose employment (II.). It closes, briefly, by asking whether the values on which activation policies are premised are still suitable for a post-carbon society, in which economic growth and the increase of productive activities can

---

[1] See also, for comparative analyses illustrating the diversity of activation models that have been pursued in different jurisdictions, P. Vielle, P. Pochet and I. Cassiers (eds.), *L'Etat social actif. Vers un changement de paradigme?*, Brussels, P.I.E.-Peter Lang (Travail & Société), 2005; S. Morel, *Les logiques de la réciprocité. Les transformations de la relation d'assistance aux États-Unis et en France*, Paris, Presses universitaires de France (Le lien social), 2000 (highlighting the difference between the "punitive" approach adopted in the United States and the more inclusive approach pursued in France); A. Serrano Pascual and L. Magnusson (eds.), *Reshaping Welfare States and Activation Regimes in Europe*, Brussels, P.I.E.-Peter Lang (Work & Society), 2007; W. Eichhorst, O. Kaufmann and R. Konle-Seidl (eds.), *Bringing the Jobless into Work? Experiences with Activation Schemes in Europe and the U.S.*, Berlin, Springer, 2008.

[2] See W. Beveridge, *Full Employment in a Free Society*, London, Allen & Unwin, 1944.

no longer be seen as the way out of all problems of social integration. Just like the human rights response to activation policies may need to be rethought in order to take into account the circumstances of today – the very circumstances that have led to the spread of activation of social and employment policies – activation policies themselves cannot ignore the need to gradually move away from our current work-centred societies, in order to encourage the exploration of alternative lifestyles that prioritise the quality of social relationships over material improvement (III.).

I. Human Rights as Part of the Bretton-Woods Consensus

Though the modern welfare state has its origins in the emergence of legislation protecting workers in the late 19th century and in the first social security schemes of the early 20th century, the institutional forms of welfare that we have inherited have their source in the Bretton-Woods era that was inaugurated at the end of the Second World War. This was an era during which social protection, economic growth and trade liberalisation were seen as mutually supportive: a virtuous cycle was established, in which trade contributed to growth and employment, which in turn could finance social protection and protect all those who were deprived of the opportunity to access gainful employment, either temporarily or permanently. The definition of welfare in the form of *rights* – benefits that individuals could claim before independent tribunals – was seen as an integral part of this compromise.

Partly reflecting the vision of U.S. President F.D. Roosevelt who called for a post-conflict world order guaranteeing "freedom from want"[3] and partly building on instruments adopted within the International Labour Organization (ILO) in the 1920s covering issues such as maternity protection, sickness, old age, invalidity, workers' compensation, occupational health and unemployment, Article 22 of the Universal Declaration of Human Rights provided in 1948 that "[e]veryone, as a member of society, has the right to social security", and Article 25 stated that "[e]veryone [...] has the right to security in the event of unemployment, sickness, disability, widowhood, old age or other lack of livelihood in circumstances beyond his control".[4] Two recommendations adopted by the ILO in 1944 sought to widen the right to social security, at the same time that this right was being recognised as an internationally protected human right.[5]

---

[3] C. Sunstein, *The Second Bill of Rights. FDR's Unfinished Revolution and Why We Need It More Than Ever*, New York, Basic Books, 2004.

[4] UN General Assembly Res. 217, UN GAOR, 3rd sess., UN doc. A/810 (1948).

[5] ILO Recommendation No. 67 concerning Income Security (12 May 1944); and ILO Recommendation No. 69 concerning Medical Care (12 May 1944).

The construction of the welfare state in advanced economies was not a radical project. Instead, it was a compromise: it sought to defuse revolutionary impulses, whether in the form of demands for the nationalisation of means of production or in the form of workplace democracy, by ensuring that the working class would share in the general increase of prosperity.[6] In the course of the 1950s, communist parties gradually ceased to exercise a major influence in most West European countries (with the notable exception of France and Italy until the 1980s), and social democratic parties abandoned the demand for the collectivisation of the economy: at its Bad Godesberg congress of 1959, the German SPD (*Sozialdemokratische Partei Deutschlands*) acknowledged that the state should "restrict itself mainly to indirect methods of influencing the economy", reflecting an evolution that all its counterparts across the continent would undergo in time.[7] The movements calling for the greater participation of workers in decision-making within the company, based on arguments of self-fulfilment initially made popular by the writings of John Dewey,[8] largely encountered the same fate: apart from the introduction of co-determination (*Mitbestimmung*) in German company law – initially in the coal and steel industries and then, after 1976, in other sectors of the economy – it was not adopted at any significant scale in other countries, though it continues to be referred to in various legislative reform proposals.

The strength of the welfare state, therefore, had largely to do with the support it gained from all parts of society, and in particular from workers and employers alike: at the same time that workers were content with their newly found security, and the promise of a constant improvement of their working and living conditions, the employers saw a robust welfare state as guaranteeing social peace, and as stimulating the continuous growth of demand for the consumer goods they were flooding the markets with. Keynesianism, in the 1950s and 1960s, was not just one economic doctrine among others: it would hardly be an exaggeration to say that it was the shared premise behind the programmes of all mainstream political parties competing for power.

---

[6] This is adequately conveyed by Alan Brinkley in his chronicle of the successive legislative programmes designed by the Roosevelt administration in the 1930s: see A. Brinkley, *The End of Reform. New Deal Liberalism in Recession and War*, New York, Vintage Books, 1995.

[7] T. Judt, *Postwar. A History of Europe Since 1945*, New York, Penguin Books, 2005, chapter XI.

[8] See especially J. Dewey, *Democracy and Education. An Introduction to the Philosophy of Education* (1916), *Middle Works 1889-1924*, Vol. 9 (ed. J.-A. Boydston), Carbondale, Southern Illinois University Press, 1980, pp. 268-269 (calling for "direct participation [of workers] in control" at factory level).

It is this consensus that is now being questioned, under the pressure of globalisation, demographics and the technological changes that accelerate skills depletion. First, the globalisation of competition, initially in the industrial sector and now increasingly in the services sector, has led to questions concerning the welfare state's ability to continue to fulfil its redistributive function, at least where this would lead to increasing the cost of labour beyond the growth of labour productivity: under the pressure of foreign competition and the competition between world regions to attract investment, the welfare state gradually has given way to what, twenty years ago, Joachim Hirsch famously called the "competitive national state",[9] in which public policies chiefly aim at improving the competitiveness of enterprises based in the jurisdiction concerned, and in which even social rights come to be defined as investments in human capital. Social security, including how unemployment benefits are defined and under which conditions they are granted, appears to form no exception in this regard.[10]

Second, over the past fifty years, life expectancy has increased significantly. This puts a particular stress on old age pension schemes, as the ratio between the active population and the total population is declining. In the EU for instance, life expectancy at birth averaged 79.7 years in 2009 (for EU-27 countries), with a slight advantage to women (82.6 years) over men (76.7 years), though this gap is narrowing. Over the period 2002-2009 alone, life expectancy increased by 1.7 years for women and 2.1 years for men. At the same time, the fertility rate has strongly declined throughout the past decades, and even taking into account the slight increase in recent years, the current fertility rate of 1.59 live births per woman in 2009 for the EU-27 remains significantly below the replacement level of 2.1.[11] In other terms, without migration, the EU population would be in slight decline, even taking into account the increased life expectancy: the population is ageing and the ratio between people of working age and people over the age of 65 is rapidly falling.[12]

---

[9] J. Hirsch, *Der nationale Wettbewerbsstaat: Staat, Demokratie und Politik im globalen Kapitalismus (The Competitive National State: State, Democracy and Politics in Global Capitalism)*, Berlin-Amsterdam, ID-Archiv, 1995.

[10] See C. Grover and J. Stewart, "'Market Workfare': Social Security, Social Regulation and Competitiveness in the 1990s", *Journal of Social Policy*, Vol. 28, No. 1, 1999, pp. 73-96.

[11] Figures from Eurostat Fertility statistics: <http://epp.eurostat.ec.europa.eu/statistics_explained/index.php/Fertility_statistics> (last consulted on 1 May 2014).

[12] The European Commission has noted that "from 2013 onwards, for the first time, the size of the population of working age in Europe will shrink, whilst the proportion of older people will expand rapidly. There are now four people to support one person over the age of 65, and this ratio is set to halve by 2040" (European Commission, Communication from the Commission, Towards Social Investment for Growth and

Third, while these developments question the *ability* of the welfare state to continue to fulfil its redistributive functions, or at least to maintain the current levels of protection it provides, other developments question the *form* in which the services and guarantees that characterise the welfare state are delivered.[13] The switch to services and information and communications technologies (de-industrialisation, in other terms, in many so-called "industrialised" countries) went hand in hand with the destandardisation of employment relations and the emergence of new social risks, primarily attributable to the acceleration of skills depletion – i.e., the fact that skills must permanently be rebuilt in order for workers to cope with the technological changes. In this changing context, the provision of unemployment benefits for an unlimited duration, or at least for a long period of time, simply in order to compensate for the loss of income that results from the loss of employment, was increasingly seen by social democrats as untenable and as threatening the very viability of the welfare state they had done so much to help establish. The alternative, it would appear, was between reforming it in order to improve its resilience against this changed background, or seeing it gradually dismantled under the assault of more conservative political parties.

The "activation" of social policies is seen by many as the answer. Since the mid-nineties, a range of reforms have been launched, often at the initiative of social democrats, to rescue the welfare systems inherited from the 1970s, albeit at the price of significantly amending how they deliver their benefits. Human rights bodies have been relatively absent from the debate that resulted from the introduction of these reforms. As described by Elise Dermine in this volume, references to the prohibition of forced or compulsory labour proved inadequate to answer the subtle pressure exercised on jobseekers, who were encouraged to accept work as a condition for being helped. As Dermine also showed, reliance on the right to work has been more promising, but much of the potential of the right to work remains untapped. The "right to work" in this discussion is often reduced to a freedom of the individual not to take up employment that is not "suitable", taking into account age, qualifications, and past remuneration.

The response of the human rights regime has been defensive, weak and generally perceived as conservative, or irrelevant in the face of today's changed circumstances. I would like to suggest how this response could be strengthened and made more relevant, without sacrificing any of the

---

Cohesion – Including Implementing the European Social Fund 2014-2020, COM(2013) 83 final, of 20.2.2013, p. 4).

[13] See A. Hemerijck, *Changing Welfare States*, Oxford, Oxford University Press, 2013, pp. 51-85.

foundational ideals of the human rights regime. The right to work, properly understood, could impose on states to pursue macroeconomic policies that promote full employment, and to provide individual counselling and support to the unemployed; and it could lead to impose on employers that they re-examine their understanding of the "qualifications" required for any particular occupation. Similarly, whereas the right to social security primarily has been invoked to oppose reforms that would reduce the level of entitlements already achieved, what is most urgently needed today is to improve the nature of the entitlements provided (building the capacities of individuals rather than simply compensating for a loss of incomes), and most importantly, to encourage individuals to experiment. The following section explores these proposals in greater detail.

II. Redefining a Human Rights Response

A number of factors seem to explain the hesitations of human rights bodies confronted with the generalisation of "workfare" reforms. In part, such hesitations stem from the fact that overly rigid prescriptions – such as an absolute prohibition on any "retrogressive" measures or on the imposition of any form of work as a condition for the continued enjoyment of unemployment benefits – would be incompatible with the answers that states are expected to provide to the complex situation they are confronted with. Changing circumstances on the employment market and in the budgetary balance of social security schemes call for adaptive solutions, well tailored to those changes.

Indeed, such adaptability of social protection schemes is a requirement of human rights law itself. Because the right to work included in human rights law includes a duty of states to take measures to promote full employment, the effectiveness of employment policies in reducing the number of unemployed must constitute an important criterion to assess their overall human rights impacts. Under Article 6 of the International Covenant on Economic, Social and Cultural Rights, the right to work requires that states parties "adopt, as quickly as possible, measures aiming at achieving full employment".[14] Therefore, to the extent that activation measures are effective in realising this objective, they will be criticised only with great reluctance, and they will be condemned only in situations where such measures are obviously restrictive of the right of the individual to freely choose employment. In the very same concluding observations addressed to Germany in 2011, in which it expresses concerns about "duty to work" impositions resulting from the Hartz

---

[14] UN Committee on Economic, Social and Cultural Rights, "General Comment No. 18: The Right to Work", 35th session, 24 November 2005, E/C.12/GC/18, § 19.

reforms,[15] the UN Committee on Economic, Social and Cultural Rights applauds "the reforms to the labour market which have made it possible to reduce unemployment to its lowest level in the past 20 years".[16] This statement provides a good illustration of the dilemma facing human rights bodies in this area. And it is significant, too, that the architects of the new welfare state generally defend the measures adopted, primarily, on the basis of the results achieved: the interests of society, they may

---

[15] The "Hartz reforms", thus named after Peter Hartz, the director of personnel of Volkswagen at the time, who chaired the "Commission for Modern Labour Market Services" set up in 2002 in order to make proposals to improve the effectiveness of employment policies, were implemented by the SPD-Greens coalition government led by Gerhard Schröder through four Acts on the Provision of Modern Services on the Labour Market (*Gesetze für moderne Dienstleistungen am Arbeitsmarkt*). In addition to raising the minimum age for early retirement from 60 to 63, the reforms shortened the duration of contributory unemployment benefits (unemployment benefit I) and created a new unemployment benefit that is a hybrid between the (formerly separate) unemployment assistance benefiting the unemployed whose right to benefits under the contributory scheme had expired and the social aid paid to the needy (unemployment benefit II). The fourth of this series of legislative reforms ("Hartz IV"), adopted in December 2003 but in force since 1 January 2005, included a broadening of the definition of "acceptable" jobs (which were now allowed to extend, for instance, to jobs that required a move to another location), and it introduced sanctions for those who refused such job offers; those who cannot find work shall be proposed "community jobs", for instance in the form of jobs to improve the social infrastructure at municipal level. In May 2011, the Committee on Economic, Social and Cultural Rights expressed its concern about "arrangements under [Germany's] unemployment assistance and social assistance, including the obligation for recipients of unemployment benefits to take up 'any acceptable job', which in practice may be interpreted as almost any job, and the assignment of long-term unemployed persons to unpaid community service work, may lead to violations of articles 6 and 7 of the Covenant"; it urged Germany to "ensure that its unemployment benefits schemes takes account of an individual's right to freely accept employment of his or her choosing as well as the right to fair remuneration" (UN Committee on Economic, Social and Cultural Rights, "Concluding Observations: Germany", 20 May 2011, E/C.12/DEU/CO/5, § 19). The views thus expressed by the Committee are consistent with earlier statements it made for instance with regard to Canada, when it expressed its concern, already in the early 1990s, that "workfare" programmes may undermine the right to work (Article 6 of the Covenant) or the right to social security (Article 9), where such programmes "constitute work without the protection of fundamental labour rights and labour standards legislation" (UN Committee on Economic, Social and Cultural Rights, "Concluding Observations: Canada", 10 June 1993, E/C.12/1993/5, § 30 ("The Committee notes with concern that at least six provinces in Canada [...] have adopted 'workfare' programmes that either tie the right to social assistance to compulsory employment schemes or reduce the level of benefits when recipients, who are usually young, assert their right to choose freely what type of work they wish to do. In many cases, these programmes constitute work without the protection of fundamental labour rights and labour standards legislation")).

[16] UN Committee on Economic, Social and Cultural Rights, "Concluding Observations: Germany", 20 May 2011, E/C.12/DEU/CO/5, § 5(a). This requirement is discussed further below.

argue, are better served when there are fewer people on welfare and more people in employment.[17]

Similarly, one of the major arguments for welfare reform is that, due to the demographic trends mentioned above,[18] maintaining the existing system unchanged may be untenable: the ratio of the employed population towards the total population cannot continuously decrease, without affecting the fiscal sustainability of the scheme. This, too, is an argument that human rights bodies cannot dismiss as irrelevant: the Committee on Economic, Social and Cultural Rights noted, in its general comment on the right to social security, that "the schemes should also be sustainable, including those concerning provision of pensions, in order to ensure that the right can be realised for present and future generations".[19]

There is a more fundamental reason, however, why the guidance human rights bodies have provided to states in this area has been relatively unhelpful. Whatever guidance was offered has been the result, for the most part, of an almost exclusively defensive posture. The *acquis* of the welfare state as they had been gradually strengthened until the late 1970s, it seemed to many, were now being threatened by the "activation" of social benefits and the tendency towards the contractualisation of the relationship between the beneficiary and the public employment services. The priority, it would seem to follow, was to preserve such *acquis*, and to build safeguards against the risks of the welfare edifice being dismantled. Indeed, that is the very premise of the principle of non-retrogression:[20]

---

[17] See, e.g., B. Clinton, *Giving. How Each of Us Can Change the World*, New York, Knopf, 2007, pp. 173-174 (noting that in the United States, since the adoption of the welfare reform act of 1996, "the welfare rolls have dropped nearly 60%, more than 7 million people, by the time I left office, and have continued to drop since. In 2000, the percentage of Americans on welfare reached its lowest point in four decades. During the economic downturn of 2001, many of those who came off the welfare rolls were able to stay in the workforce in part due to policies designed to help them succeed").

[18] See above, text corresponding to footnotes 11-12.

[19] UN Committee on Economic, Social and Cultural Rights, "General Comment No. 19: The Right to Social Security", 37th session, 23 November 2007, E/C.12/GC/19, § 11.

[20] The Committee on Economic, Social and Cultural Rights made it explicit that retrogressive measures taken in relation to the right to social security are presumptively a violation of the duty of progressive realisation: "If any deliberately retrogressive measures are taken, the State party has the burden of proving that they have been introduced after the most careful consideration of all alternatives and that they are duly justified by reference to the totality of the rights provided for in the Covenant, in the context of the full use of the maximum available resources of the State party. The Committee will look carefully at whether: (a) there was reasonable justification for the action; (b) alternatives were comprehensively examined; (c) there was genuine participation of affected groups in examining the proposed measures and alternatives; (d) the measures were directly or indirectly discriminatory; (e) the measures will have

if there is only one direction of social progress, it follows that any change in the system of social protection that would result in weakening the position of some members of the community should be treated with suspicion, and should only be accepted in limited circumstances.

Yet, this conveys the impression that rights are conservative, not transformative. It is telling that one of the most perceptive commentators of the transformation of the welfare state includes as one of the key reasons why needed reforms cannot be achieved the fact that governments have pre-committed themselves to provide certain advantages, making it difficult for them, or even impossible where such benefits have been codified in the form of rights, to re-examine past choices.[21] Even more important, this defensive position risks protecting those who already are recognised as having certain entitlements (the "insiders", who are employed or have been employed, and the more senior workers), at the expense of those who have only been recognised as having limited protection hitherto, and are in a comparatively much more marginal position (the "outsiders", who have never been in employment, and the young workers).[22]

---

a sustained impact on the realisation of the right to social security, an unreasonable impact on acquired social security rights or whether an individual or group is deprived of access to the minimum essential level of social security; and (f) whether there was an independent review of the measures at the national level" (UN Committee on Economic, Social and Cultural Rights, "General Comment No. 19: The Right to Social Security", cited above, § 42). This requirement explains, for instance, why the Committee was particularly critical of the introduction in Canada of "successive restrictions on unemployment insurance benefits, [which] have resulted in a dramatic drop in the proportion of unemployed workers receiving benefits to approximately half of previous coverage, in the lowering of benefit rates, in reductions in the length of time for which benefits are paid and in increasingly restricted access to benefits for part-time workers" (UN Committee on Economic, Social and Cultural Rights, "Concluding Observations: Canada", 10 December 1998, E/C.12/1/Add.31, § 20). This was the Committee's answer to measures that the Canadian government was presenting as intended to "promot[e] improved skills in the workforce and [to reduce] the disincentives to work" (see third report submitted by Canada in accordance with Articles 16 and 17 of the International Covenant on Economic, Social and Cultural Rights, E/1994/104/Add.17, § 125).

21 See A. Hemerijck, *Changing Welfare States*, op. cit., p. 24 ("pre-committed resources of past policy choices, such as old age pensions, 'lock in' social provisions, which in turn come to constrain budgetary leeway for present-day social policy innovation"). Although this comment does not refer explicitly to the consequences of defining social benefits as legal rights that the beneficiaries may claim, defining them thus of course only reinforces this 'lock-in', forcing governments to remain bound to past policy choices.

22 For a similar critique focused on the role of courts in protecting social rights in developing countries, see D. Landau, "The Reality of Social Rights Enforcement", *Harvard International Law Journal*, Vol. 53, No. 1, 2012, pp. 189-247 (noting that remedies typically used by courts in litigation concerning social rights, which either

Instead, a more positive approach can be taken: one that accepts the constraints that states face and acknowledges the need for reform, but broadens the political imagination of governments in order to ensure that their responses to the predicament they are facing will be guided by human rights. Three proposals could be explored in this regard. None of them condemns activation absolutely. Each of them builds on a reading of human rights, however, to clarify the framework under which the activation of unemployment benefits or social assistance could be envisaged.

A. Providing a Supportive Macro-economic Environment, Individualised Counselling and Support to the Unemployed

As already mentioned, and as emphasised throughout this volume,[23] the "activation" of benefits granted to the unemployed may take different forms: some are clearly penalising; others strengthen the capacity of the unemployed by developing his or her skills, equipping the beneficiary to meet the exigencies of employment market. Similarly, the "activation" can be understood as a two-way process: while it can mean improving the employability of the individual jobseeker, it can also mean encouraging employment services to be more proactive, to provide more individualised counselling and training, rather than to limit themselves to the provision of financial support.

The relationship between the right to work and the duties of the public authorities to provide "active" support is well-established in certain human rights instruments. In Article 1 of the European Social Charter (ESC), the right to work includes the obligation on the state to maintain "as high and stable a level of employment as possible, with a view to the attainment of full employment" (§ 1 of Article 1); its obligation to provide "free employment services" to all (§ 3); and its obligation, finally, to "provide or promote appropriate vocational guidance, training and rehabilitation" (§ 4). The right to work under Article 1 of the ESC does refer, of course, to the effective protection of "the right of the

---

protect individual rights of claimants or prohibit the executive or the legislator from removing certain benefits that were formerly granted, "benefit primarily upper income groups" (p. 201) rather than the poorest groups of the population).

[23] See also, for comparative overviews, in addition to the sources mentioned in footnote 1, G.J. Van den Berg, B. van der Klaauw and J.C. van Ours, "Punitive Sanctions and the Transition Rate from Welfare to Work", *Journal of Labor Economics*, Vol. 22, No. 1, 2004, pp. 211-241; J.T. Weishaupt, *From the Manpower Revolution to the Activation Paradigm. Explaining Institutional Continuity and Change in an Integrating Europe*, Amsterdam, Amsterdam University Press, 2011; A. Hemerijck, "Two or Three Waves of Welfare State Transformation?", in N. Morel, B. Palier and J. Palme (eds.), *Towards a Social Investment Welfare State? Ideas, Policies and Challenges*, Bristol, Policy Press, 2012, pp. 33-60.

worker to earn his living in an occupation freely entered upon" (§ 2), but this "negative" freedom (that essentially imposes on the state not to obstruct efforts by individuals to be employed) is thus complemented by positive duties imposed on the state to support the individual's efforts by providing an appropriate macro-economic environment, as well as by providing guidance and training.

Similarly, the right to work in article 6 of the International Covenant on Economic, Social and Cultural Rights is not limited to the freestanding freedom of the individual to take up whichever employment he or she may happen to find: it imposes on the state an active duty to pursue policies that create employment opportunities, and to equip individuals in order to ensure that they can seize such opportunities. This is what the Committee implies when referring to the *availability* of work ("States parties must have specialised services to assist and support individuals in order to enable them to identify and find available employment"), which together with the dimensions of *accessibility* (non-discrimination) and *acceptability* and *quality* ("Protection of the right to work has several components, notably the right of the worker to just and favourable conditions of work, in particular to safe working conditions, the right to form trade unions and the right freely to choose and accept work") form the normative content of the right to work.[24]

Rebalancing the duties between the individual and the State, as required under human rights law, is especially important today given the current tendency to reduce the right to work to an economic freedom – that of the individual to seek work and to engage in work of his or her choosing – while omitting correlative state duties. Article 15 of the EU Charter of Fundamental Rights is typical of this shift.[25] That provision states in § 1 that "Everyone has the right to engage in work and to pursue a freely chosen or accepted occupation".[26] But it is silent on any duty of the state to strive towards full employment, by creating appropriate macro-economic conditions; as well as on any duty to support the individual's quest towards "employability".[27]

---

[24] UN Committee on Economic, Social and Cultural Rights, "General Comment No. 18: The Right to Work", cited above, § 12.

[25] *Official Journal*, No. C 303 of 14.12.2007, p. 1.

[26] The second and third paragraphs of Article 15 of the Charter relate the freedom to choose an occupation and the right to engage in work to the freedom of citizens of the Union to seek employment in another EU Member State, or to exercise his or her freedom of establishment or freedom to provide services (§ 2), and to the right of third country nationals authorised to work in the territory of the EU Member States to working conditions equivalent to those of citizens of the Union (§ 3).

[27] See D. Ashiagbor, "Article 15", in S. Peers, T. Hervey, J. Kenner and A. Ward (eds.), *The EU Charter of Fundamental Rights. A Commentary*, Oxford-Portland (OR),

This is a surprising omission, since the European Employment Strategy (EES), which has been developed by the EU since the Luxembourg Summit of 1997, has systematically referred to the need to create jobs, an objective mentioned in Article 3, § 3 of the Treaty on the European Union (which stipulates that the Union shall aim at full employment), and since the employment guidelines adopted within the EES emphasise the need to develop skills that correspond to labour market needs so as to increase the employability of workers.[28] The deliberate reluctance to formulate these objectives in rights-based terms – as a duty that the state owes to individuals, who in turn should have a right to claim certain forms of support in order to move towards increased "employability" – betrays either a misunderstanding about what the "right to work" entails, for it means not that unemployment is *per se* a violation of the said right, but rather that the absence of any effort by the state to move towards full employment may engage its responsibility,[29] or, more plausibly, a framing of the issue of the unemployment that places almost all the burden on the individual to "adapt" to the exigencies of the labour market, and much less on the collectivity to provide an environment that enables those individual efforts and rewards them.

Indeed, one of the major concerns associated with the discourse of "activation" has to do with the *framing* it suggests of the issue of unemployment – i.e., the implicit understanding of the causes of unemployment that this discourse conveys. To a large extent, it was

---

Beck-Hart-Nomos, 2014, p. 428 (noting that "the most prominent dimension of the [European Social Charter's] understanding of the right to work – namely, the right to have work made available, implying a duty on the state to provide work – is missing from the EU's version of this right").

[28] See, in particular, Recital 11 of the Preamble to the guidelines for the employment policies addressed to the EU Member States (Council Decision 2010/707/EU of 21 October 2010 on guidelines for the employment policies of the Member States, *Official Journal*, No. L 308 of 24.11.2010, p. 46) ("Ensuring the effective functioning of the labour markets through investing in successful transitions, education and training systems, appropriate skills development, raising job quality, and fighting segmentation, structural unemployment, youth unemployment, and inactivity while ensuring adequate, sustainable social protection and active inclusion to prevent and reduce poverty, with particular attention to combating in-work poverty and reducing poverty amongst the groups most at risk from social exclusion, including children and young people, while at the same time adhering to agreed fiscal consolidation, should […] be at the heart of Member States' reform programmes") and guideline 8 ("Developing a skilled workforce responding to labour market needs and promoting lifelong learning").

[29] See, for instance, D. Ashiagbor, "The Right to Work", in G. de Búrca and B. de Witte (eds.), *Social Rights in Europe*, Oxford, Oxford University Press, 2005, pp. 241-259; or P. Harvey, "Benchmarking the Right to Work", in S. Hertel and L. Minkler (eds.), *Economic Rights. Conceptual, Measurement, and Policy Issues*, Cambridge, Cambridge University Press, 2007, pp. 115-141.

this new narrative about the causes of unemployment that exercised the strongest influence on policy-makers. The intellectual foundations on which Tony Blair's New Labour programme rested provide a vivid illustration. In a series of papers published since the mid-1980s, Richard Layard and Stephen Nickell, together with some others, argued that it was essential in order to reduce unemployment to link benefits to active labour market policies, in order to move people from welfare to work.[30] Writing in 1996, just before an exhausted Tory government would cede power in Britain to the reformed Labour Party, these authors invoked the factors that explained the low levels of unemployment (less than 2 per cent) in Sweden until the late 1980s, to conclude that "what is needed is in fact a change of regime. When people enter unemployment they need to understand that there will be no possibility of indefinite life on benefits. Instead it should be made clear that, after a period of say one year, public support will be provided only through participation on a programme. But access to the programme is guaranteed. This will have the twin effect of (a) helping those who really need help and (b) driving off the public purse those who only want help in the form of cash".[31]

This was not a neoliberal proposal. Indeed, Layard and Nickell are quite explicit in rejecting the relaxation of employment protection legislation as a solution to unemployment. At the same time however, they quite deliberately do not adopt the keynesian view that unemployment is the result of macroeconomic policies that fail to support demand by generous levels of redistribution (through progressive taxation and high levels of social protection). The key obstacle they see to a durable reduction of unemployment is in the failure to build human capital in a way that corresponds to the exigencies of the labour market, and in the availability of generous unemployment benefits for long periods of time without such benefits being made conditional upon the active search for employment and/or retraining. The message that is conveyed is that the "problem" is located in the individual, or at least in the mismatch between the individual's efforts and qualifications and the demand side

---

[30] R. Layard and S. Nickell, "Unemployment in Britain", *Economica*, Vol. 53, No. 210, 1986, pp. S121-S169; R. Layard and S. Nickell, "The Thatcher Miracle?", *American Economic Review*, Vol. 79, No. 2, 1989, pp. 215-219; R. Jackman, R. Layard and S. Nickell, "Combatting Unemployment: Is Flexibility Enough?", CEP Discussion Paper No. 293, 1996; R. Layard and S. Nickell, "Labour Market Institutions and Economic Performance", in O. Ashenfelter and D. Card (eds.), *Handbook of Labor Economics*, Vol. 3, Amsterdam, Elsevier, 1999, pp. 3029-3084.

[31] R. Jackman *et al.*, "Combatting Unemployment: Is Flexibility Enough?", cited above, p. 12.

of the labour market, rather than in the macroeconomic choices made by society as a whole.[32]

There is a symbolic value to law and public policies: legislation and governmental practices convey a worldview and a message about citizenship and the respective roles of the individual and the collectivity. The keynesian diagnosis about unemployment saw it as a macroeconomic problem, to be addressed by growing the economy and stimulating demand. The new message about unemployment sees it as a microeconomic problem, to be addressed by reforming the individual in order to better satisfy the needs of the market. Coercive activation policies send the message that unemployment is a problem of the individual, not of the collectivity, despite ample evidence that the growth of unemployment since the 1970s is the result of the reduction in employers' demands for low-skilled labour, itself largely the result of technological change.[33] This may be problematic where jobs are scarce, especially where this scarcity is not simply the result of a lack of qualifications, but also of growing inequalities lowering the demand for goods and services: it may be a source of discouragement for the jobseekers; it may exercise a downward pressure on wages; and in certain contexts, it may reinforce racial stereotypes.[34] Imposing on the state that it fulfils the right to work

---

[32] See also E. Carmel and T. Papadopoulos, "The new governance of social security in Britain", in J. Millar (ed.), *Understanding Social Security. Issues for Social Policy and Practice*, Bristol, Policy Press, 2003, pp. 5-6 of the online version (<http://people.bath.ac.uk/hsstp/TP-Publications/EC-TP-New-Governance-of-Soc-Sec_2003.pdf> (last consulted on 20 July 2014)) (noting that an approach emphasising the duty of the government to promote full employment is "markedly different from the New Labour approach of 'work for those who can'. [Where 'full employability' is emphasised rather than 'full employment',] the reason for unemployment is [...] firmly anchored to an individual's capacities and capabilities, implying that they themselves are responsible for their employment status. The state's responsibilities are to provide only opportunities for training and skills development, which the risk-taking individual is required to take up. [...] The individual of working age is made responsible for their employment status, and for the provision of their own security, including in old age").

[33] See for instance for studies concerning the United States: R. Freeman and P. Gottschalk (eds.), *Generating Jobs. How to Increase Demand for Less-skilled Workers*, New York, Russell Sage Foundation, 1998; or F. Levy and R. Murnane, "U.S. Earnings Levels and Earnings Inequality: A Review of Recent Trends and Proposed Explanations", *Journal of Economic Literature*, Vol. 30, No. 3, 1992, pp. 1333-1381.

[34] Indeed, some authors have linked this shift in the framing of the question of poverty to racial politics: in the U.S., the emergence of a discourse about individual "responsibility" went hand in hand with the mostly implicit, but nevertheless powerful idea that certain groups of the population, particularly among the African-American community, were illegitimately benefiting from a system that others, "hard-working" average (White) Americans, were financing. This is what some sociologists have called the "story of illegitimate takings": see J. Soss, R. Fording and S. Schram, *Disciplining the Poor.*

by adopting pro-employment macroeconomic policies and by providing strong support to jobseekers is one way to counter these risks.

B. Clarifying the Duties of Private Employers to Contribute to the "Employability" of Jobseekers

Within the approach to unemployment that sees it as primarily a microeconomic problem, a further shift has taken place in recent years: it is not the structures that must be adapted to the individual, it is he, or she, who is expected to adapt. It is true that some lip service is being paid to the duties of employers. Thus, guideline 8 of the EU's employment guidelines include a paragraph referring to the contribution of the private sector to the objective of "Developing a skilled workforce responding to labour market needs and promoting lifelong learning":

In cooperation with social partners and firms, Member States should improve access to training, strengthen education and career guidance. These improvements should be combined with the provision of systematic information on new job openings and opportunities, the promotion of entrepreneurship and enhanced anticipation of skill needs. Investment in human resource development, up-skilling and participation in lifelong learning schemes should be promoted *through joint financial contributions from governments, individuals and employers*. To support young people and in particular those not in employment, education or training, *Member States, in cooperation with the social partners*, should enact schemes to help those people find initial employment, job experience, or further education and training opportunities, including apprenticeships, and should intervene rapidly when young people become unemployed (emphasis added).[35]

It is unclear whether these references to the role of employers are intended to impose on them a form of burden-sharing, or whether they primarily should be interpreted as requiring that the private sector be involved, and its needs taken into account, in defining the characteristics that the workforce should present. What is clear, however, is that there is no reference in this paragraph, nor in the employment guidelines as a whole, to the need to question the definition of "qualifications" the prospective workers are supposed to possess, in order to shift to more inclusive employment markets – employment markets that could, in particular, reward and value difference. The one exception to this is the reference, in the same paragraph of the employment guidelines, to the

---

Neoliberal Paternalism and the Persistent Power of Race, Chicago, University of Chicago Press, 2011.

[35] Council Decision 2010/707/EU of 21 October 2010 on guidelines for the employment policies of the Member States, cited above.

need to put in place "systems for recognising acquired competencies", in other terms, for overcoming the rigidities that may result from overvaluing diplomas and the acquisition of competencies through formalised channels, while competencies acquired through informal means, including through past professional experience, would remain undervalued. But this is only a minor admission, of relatively minor importance. For the most part, the discussion on "activation" assumes that employers know whom they need – that they are irreproachably "objective" in defining which "competences" or "qualifications" are required from the jobseeker. Employers, of course, are prohibited from practicing discrimination. Beyond that minimum requirement however, which only serves to screen out the most irrational forms of exclusion (and generally protects jobseekers to the extent that they present certain "suspect" characteristics or belong to certain traditionally disadvantaged groups), employers remain free to set requirements for access to employment as they see fit.

"Merit" as defined by the employer, thus, is fetishized. Two implications follow. First, because of this reification of what it means to be "qualified" – and the reference to an impersonal and anonymous "employment market" that rewards certain "qualifications" only serves to reinforce this impression – any active intervention by the state to strengthen access to employment is seen as paternalistic. It is seen both as creating a risk that the "market signals" will be distorted (a classic ordoliberal theme),[36] and as resulting in individuals not gaining "self-respect" by obtaining employment under conditions that are not those imposed by "the market". It is perhaps worth noting in this regard that Jon Elster, because of his strong emphasis on work as a means for the individual to gain self-respect, rejects on that basis a duty of the state to provide work: such support by the state, he reasons, would negate the very idea of satisfaction and self-respect that the individual should gain through work.[37] Yet, his argument presupposes that the market is somewhat neutral; that the competencies as defined by employers in accordance with business necessities are somehow immune to challenge; and that if one is excluded from access to employment, this has to do

---

[36] The "social market economy" as promoted initially by Alfred Müller-Armack, one of the most influential figures of ordoliberalism, was premised on the idea that any social measures should be strictly "in conformity with the market" (*marktkonform*); otherwise it would be disruptive to the market's equilibrium and it would distort the signals the market sends to economic actors through "normal" price mechanisms. See A. Müller-Armack, "The Meaning of the Social Market Economy", in A. Peacock and H. Willgerodt (eds.), *Germany's Social Market Economy: Origins and Evolution*, London, Macmillan, 1989, pp. 82-86 (initially published in 1956 in *Handwörterbuch der Sozialwissenschaften*, Vol. 9).

[37] J. Elster, "Is There (or Should There Be) a Right to Work?", in A. Gutmann (ed.), *Democracy and the Welfare State*, Princeton, Princeton University Press, 1988, p. 74.

with one's failure to make the right choices, rather than to a definition of qualifications that is unnecessarily demanding, or culturally biased, or simply the result of unchecked assumptions about certain "normal" ways of performing a function.

A second implication is that we miss the opportunity, with such an approach, to "activate" the employer. Yet, a number of studies originating in the field of institutional (or, in the French version, "conventionalist") economics have highlighted the importance of how qualifications are defined – what François Eymard-Duvernay calls "assessments proofs" (*épreuves d'évaluation*) – in order to understand the sources of unemployment.[38] Understanding the right to work as a human right should lead us to question the principles of allocation of employment as a scarce social good. How jobs are being allocated should not be left to the magic of whichever preferences are stated by employers: it should be asked, in each case, whether the working environment should not be accommodated to fit the need to accelerate the inclusion of jobseekers, especially those that are long-term unemployed or that belong to a category (young or old workers, women, minorities, etc.) which has traditionally been disadvantaged.

C. *Respecting the Choice of Alternative Lifestyles*

There is, finally, a third direction in which a human rights response to the activation of social policies could be improved: it is as a safeguard against the risk of imposed uniformity. In political philosophy, this risk is seen as a threat to the plurality of conceptions of the "good life".[39] In human rights law, it may be seen as a threat to the right to privacy.

It has been once remarked that the right to privacy is perhaps best understood not as a protection of the individual against what the law may prohibit, but rather as a protection against what the law imposes: the distinguishing feature of the laws struck down in privacy cases, it was noted in support of this approach, has been "their profound capacity to direct and to occupy individuals' lives through their affirmative

---

[38] See in particular, in chronological order, O. De Schutter, *Discriminations et marché du travail. Liberté et égalité dans les rapports d'emploi*, Brussels, P.I.E.-Peter Lang (Travail & Société), 2001; C. Bessy, F. Eymard-Duvernay, G. de Larquier et E. Marchal (eds.), *Des marchés du travail équitables? Une approche comparative France – Royaume-Uni*, Brussels, P.I.E.-Peter Lang, 2001; F. Eymard-Duvernay, "Conventions de qualité du travail et chômage", *Economies et sociétés*, AB, *Socio-économie du travail*, No. 26, 2005, pp. 1381-1410; F. Eymard-Duvernay (ed.), *Epreuves d'évaluation et chômage*, Toulouse, Octarès, 2012.

[39] See, for instance, J. Habermas, "Equal Treatment of Cultures and the Limits of Postmodern Liberalism", *Journal of Political Philosophy*, Vol. 13, No. 1, 2005, pp. 1-28.

consequences".[40] The right to privacy is not simply about confidentiality, or preserving from public scrutiny information that an individual wishes to keep for himself: it is fundamentally about the freedom of each individual to express his or her identity, be it by entering into relationships with others, or alone.[41] Such freedom in turn depends on the creation of conditions that allow an individual to reflect on the reasons why he or she entertains certain desires, or as expressed by Gerald Dworkin, to "reflect upon one's motivational structure and to make changes in that structure".[42] Only by being confronted with a plurality of life options and with various understandings of the "good life" can an individual make a fully informed choice as to which life he or she wants to lead. The importance of the freedom of choice has been rightly highlighted by Jean-Michel Bonvin and Eric Moachon in their presentation of the "capability approach" to activation policies.

This, indeed, may be the ultimate challenge posed to human rights by the activation of social policies. It is often said that activation policies encourage a "work ethic", and that individuals should be active members of society in order to share in its advantages; to which it is added that moving people from welfare to work ensures their social integration. It is important to note, however, that such a reasoning presupposes that in order to achieve social integration, individuals should succeed as market participants. This is a much narrower and more materialistic definition of "work" than is useful to society and than could in fact ensure social integration; and it robs individuals of the possibility to choose alternative means of self-fulfilment. As remarked by Emma Carmel and Theodorus Papadopoulos:

---

[40] J. Rubenfeld, "The Right of Privacy", *Harvard Law Review*, Vol. 102, No. 4, 1989, p. 740.

[41] This of course paraphrases the definition provided by the Human Rights Committee of the United Nations under Article 17 of the International Covenant on Civil and Political Rights: see UN Human Rights Committee, *Raihman v. Latvia*, communication No. 1621/07, decision of 30 November 2010, CCPR/C/100/D/1621/2007, 2010, § 8.2 (where the Committee notes: "the notion of privacy refers to the sphere of a person's life in which he or she can freely express his or her identity, be it by entering into relationships with others, or alone"). This also echoes the approach of the European Court of Human Rights under Article 8 of the European Convention on Human Rights, which it sees as protecting "a right to personal development", described as "the right to establish and develop relationships with other human beings and the outside world", and the interpretation of which should be guided by the notion of "personal autonomy" (see, e.g., Eur. Ct. HR, *Pretty v. the United Kingdom*, 29 April 2002 (app. No. 2346/02), § 61).

[42] G. Dworkin, *The Theory and Practice of Autonomy*, Cambridge, Cambridge University Press, 1988, p. 108.

[The] narrow definition [of work as security] as paid work in a labour market underlines an exclusionary vision. Important welfare-creating activities that are not part of the cash/market nexus and thus are not 'registered' as productive are absent from such definition – two obvious examples here being care-work or voluntary work. Further, work seen in this way potentially enhances the social differences between able-bodied and disabled-bodied people of working age, and echoes a rather narrow vision of social life – we do not work to live but rather live to work.[43]

In this volume, it is perhaps R. Hoop who comes closest to expressing this critique, where he argues:

When activation policies are stimulated under reference to a work ethic or to a balance between rights and duties, we should be aware of this nuance because this discourse could be misleading. Indeed, this discourse may suggest that, by receiving and accepting a benefit, a debt arises that has to be paid off towards society. In other words, the principle of reciprocity is put forward. Responding to this principle should be possible by every contribution that is judged valuable to society, especially in social assistance schemes where there is no predetermined link with paid labour. But this will not be the case when the invoked work ethic appears to be a materialistic one, when the underlying norm is not to give something back to society, but is on the contrary not having to rely on society. Only paid work can correspond to this type of work ethic; informal unpaid work cannot. The proclaimed norm of reciprocity will then miss its target. Rather than creating among citizens a sense of duty, it will probably only evoke feelings of frustration, powerlessness or even humiliation, since a lot of people will feel excluded from the possibility of giving something in return.

Must work necessarily remain so central to our lives, and almost the only channel through which to achieve social integration? Historically, the centrality of waged employment has gone hand in hand with the

---

[43] E. Carmel and T. Papadopoulos, "The New Governance of Social Security in Britain", *op. cit.*, p. 5 (internal citations omitted). See also, formulating a similar critique, B. Lund, *Understanding State Welfare. Social Justice or Social Exclusion?*, London, Sage, 2000, pp. 202-203; or J. Hills, "Thatcherism, New Labour and the Welfare State", CASE Paper No. 13, London, London School of Economics, Centre for Analysis of Social Exclusion, 1998, p. 27 (noting that "the Government has started using language borrowed from Continental Europe of 'social exclusion' and 'social inclusion', but much of the way in which it uses it implies that the main way in which inclusion is achieved is through paid work, rather than other activities. Its Green Paper on welfare reform has for instance been criticised by social policy academics for ignoring 'other forms of work, most notably care work undertaken in the home, still mainly by women. [This] has left the impression that the Government does not value care work as an expression of citizenship responsibility'" (citing open letter from Professor Peter Alcock and others to the new Secretary of State for Social Security, Alistair Darling, published in the *Guardian*, 29 July 1998)).

dismantling of informal networks of solidarity, at local levels, through neighbourhood communities, or through professional corporations.[44] Today however, a new range of social innovations seek to re-establish these networks of solidarity, reducing the dependency of the individual both on access to waged employment and on protection through state-led social security schemes. For these innovations to prosper, citizens wishing to invest in them should be given time, and they should be given support. Should we not seek to make activation policies "social innovation-friendly", by maintaining a right to unemployment benefits or, as the case may be, to social assistance, to all those who are pursuing socially useful activities, whether or not such activities measurably contribute to economic growth?[45]

It is this profound intuition, of course, that provides the key motivation to the proponents of a universal basic income, represented in this volume by Yannick Vanderborght.[46] Quite apart from the controversial nature of this proposal and whether or not, as argued here by Philip Harvey, such a guaranteed and unconditional basic income to all is the best way to achieve social inclusion,[47] one clear benefit that would result from even a partial implementation of this idea would be in its encouragement to sociodiversity: to the coexistence, within society, of different life choices, that will not all necessarily be guided by the imperative to meet essential needs. This will reward experimentation, and it will contribute to the autonomy of the individual. Real choice can only flourish in the context of a society in which a variety of life options are open to the individual.

III. Conclusion

The human rights response to activation policies can redefine itself, without either renouncing the principles on which human rights were built in the post-Second World War period, nor ignoring the very real

---

[44] See especially R. Castel, *Les métamorphoses de la question sociale. Une chronique du salariat*, Paris, Fayard, 1995.

[45] In this perspective, J. Peck and N. Theodore mention the failure to take into account the potential of the social economy in the New Deal implemented in 1998-1999 by the Blair government (J. Peck and N. Theodore, "Beyond 'Employability'", *Cambridge Journal of Economics*, Vol. 24, No. 6, 2000, pp. 729-749). However, social innovations that can support the shift to more inclusive societies go beyond the social economy alone.

[46] See, notably, P. Van Parijs (ed.), *Arguing for Basic Income. Ethical Foundations for a Radical Reform*, London, Verso, 1992; and P. Van Parijs, *Real Freedom for All. What (If Anything) Can Justify Capitalism?*, Oxford, Oxford University Press, 1995.

[47] *Contra* the proposal for a basic income guarantee, see also P. Harvey, "Basic Income and the Right to Work: Competing or Complementary Goals?", *Rutgers Journal of Law and Urban Policy*, Vol. 2, No. 1, "Basic Income", 2005, pp. 2-59.

challenges that welfare states are facing and to which social-democrats have sought to answer. I have argued here that such a response should take into account two considerations.

First, it should focus not only on the jobseeker or on the recipient of social benefits him- or herself (and on the need for a balance between the right to freely chosen employment and the duty to work), but also on the duties of other actors: the state itself, which should be held accountable for the adoption of macro-economic policies that seek to achieve full employment and provide opportunities to all; and the prospective employer, whose definition of the qualifications required from the jobseeker should be critically examined in order to ensure that such a definition shall not result in unnecessarily exclusion from work. The right to work, including the right not to face discrimination in access to employment, requires such a triangulation: responsibility for delivering opportunities for decent work should be made mutual, in order for work, as a scarce social good, to be equitably shared. Second, the human rights response should take into account the need to allow the individuals to choose lifestyles that are not exclusively employment-centred, and whose contribution to the community may take forms other than that of entering into an economically "productive" activity. Ultimately, the objective should be to encourage individuals to seek personal fulfilment by providing them with a range of alternatives from which to choose, provided the choices remain within the right balance between what an individual contributes to the community and the level of support he or she receives from the community.

This latter component of the human rights response to activation leads, almost inevitably, to more fundamental questions about the world we intend to shape for ourselves. Our societies are trapped into a race in which technological progress results in improved labour productivity, thus reducing the volume of work required per unit of output. Labour-saving technologies manufacture unemployment, as people are being replaced by machines and become redundant. The solution to this has been, historically, twofold. First, a range of activities or resources that, formerly, had not been part of the "market", were commodified. This, for instance, is how the services industry emerged: to a large extent, the growth of this industry has resulted in services being provided by paid professionals, who are now delivering services that, in the past, were free, as they were provided through family and community networks.[48] Second, new "needs" were created by advertising, by certain mirages of

---

[48] See R. Heilbroner, *The Nature and Logic of Capitalism*, New York-London, W.W. Norton, 1985, p. 60: "Much of what is called 'growth' in capitalist societies consists in this commodification of life, rather than in the augmentation of unchanged, or even improved, outputs".

happiness based on material well-being, and by mimicry of the lifestyles of the most affluent classes – what Veblen referred to as "conspicuous consumption".[49] Thus, we seek to compensate for the destruction of jobs by displacing the frontiers of the market and by making people feel unhappy if they do not consume more (though often unnecessary) stuff. This futile and never-ending quest for more, based on a deliberately entertained confusion between "more" and "better", has been responsible for the spectacular increase in our ecological footprint, both in the form of the rapid depletion of natural resources and of the destruction of the natural balances of the ecosystems. Yet, we continue to destroy jobs in the name of allowing each job to produce more, and to encourage people to consume more in order to ensure that this superfluous production with be absorbed.

This is not peripheral to the debate about the activation of social policies. Instead, it highlights that the solution that "activation" proposes as a remedy to unemployment, however revolutionary it looks to some commentators, is not radical enough, in that it does not question the perverse trajectory in which we seem to be trapped. The startling increases in labour productivity over the past century could have provided an opportunity, for the first time in human history, to allow whole societies to escape, for most people during most of their active lives, from the drudgery of having to work for a living: they could have enjoyed music, conversation, reading, or walking around in parks. To avoid gaps from emerging between members of society, work could have been shared more equitably, and robust redistributive social programmes implemented to ensure that inequalities would remain within reasonable margins. Instead, more people were put to work, often for too long hours to compensate for low wages – low, that is, in comparison to what kind of wages they should receive in order to have access to the cornucopia of goods in the acquisition of which, they are told, resides the secret to felicity. This chapter has proposed to rely on human rights to broaden our political imagination about unemployment and what to do about it. Much more remains to be done in this regard.

---

[49] See T. Veblen, *The Theory of the Leisure Class. An Economic Study of Institutions* (1899), New York, Dover, 1994 (noting that "the standard of expenditure which commonly guides our efforts is not the average, ordinary expenditure already achieved; it is an ideal of consumption that lies just beyond our reach, or to reach which requires some strain. The motive is emulation – the stimulus of an invidious comparison which prompts us to outdo those with whom we are in the habit of classing ourselves").

Contributors

Jean-Michel Bonvin is professor of sociology and social policy at the University of Applied Sciences and Arts – Western Switzerland (HES-SO). His main fields of expertise include social and employment policies and organisational innovation in public sector management. He is currently a member of the management committee of the SOCIETY project funded by the European Union's 7th framework programme.

Olivier De Schutter is professor of human rights law at the Université Catholique de Louvain and at Sciences Po Paris. A specialist in economic and social rights and globalisation, he was between 2008 and 2014 the United Nations special rapporteur on the right to food, and he will join the UN Committee on Economic, Social and Cultural Rights in 2015.

Elise Dermine is research fellow of the Belgian National Fund for Scientific Research, within the Université Catholique de Louvain. She is completing a doctorate on activation policies for the unemployed and international human rights law. Previously, she has been a lawyer and a teaching assistant in social security law.

Daniel Dumont holds a doctorate in law as well as a degree in philosophy. He is professor of social security law at the Université Libre de Bruxelles. In 2011-2012, he was visiting scholar at UCLA school of law. His research mainly focuses on social security systems and employment policies.

Philip Harvey is professor of law and economics at Rutgers University. He received his PhD in economics from the New School for Social Research in New York and he graduated in law at Yale school of law. His research focuses on policy options for securing the right to work.

Renaat Hoop obtained a doctorate in law at the University of Utrecht and worked as a researcher in the field of social security at the Vrije Universiteit Brussel and the University of Maastricht. He is currently professor of labour law and social security law at VIVES University College in Bruges.

Eric Moachon holds a degree in sociology and will soon defend a doctoral thesis in political science. He has been a researcher in social policy at the University of Geneva and at the University of Applied Sciences and Arts – Western Switzerland (HES-SO). Since 2012, he has directed policy evaluations for the canton of Geneva. His main research interests are policy implementation, accountability processes and active labour market policies.

Diane Roman is professor of law at the Université François-Rabelais de Tours and a member of the Institut universitaire de France. Since receiving her doctorate from the Université Paris I Panthéon-Sorbonne, she has become an expert in the field of human rights and social welfare and has published numerous books and articles dealing with human rights, poverty and social justice in French and European law. From 2008 to 2011, she led a collective research project focusing on the justiciability of social and economic rights. She has also been appointed as an expert for the Council of Europe and the European Commission.

Fernand Tanghe is emeritus professor of philosophy of law and political philosophy at the University of Antwerp. His main research interests are human rights, and in particular social rights, theories of the welfare state and equality, multiculturalism, marxism and the origins of modern political thought.

Yannick Vanderborght is professor of political science at Université Saint-Louis – Bruxelles, where he currently directs the Research Centre in Political Science (CRESPO). He is also a member of the Hoover Chair at the Université Catholique de Louvain and an associate editor of *Basic Income Studies*. He has published several articles on basic income and related issues.

"Work & Society"

The series "Work & Society" analyses the development of employment and social policies, as well as the strategies of the different social actors, both at national and European levels. It puts forward a multi-disciplinary approach – political, sociological, economic, legal and historical – in a bid for dialogue and complementarity.

The series is not confined to the social field *stricto sensu*, but also aims to illustrate the indirect social impacts of economic and monetary policies. It endeavours to clarify social developments, from a comparative and a historical perspective, thus portraying the process of convergence and divergence in the diverse national societal contexts. The manner in which European integration impacts on employment and social policies constitutes the backbone of the analyses.

Series Editor: Philippe Pochet, General Director ETUI-REHS (Brussels) and Digest Editor of the Journal of European Social Policy

Published books

No. 78 – *The Transnationalisation of Collective Bargaining. Approaches of European Trade Unions*, Vera GLASSNER, 2014, 978-2-87574-167-7.

N° 77 – *L'Europe entre marché et égalité. La politique européenne d'égalité entre les femmes et les hommes, de l'émergence au démantèlement*, Sophie JACQUOT, 2014, 978-2-87574-159-2.

N° 76 – *Représenter le patronat européen. Formes d'organisation patronale et modes d'action européenne*, Hélène MICHEL (dir.), 2013, 978-2-87574-057-1

No. 75 – *The Wage under Attack. Employment Policies in Europe*, Bernadette CLASQUIN & Bernard FRIOT (eds.), 2013, 978-2-87574-029-8.

No. 74 – *Quality of Employment in Europe. Legal and Normative Perspectives*, Silvia BORELLI & Pascale VIELLE (eds.), 2012, 978-90-5201-888-1.

No. 73 – *Renewing Democratic Deliberation in Europe. The Challenge of Social and Civil Dialogue*, Jean DE MUNCK, Claude DIDRY, Isabelle FERRERAS & Annette JOBERT (eds.), 2012, 978-90-5201-875-1.

No. 72 – *Democracy and Capabilities for Voice. Welfare, Work and Public Deliberation in Europe*, Ota DE LEONARDIS & Serafino NEGRELLI (eds.), 2012, 978-90-5201-867-6.

N° 71 – *Trajectoires des modèles nationaux. État, démocratie et travail en France et en Allemagne*, Michèle DUPRÉ, Olivier GIRAUD et Michel LALLEMENT (dir.), 2012, ISBN 978-90-5201-863-8.

No. 70 – *Precarious Employment in Perspective. Old and New Challenges to Working Conditions in Sweden*, Annette THÖRNQUIST & Åsa-Karin ENGSTRAND (eds.), 2011, ISBN 978-90-5201-730-3.

No. 69 – *Europe 2020: Towards a More Social EU?*, Eric MARLIER and David NATALI (eds.), with Rudi VAN DAM, 2010, ISBN 978-90-5201-688-7.

No. 68 – *Generations at Work and Social Cohesion in Europe*, Patricia VENDRAMIN (ed.), 2009, ISBN 978-90-5201-647-4.

No. 67 – *Quality of Work in the European Union. Concept, Data and Debates from a Transnational Perspective*, Ana M. GUILLÉN and Svenn-Åge DAHL (eds.), 2009, ISBN 978-90-5201-577-4.

No. 66 – *Emerging Systems of Work and Welfare*, Pertti KOISTINEN, Lilja MÓSESDÓTTIR & Amparo SERRANO PASCUAL (eds.), 2009, ISBN 978-90-5201-549-1.

No. 65 – *Building Anticipation of Restructuring in Europe*, Marie-Ange MOREAU (ed.), in collaboration with Serafino NEGRELLI & Philippe POCHET, 2009, ISBN 978-90-5201-486-9.

No. 64 – *Pensions in Europe, European Pensions. The Evolution of Pension Policy at National and Supranational Level*, David NATALI, 2008, 290 p., ISBN 978-90-5201-460-9.

No. 63 – *Building Anticipation of Restructuring in Europe*, Marie-Ange MOREAU (ed.), 2008, 234 p., ISBN 978-90-5201-456-2.

No. 62 – *Jobs on the Move. An Analytical Approach to 'Relocation' and its Impact on Employment*, Béla GALGÓCZI, Maarten KEUNE & Andrew WATT (eds.), 2008, 245 p., ISBN 978-90-5201-448-7.

N° 61 – *Les nouveaux cadres du dialogue social. Europe et territoires*, Annette JOBERT (dir.), 2008, 267 p., ISBN 978-90-5201-444-9.

No. 60 – *Transnational Labour Regulation. A Case Study of Temporary Agency Work*, Kerstin AHLBERG, Brian BERCUSSON, Niklas BRUUN, Haris KOUNTOUROS, Christophe VIGNEAU & Loredana ZAPPALÀ, 2008, 376 p., ISBN 978-90-5201-417-3.

No. 59 – *Changing Liaisons. The Dynamics of Social Partnership in 20th Century West-European Democracies*, Karel DAVIDS, Greta DEVOS & Patrick PASTURE (eds.), 2007, 265 p., ISBN 978-90-5201-365-7.

No. 58 – *Work and Social Inequalities in Health in Europe*, Ingvar LUNDBERG, Tomas HEMMINGSSON & Christer HOGSTEDT (eds.), SALTSA, 2007, 538 p., ISBN 978-90-5201-372-5.

Peter Lang - The website
Discover the general website of the Peter Lang publishing group:
www.peterlang.com